Racism and Education

Education policy is not designed to eliminate race inequality but to sustain it at manageable levels.

This is the inescapable conclusion of the first major study of the English education system using 'critical race theory'.

David Gillborn has been described as Britain's 'most influential race theorist in education'. In this book he dissects the role of racism across the education system; from national policies to school-level decisions about discipline and academic selection.

Race inequality is not accidental and things are not getting better.

Despite occasional 'good news' stories about fluctuations in statistics, the reality is that race inequality is so deeply entrenched that it is effectively 'locked in' as a permanent feature of the system.

Built on a foundation of compelling evidence, from national statistics to studies of classroom life, this book shows how race inequality is shaped and legitimized across the system. The study explores a series of key issues including:

- The impact of the 'War on Terror' and how policy privileges the interests of White people;
- How assessment systems produce race inequality;
- How the 'Gifted and Talented' programme is a form of eugenic thinking based on discredited and racist myths about intelligence and ability;
- The Stephen Lawrence case, revealing how policymakers have betrayed earlier commitments to race equality;
- How 'model minorities' are created and used to counter antiracism;
- How education policy is implicated in the defence of White power.

Racism and Education: Coincidence or Conspiracy? takes critical antiracist analyses to a new level and represents a fundamental challenge to current assumptions in the field. With a foreword by Richard Delgado, one of the founders of critical race theory.

David Gillborn is Professor of Education at the Institute of Education, University of London, and editor of the international journal *Race Ethnicity and Education*.

Richard Delgado is University Distinguished Professor of Law and Derrick Bell Fellow at the University of Pittsburgh.

Racism and Education:
Coincidence or Conspiracy?

David Gillborn

 Routledge
Taylor & Francis Group

LONDON AND NEW YORK

First published 2008
by Routledge
2 Park Square, Milton Park, Abingdon, Oxon, OX14 4RN

Simultaneously published in the USA and Canada
by Routledge
270 Madison Ave, New York, NY 10016

Routledge is an imprint of the Taylor & Francis Group, an informa business

© 2008 David Gillborn

Typeset in Galliard by
Saxon Graphics Ltd
Printed and bound in Great Britain by
Antony Rowe Ltd, Chippenham, Wiltshire

British Library Cataloguing in Publication Data
A catalogue record for this book is available
from the British Library

Library of Congress Cataloging in Publication Data
Gillborn, David.
    Racism and education : coincidence or conspiracy? / David Gillborn.
        p. cm.
    Includes bibliographical references.
    1. Racism in education—Great Britain. 2. Discrimination in education—Great Britain. 3.
Race discrimination—Great Britain. I. Title.
    LC212.3.G7G453 2008
    371.82900941—dc22   2007042195

ISBN10: 0-415-41897-6 (hbk)
ISBN10: 0-415-41898-4 (pbk)
ISBN10: 0-203-92842-3 (ebk)

ISBN13: 978-0-415-41897-3 (hbk)
ISBN13: 978-0-415-41898-0 (pbk)
ISBN13: 978-0-203-92842-4 (ebk)

To Joyce and Jim for their love and inspiration

Contents

Exhibits

Acknowledgements

My first thanks must go to my family, who tolerate my excessive focus on work, support me without question and love me no matter how much I'm away. Dad, you're my hero and my best mate; Mum, you're a constant inspiration, thank you for always being there; Dorn, your love keeps me going, thanks for not mentioning all those great (unrealized) plans we had for my study leave; Becky, you're an incredible young woman who makes me proud every day; Sarah, a big thank you for your help with Photoshop: a musician and a Forest fan – what more could I ask for?

This book has taken me to places that I could only dare explore with the guidance and support of many close friends. Deborah Youdell encouraged, challenged and refined many of the ideas – thanks for your scholarship, your friendship and the numerous beers! Richard Aldrich took me under his wing and helped me see the long view with grace and humour; Mike Apple is a true friend, an inspiration and the best teacher I ever met (in and out of the classroom); Stephen Ball has encouraged me for more than 20 years and there have been times when, without him, I might have given up; James A. Banks has shown me kindness and wisdom that continue to inspire; Gregg Beratan introduced me to CRT and continues to add to my understanding; Anna Clarkson for believing in the idea and never flinching no matter where the work took me; Richard Delgado and Jean Stefancic showed me a world of scholarship that changed my ideas about what was possible – their warmth and encouragement made this book possible; Kal Gulson was a great sounding board for ideas who pushed me further; Gus John for his laser sharp insight and unfailing willingness to fight on; Gloria Ladson-Billings, a world-class scholar who shows that serious critical work can enlighten and enliven; Doreen Lawrence towers above the race field in the UK as a model of grace, strength and determination; Marie Lall for her friendship, support and the chop-stick lessons; Zeus Leonardo – my brother in Berkeley – keeps giving me good ideas and convincing me that I thought of them; Grace Livingston has much better things to do than help me, but she's always there to encourage and offer insight; Larry Parker's help and support were very important as I got to grips with CRT; Claudine Rausch commented incisively on every chapter and with only one hand – with babe in arms and despite sleep deprivation; Brian Richardson is the model organic intellectual and my legal inspiration;

Nicola Rollock understood my arguments before I did and helped me explain them better; Christine Sleeter for her scholarship and encouragement; Ed Taylor for befriending me, inspiring me and sharing his b-ball knowledge; Sally Tomlinson for sharing her experience and always believing in me; Carol Vincent for her calm confidence and great ideas; Geoff Whitty for giving me a job and helping me outgrow my own expectations; and Terezia Zoric for her warmth, insight and encouragement, even when she disagreed with me.

In addition, there are countless friends and colleagues who have helped me refine my ideas; shown me new insights; kept me sane; and pushed me to have the courage to say the unsayable. My thanks especially to Len Barton, Alastair Bonnett, David Buckingham, Chamion Caballero, Neal Carr, Roger Dale, Joseph Flessa, Thomas Gitz-Johansen, Helen Green, Jo Haynes, John Hill, Lauri Johnson, Reva Joshee, Jan Kampmann, Anjali Kothari, Cate Knowles, Jette Kofoed, Drego Little, Carl Maki, Jacqui Macdonald, Heidi Safia Mirza, Stephen Pickles, Peter Ratcliffe, Jessica Ringrose, Gordon Stobart, David Omotoso Stovall, Leon Tikly, Joy Warmington, Alan Wieder and Sarah Wishart.

While writing this book I was also part of a team working on policy/practice issues. I was privileged to work closely with a group of activists drawn from a range of Black community-based groups and professional associations. It has been one of the most exciting and educative experiences of my life. My thanks to all those who took part in the enterprise, especially Bisi Akiwumi-Jones, Ken Barnes, Enrima Bell, Lorna Cork, Melvyn Davies, Lorna Downer, Paul Elliot, Clive Lewis, Josef Norford, David Okoro, Paul Olaitan, Ann Palmer, Bevan Powell, Conrad Sackey and Simon Woolley.

The ideas in this book have also benefited from the support, interrogation and collegiality of staff and students at the following seats of learning: Center for Multicultural Education at the University of Washington, Seattle; Institute of Education, University of London; Havens Center for the Study of Social Structure and Social Change at the University of Wisconsin, Madison; and Ontario Institute for Studies in Education (OISE) of the University of Toronto. Finally, a special thanks to Mike Apple's Friday Seminar – you're even better than you think you are!

All of the radio broadcast transcripts included herein are my own. With the exception of programme hosts and public figures, all names of people and places have been changed.

Copyright Acknowledgements

Twomey, J. and Pilditch, D. (2005) 'It was just a tragic mistake: why the police should NEVER face murder charges over shot Brazilian', *Daily Express*, 18 August 2005, is reproduced by permission of the *Daily Express*.

Waterhouse, R. (1997) 'British schools are second rate say the volcano island refugees', *Mail on Sunday*, 30 November, is reproduced by permission of the *Mail on Sunday*.

Chapters 4, 5 and 8 build on ideas and data that have appeared previously: my thanks, therefore, to the copyright holders for permission to draw on my earlier work:

Gillborn, D. (2005) 'Education policy as an act of white supremacy: whiteness, critical race theory and education reform', *Journal of Education Policy*, 20(4): 485–505. My thanks to Taylor & Francis and to Stephen Ball for his friendship and unfailing support.

Gillborn, D. (2006) 'Critical Race Theory and education: racism and anti-racism in educational theory and praxis', *Discourse: Studies in the Cultural Politics of Education*, 27(1): 11–32. My thanks to Taylor & Francis and to Bob Lingard for his encouragement.

Gillborn, D. (2006) 'Public interest and the interests of white people are not the same: assessment, education policy, and racism'. Reprinted by permission of the publisher. From Gloria Ladson-Billings and William F. Tate (eds), *Education Research in the Public Interest: Social Justice, Action, and Policy*, New York: Teachers College Press, © 2006 by Teachers College, Columbia University. All rights reserved. My thanks to Gloria Ladson-Billings and William Tate for permission and, especially, their inspirational work.

Gillborn, D. (2006) 'Rethinking white supremacy: who counts in "Whiteworld", *Ethnicities*, 6(3): 318–40. *Special Issue: Rethinking Race and Class in a Time of Ethnic Nationalism and The New Imperialism* (eds) Peter McLaren and Nathalia E. Jaramillo. My thanks to Tariq Modood and Sage for permission to re-use these data, and to Peter and Nathalia for including me in such an important volume.

Foreword by Richard Delgado

You are about to encounter a wonderful, rich book with a bold, audacious premise, clear writing, and a reader-friendly structure and plot line.

In the early pages, you meet Steve, a brilliant young law student of color, social activist, and budding lawyer, and 'the Professor', an older figure who is both the young man's straight man and the author's alter ego. Stephen uses the Professor as a foil for his thoughts, and the Professor, in the manner of all academics since time immemorial, borrows the young man's ideas and expands on them.

The two outline their main points, after which the book unfolds in standard expository prose, touching on each of the matters the two protagonists agreed needed documentation, on the way to proving their astonishing thesis about Whiteness and power.

That premise is easily stated: White privilege and supremacy exhibit the structure of a conspiracy. Not an ordinary conspiracy, hammered out between business rivals, for example, who agree to sell their products at the same price, but a more complex hub-and-spoke variety seen in some criminal settings in which each member of the conspiracy only knows and deals with a central element or figure. For Gillborn, that central figure is Whiteness, and the individual spokes are powerful Whites in the educational establishment and elsewhere.

Gillborn shows how the conspiracy works and traces its constituent elements, including standardized high-stakes testing, biological theories of racial inferiority, racist disciplinary procedures in schools, and, in society at large, whipped-up fear of immigrants, police profiling, the myth of model minorities, and a perverse form of free speech that tolerates racial hatemongering while deeming the speech of minority defenders deranged and irresponsible.

On the way to making its point about the British educational establishment, the book introduces a movement, Critical Race Theory, that may be new to some of Gillborn's readers. Critical Race Theory began as a movement in US legal circles in the late 1970s, when a number of progressive lawyers and legal scholars realized that the heady gains of the 1960s civil rights movement had stalled and were, in some cases, being rolled back. New approaches were necessary to cope with the more subtle forms of institutional and unconscious racism that were emerging and a public newly indifferent ('colour blind') to matters of race.

After a gestation period in the law, Critical Race Theory took hold in a number of other fields, including sociology and education, where scholars used its ideas to analyze hierarchy in the schools, high-stakes testing, school discipline, migrant and bilingual education, affirmative action, and the debate over the Western canon. Critical race theorists in schools of education teach courses and seminars in this discipline, supervise PhD students, and hold conferences and panels on how to use its precepts in their work. The burgeoning Critical-Race-Theory-in-education literature now includes dozens of articles, two anthologies, and half a dozen books.

With the present volume, the movements jumps the Atlantic and lands in Great Britain, where it seemingly has found fertile ground. Although the history of the two countries differs in some respects (for example, the USA applied racial ideas early in its history to justify slavery and, later, empire; Great Britain, first to justify empire and only later as a basis for domestic stratification), the two are beginning to confront very similar racial problems. The citizenry of both countries are largely in denial about the extent of their racial problems. Both are fearful of foreigners, especially ones of color. Both use many of the same rationalizations, including the insistence that they are colour blind.

Both countries guard, but hide, White privilege and use hate speech as an instrument of social control, justifying it by invocation of principle ('I may disagree with what you say, but...'). They both exhibit locked-in racism that, once in place, maintains itself effortlessly though a thousand mechanisms, rules, and habits. Each operates an educational system that, year after year, turns out under-prepared students of color, yet deems itself to have offered a fair opportunity to all.

After chapters devoted to inequality and the racial gap, official policy and rhetoric, testing, the Stephen Lawrence case, model minorities, and White privilege and normativity, the two characters re-emerge from the measured, endnoted prose in which the book unfolds to greet each other and conclude their conversation. The younger man observes that a pessimistic philosophy need not be enervating; indeed may inspire one to try even harder. The older man agrees, positing that merely because a concerted practice is hard to crack, it highlights the need for a more strenuous form of resistance.

The two part on the best of terms. The book ends with the reader wishing for more.

1 Introduction

If you have a commitment to educational equality, and a society where people have equal chances of success regardless of their skin tone or ethnic background, this book's detailed research-based accounts of systematic and deep rooted racism will sadden and shock you. Alternatively, perhaps you believe that race issues are a peripheral matter, much less pressing than class or gender, or that things are gradually improving as policy makes incremental step-by-step improvements; if so, this book offers a direct challenge by arguing that race inequality should be placed centre-stage as a fundamental axis of oppression.

Most of the arguments in the book are constructed on the basis of research in England, but many of the key strands in the analysis are just as applicable to the education systems in the US, Canada, Europe and Australasia – where I have benefited from the collegiality and critical support of many friends and colleagues. The book is the first major study to examine the English education system[1] using an approach known as Critical Race Theory (CRT). To date, CRT has remained an almost exclusively North American approach but there is no reason why the conceptual tools and techniques developed by critical race scholars elsewhere cannot be adopted and refined through their application in other nation states. The next chapter offers a detailed guide to CRT but, for those readers who prefer to skip from one part of the book to another, there are a few points that I should make clear at the outset.

First, every chapter develops a key set of arguments that can stand in isolation but which build into a damning critique of the racist nature of the education system. Although they are best appreciated as a whole, the chapters are written to be relatively self-contained with plenty of cross-referencing to other parts of the book that complement the analysis. Judicious use of the index should enable you to find anything you need straight away and I use subheadings throughout the text to signal the topics under debate and new issues as they arise. Most chapters begin with a clear indication of the issues that they address and conclude by summarizing their main findings.

In addition, this introduction ends with a clear chapter-by-chapter guide to what is in store, although the format (a discussion between invented characters) will be unfamiliar to many readers. This is one of several aspects of the book that will be new to people who have not encountered CRT before. At certain points, for example, I use imaginary dialogues, storytelling and other narrative techniques to develop new lines of analysis. As I explain in greater detail later in this introduction, these are a key part of the CRT armoury, but they are also familiar to writers working in fields such as poststructuralist Feminism.

At no stage is there a substantive statement about research on racism and inequality that is not backed by referenced studies and/or empirical evidence. Critical race scholars use storytelling to throw issues into relief but they do not invent the realities of racism that their stories explore. The evidence is laid out in the body of each chapter and references are cited through the use of endnotes rather than the usual Harvard style of academic citation, which constantly breaks up text by inserting authors' names and publication dates. Various tables and illustrations are presented as 'exhibits', as I build my case in each chapter.

The language of race and racism

In this study I draw on a great deal of research from the US (where CRT originates) and the UK (where most of my work is based). This can cause confusion because similar terms have dramatically different meanings on either side of the North Atlantic.[2] For example, in the US 'people of color' is generally accepted as an appropriate collective term for people who would probably be termed 'Black and Minority Ethnic' (BME) in the UK, where the word 'coloured' is seen as an out-dated and derogatory hangover from the late 1950s and 1960s. In many instances I use the term 'minoritized' as a general descriptor. I first heard this term at a Canadian conference and it is useful in highlighting the constructed nature of the minority/majority relations that are taken for granted in many societies.[3] For example, globally speaking White people are very much a demographic minority but they are most certainly in a majority position when it comes to wealth and power.

The word 'Black' has a similarly complex history. Some activists and academics use the term collectively to include *all* minoritized groups that are subject to White racism. Although this can have a politically useful unifying purpose, in research this approach can obscure important social, historical, cultural and economic differences between groups. In the US the term is usually taken to denote people of African American ethnic heritage; in the UK it usually describes those who would identify their family origins in Black Africa and/or the Caribbean: this is how I use the term in this book.

Part of the reason for the ever-changing series of labels that are used in this field is the nature of the issues that are at stake. Language not only describes an issue, it helps to define the issue: it can make certain understandings seem natural and commonsensical, while others are presented as outrageous or unworkable. The role of discourse is central to many of the arguments in this book but, before moving on, it is useful to briefly clarify two more key terms.

Race

It is widely accepted that there is no such thing as separate human races in the traditional biological sense.[4] Those characteristics that are usually taken to denote 'racial' phenomena (especially physical markers such as skin tone) are assigned different meanings in particular historical and social contexts. Far from being a fixed and natural system of genetic difference, 'race' is a system of socially constructed and enforced categories that are constantly recreated and modified through human interaction. In the US, for example, any physical marker of African American ancestry is usually taken as sufficient to identify a person as 'Black'; that same person, however, could board a flight to Brazil and, on disembarking, would find that they were viewed very differently by most Brazilians because the conventional categories in that society are markedly different to the 'commonsense' assumptions in North America.

This is a fairly simple point that the majority of scientists (in the natural- and social sciences) now accept. It is, however, necessary to make this point very clearly because there are still powerful voices that repeat the falsehood of separate, fixed and deterministic human races. Politicians on the extreme right trade in these beliefs but so too do those writers on intelligence and 'cognitive abilities' who would have you believe that there is something in our genes that determines significant differences in intellectual, sporting and criminal behaviour.[5]

Racism/s

Racism is a highly contested term and one that is almost always controversial. To be labelled a 'racist' is generally a highly derogatory slur and this can be an advantage for those of us working for greater race equality because we begin from a position where most people will be broadly sympathetic to our aims (at least in public). However, the force of the label can also be a hindrance: racism is such a harsh word that some people feel uneasy about using it. In addition, the term is so forceful that most people react very defensively against any suggestion that they might possibly be involved in actions or processes that could conceivably be termed as 'racist'. Such reactions show a failure (sometimes a refusal) to engage with the different ways in which racism can operate. There are multiple forms of racism: it is not unusual to see writers talking about racism*s* in the plural.[6]

Traditionally, racism has often been viewed as involving two key characteristics: a belief in the existence of discrete human races and the idea that those 'races' are hierarchically ordered. Although these views are by no means extinct, it is rare to hear them espoused directly in mainstream politics or educational discussions. This is, therefore, an extremely limited understanding of racism and it has been argued that there are other forms of racism that are both more subtle and more common.

In particular, it is now common in the UK to hear talk of institutional and/or unintended racism. The term 'institutional racism' has been around for a long time. It was originally used to draw attention to the ways in which US society is saturated with assumptions and practices that have the routine effect of privileging White people over minorities.[7] A great deal of this book explores this form of racism and it is important to state clearly that such forms can operate regardless of people's conscious intentions. In this way, even well-intentioned actions can be said to have racist consequences if they unfairly discriminate against members of one or more minoritized groups. Every chapter in the book looks at the operation of racism in one form or another.

Coincidence or conspiracy?

This book's title proposes a question. Is racism in education a form of conspiracy? To some readers this may seem immediately ridiculous and, I must admit, my initial work with the notion of conspiracy did not interrogate the term.[8] As I discussed the idea with colleagues and conference-goers around the world, however, I started to rethink my approach.[9] Buoyed by the freedom of my first sabbatical in a decade, and as a means of exploring the pros and cons of the idea, I drafted an imaginary discussion between two scholars. Although struck by the force of such writing when authored by others, I had never seen the need myself nor felt able to adopt such a style. As I bounced ideas between my imaginary characters, however, I appreciated the usefulness of the approach as a means of exploring difficult and contradictory issues.

I use these fictional characters in this introduction and for the conclusion where, I hope, they will help bring life to some real-world dilemmas. The first episode, or chronicle, introduces the key issues that shape the book, especially concerning the non-accidental nature of racism as a structure of domination patterned historically, culturally, socially and economically. It also sets out some initial problems with the notion of conspiracy as a way of highlighting the agency of White people in actively (although not always knowingly) constructing and legitimating racist inequalities in education. Finally, the characters describe the contents of each of the coming chapters. The characters are reunited in the book's conclusion where they identify the nature of the conspiracy that they are trying to understand and oppose.

Chronicles and characters: real issues in imaginary lives

The use of imagined characters to debate issues and exemplify real-world problems has become a hallmark of some of the best legal CRT. Derrick Bell, the visionary African American scholar/activist, coined the term 'chronicle' for this approach when he used it as the format for one of the most prestigious invitations that can be offered to a legal scholar, authoring the foreword to the annual Supreme Court issue of the *Harvard Law Review*.[10] The approach has been developed further by numerous critical race scholars, perhaps most brilliantly by Richard Delgado and Patricia Williams.[11] Both Bell and Delgado frequently return to a small number of characters, usually a law professor (men of color combining legal scholarship and civil rights activism) and a younger alter-ego: Geneva Crenshaw is the star of Bell's works, while her half-brother Rodrigo is Delgado's foil.[12] Gloria Ladson-Billings has recently explored the medium in her educational research[13] and similar imaginative writing is becoming more familiar in UK educational scholarship, especially among feminist authors.[14]

Taking my inspiration from the two men most responsible for the development of CRT, it seems fitting that my two characters are also a professor and a younger scholar/activist. *The Professor* is a 50-something White academic who works on race inequalities in education. Originally from a working-class background in the English Midlands, he was one of the first cohort of students in his city to attend a non-selective comprehensive school. *Stephen Freeman* was born on 12 September 1977 and named for Steve Biko, who died that day at the hands of White racists.[15] Also a working-class product of a comprehensive school, Steve is a Black Londoner who left school with minimal qualifications but worked hard through night school and completed an Open University degree.[16] Steve and the Professor first met through an antiracist campaign that the younger man was organizing and the two soon became firm friends. Despite the Professor's encouragement, Steve chose not to pursue doctoral research because of his frustration with Ivory Tower academia and especially with the posturing of some self-proclaimed radical academics. He is currently working for a major labour trade union while studying law part-time.

Unlike Sara Delamont, whose principal fictional characters (Eowyn and Sophonisba) 'are two aspects of my scholarly identity',[17] the Professor and Steve are not me. They share some of my thoughts, fears and experiences but they are also free to say and think things that I would not necessarily support and to do things that are outside my experience.[18] Hence, both characters draw heavily on the ideas and experiences of friends, colleagues, students and comrades in the antiracist struggle.

Chronicle I: Racism, non-accidents and conspiracies

'Steve! What are *you* doing here?'

The Professor's face lit up as he recognized his young friend across the crowded room. The older man had just given a public lecture and, until he spied Steve, was deep in conversation with a group of audience members who had come to the lectern to informally discuss the ideas he had set out.

Steve knew the Professor would be some time yet and, aware that his voice wouldn't carry across the melee of animated discussion in the lecture theatre, he silently mouthed 'I'll – wait – here' and indicated a space by the exit.

The older man nodded and returned to the discussion with a new sense of purpose.

An hour later the two friends emerged from the university building onto the London street. The lunchtime lecture series was part of the university's outreach programme, offering the public a chance to hear and debate new ideas in education. The Professor had drawn a larger audience than was usual for such events and the discussions had kept him back so long that the early evening rush hour was already underway.

'I thought you had exams this week and next: what are you doing here?' the Professor asked.

Steve smiled and waited for a break in the traffic before the two men made a dash for the other side of the road and headed away from the university.

'I've got a couple days between papers,' Steve began, 'and I saw your lecture mentioned online. So I thought I'd see whether I could grab some R&R away from the law books.'

'It's great to see you. I was hoping to get a chance to talk to you about how my new book's shaping up – there are a few ideas I'd like your thoughts on – but I didn't want to intrude on your studies.'

'No problem,' Steve laughed. 'It's a relief to get away from the textbooks for once. You remember I said that law appealed to me so much because it's *real*: it gives me a chance to get to grips with real problems and make a difference?'

'Yeah.' The older man nodded, remembering his attempts a couple of years earlier to talk Steve into post-doctoral work in education.

'Well, all of that disappears when there's a test to take', Steve announced. 'Law exams are just as boring as the sociology exams at the OU.'

'Sociology *boring*?' The Professor feigned disgust but stopped in his tracks. The two men gazed up at the building in front of them – the imposing Portland stone structure of Senate House, the administrative centre of London University. The tower loomed more than 200 feet into the air, its myriad windows reflecting the setting sun in a dazzling show that for once made the structure less imposing than usual. It is rumoured that Hitler selected the building as his London headquarters in the event of an invasion. Fortunately, neither Hitler nor Oswald Mosley (the British fascist leader also favoured the building) had the opportunity to move in. Now, with the countless windows reflecting the sun, the tower looked almost magical.

'Nice,' Steve commented with deliberate understatement.

'Nineteen eighty-four,' said the Professor. Then, seeing Steve's puzzled expression, he explained, 'During the war the building was used by the Ministry of Information – the propaganda department. It's said to have been the model for Orwell's "Ministry of Truth": you know, the fictional government department that peddled lies like "War is Peace"?'[19]

'Doesn't sound very fictional to me,' Steve observed. 'Which reminds me – I want to ask you a question about the lecture you just gave. I think I'm missing something.'

The Professor fixed his friend with a knowing stare and smiled. 'That probably means you think *I'm* missing something? Right?'

Steve smiled and indicated that they should take a left at the next street corner. 'I'll make you a deal, Prof: I'll show you one of George Orwell's favourite drinking spots if you answer a couple of questions.'

The non-accidental nature of race inequality

'First, I have to say that I really enjoyed your lecture,' Steve began.

'Now I *know* I'm in trouble,' the Professor joked. 'Cut to the chase.'

Steve ignored the interruption. 'I loved the part about the non-accidental nature of racism,' he enthused. 'I hadn't heard that bit before.'

'Ha! Well I do have a new idea every now and again you know,' the Professor joked. 'I thought it was a nice way of introducing a complex set of arguments to an audience who didn't necessarily have two degrees under their belt. The more I looked at the idea, the more useful it became.'

'Well, that's what I want to talk to you about.' Steve was suddenly very serious. 'You ran through the evidence on lots of different race inequalities in education and you said they were deliberate.'

'No, I didn't,' the Professor interrupted. He knew that his friend's legal training was already shaping him into a formidable tactician in an argument and decided to be careful about how his words were recalled. 'I said they weren't an accident.'

Steve looked at him quizzically, seeking an explanation of the difference between a non-accident and a deliberate action.

'Is this pub much further?' the Professor complained. 'If we sit down we can go over my notes – they're in my bag. I'd really welcome some feedback on the ideas before I write them up.'

'It's just around the corner,' Steve assured his friend. 'So, something can be a non-accident *without* being deliberate?'

A few minutes later, inside The Dog and Duck, the Professor bought the drinks while Steve found a place to sit in the corner of the bar. The older man was amazed that he'd never seen the place before. The main seating area was only big enough to house around 20 people and the decor was an odd mix of aged timbers and antique tiles dating back to 1897. As he paid for the round the Professor noticed a sign indicating 'The George Orwell Bar' upstairs but, keen to return to the conversation with his friend, he decided to investigate later.

The Professor made his way through the early evening crowd and placed the drinks on the table. He fell into his chair with a sigh and began searching for his lecture notes in the large old leather bag that was his constant companion.

Steve took a gulp of his beer and watched in gentle amusement while the Professor flipped through the pages of his lecture. 'Ah, here we are,' the older man exclaimed: 'These patterns are not accidental: an *accident* would suggest that the outcomes were somehow unpredictable and random, but these consequences were wholly predictable.'

'*Absolutely*,' Steve agreed. 'Years ago antiracists warned that increasing the use of selection in schools would create even deeper race inequalities. Politicians claim to be interested in "evidence-informed policy".[20] We give them lots of evidence – from decades of research in the US and UK – but they still go ahead and time after time a few years later they release official statistics that prove us right.[21] And to drive home your point,' Steve continued, 'you put up a slide showing a dictionary definition.'

---

accident

Anything that happens without foresight or expectation; an unusual event, which proceeds from some unknown cause, or is an unusual effect of a known cause.

Oxford English Dictionary[22]

The Professor nodded. 'Antiracists aren't psychic; we don't have crystal balls that predict the future. Numerous research projects show that if you ask teachers – most of whom are White – to rank kids by some notion of ability or motivation, you're almost certain to get a disproportionate number of Black kids in the bottom groups.'

'Right, so it's not an accident,' Steve summarized. 'The patterns of race inequality are wholly predictable. The situation violates every aspect of that definition.' He emphasized his speech by counting off each element on a newly raised finger:

'One: it happens without foresight? *No.* We saw the inequalities coming and we warned them.

'Two: an unusual event or effect? *Hardly*: Bernard Coard highlighted this more than 30 years ago and the same thing is still being documented in study after study. The precise dynamics change but the outcomes are the same.[23]

'Three: an unknown cause? *Only unknown if you ignore the research, blindfold yourself and stick your fingers in your ears.* How many times do they need to be told that White teachers see Black kids as more likely to cause trouble than excel in class? All those countless studies show that – whatever the teachers tell themselves – White teachers tend to be systematically more controlling and have lower expectations of Black students?'[24]

'Ah, but you're missing an important element,' the Professor interjected. 'You said it yourself: *whatever the teachers tell themselves.* I'm convinced that the vast majority of White teachers genuinely don't know they're doing this.'

'But, Professor,' Steve protested, 'the policymakers *must* know what they're doing when they ignore the warnings of antiracists. And teachers must know what's happening when they look at their school's exam results and year after year the same groups of kids are at the bottom – Black kids (boys *and* girls),[25] and Pakistani and Bangladeshi kids.'

'That's what I meant when I said it's not a conspiracy,' the Professor tried to explain.

'Okay,' Steve interrupted, 'I'll get the next round of drinks while you find that part of the lecture, because *that's* what was worrying me.'

Racism, ignorance and the 'motivated inattention' of White people

The Professor found the relevant page of his notes long before Steve managed to fight his way through the crowds and get served. To pass the time waiting, he flicked through a bar menu and read that the pub boasted John Constable, Dante Gabriel Rossetti and Madonna among its past and present customers. George Orwell was such a fixture at one time that they named the upstairs bar for him. The Professor wondered whether any of Orwell's great works had taken shape in the room that, even now, was bursting at the seams with the kind of diversity of cultures, class background, fashion and accent that only Soho can blend into a seamless mass of uncomfortable souls, all feeling too tightly packed in but having too good a time to consider going anywhere else.

'Sorry for the delay,' Steve apologized as he finally arrived with the drinks. 'You should see this place on Friday night.'

'Cheers!' The Professor raised his glass. 'If Rossetti can put up with it, who are we to complain?'

'Rossetti? Is he Chelsea's new winger?' Steve joked as he raised his glass, but before the conversation was fatally mauled by the intrusion of football, he swiftly returned to his earlier thread. 'So, you were saying it's not a conspiracy?'

The Professor looked at his notes: 'I said, "I want to make it clear that I don't think this is a deliberate conspiracy. It's not a conspiracy; it's *worse* than that!"'[26]

'That's the bit that threw me,' Steve confessed. 'I was chatting with some people afterwards and they asked me what that meant and the more I tried to explain, the more confused I became.'

The Professor was disappointed – he thought it was quite a striking line. 'I was trying to highlight how deeply rooted *Whiteness* is throughout the education system. What I mean is that it's not as simple as a conspiracy. If race inequality was the result of a few Whites getting together and deciding to stick it to Black kids we could expose the plot and do away with it. But there is no conscious plot; there doesn't need to be because White people learn to act and think in ways that have *exactly* the same outcomes, but they do it almost automatically.'

Steve put his glass down but chewed his bottom lip, looking pensive. The Professor continued, 'There's been an explosion of writing about Whiteness but lots of it lacks any critical edge at all.'

Steve nodded. 'I was talking to some people at law school about it and they just had no conception of what I was talking about. One guy thought I was saying that White people are an ethnic group with a separate culture.'

'Yes, it's very difficult,' the Professor agreed, 'to explain that White*ness* relates to the ways of knowing and being, the assumptions and actions that characterize White people in this racist society. Were *they* White?'

'Yes,' Steve nodded. 'I find that White people are the only ones who have a hard time imaging that Whites are anything other than *normal* people: it's only *Other* people who have ethnicity or race. Present company excepted.' He winked at the Professor, who accepted the compliment with a smile.

'So what did you do?' the Professor asked.

'I told them about Peggy McIntosh's paper, which lists all the ways that White people gain from being White on a moment-by-moment basis and is about the constant unrecognized privileges that they experience every single day.' [27]

'Any luck?' the Professor queried.

'Not much,' Steve laughed. 'Even White middle-class law students have a hard time thinking of themselves as *privileged*.'

'I know what you mean,' the Professor agreed, 'and there's the additional problem with how some of the White privilege literature has developed. As if White people gain all these advantages but remain innocent.'

'Zeus Leonardo has a great line for that,' Steve observed. 'He says that privilege "conjures up images of domination happening behind the backs of whites, rather than on the backs of people of color".'[28]

'I use Zeus's work in a book outline I'm putting together,' the Professor revealed. 'He's absolutely right to say the term "privilege" doesn't do justice to the real scope and deep effects of White power. Zeus is very clear that he's talking about White racial domination – *White Supremacy*.'

'Now *there's* a term that raised a few eyebrows!' Steve laughed.

The Professor smiled, remembering the conference when he first described the English education system as based on White Supremacy: he was met with total silence and later told by a White colleague that he must have 'gone mad'.[29]

'Do you have a note of that quote you used from Charles Mills?' Steve asked, pulling the Professor back from one of his stranger conference memories. 'You know, the one about White people and deception?'

The Professor delved into the chasm of his bag and fished out some background notes to the lecture. 'Is this the one? Mills says that White Supremacy is characterized by "pervasive patterns of not seeing and not knowing – structured white ignorance, motivated inattention, self-deception, historical amnesia, and moral rationalization".'[30]

Steve nodded silently as he stared at his drink and slowly repeated the quotation:

'Pervasive patterns of not seeing and not knowing …
   structured White ignorance …
      motivated inattention …
         self-deception …
            historical amnesia …
               moral rationalization.'

Steve looked at the Professor. 'And you think it's *not* a conspiracy?'

If it looks, feels and operates like a conspiracy…

There was a moment's pause while the two men looked at each other.

A barman reached across the table to collect their empty glasses and his intrusion broke the silence. 'One of the people who spoke to me after the lecture raised the same point,' the Professor began. 'They said, "If race inequality isn't an accident, doesn't that mean that it's deliberate?" I explained that it's not an either/or question. It's not that race inequality is *either* a complete accident *or* a deliberate conspiracy. I'm not suggesting that policymakers and teachers sit around at night trying to work out new ways of blaming Black kids for their own failure and ensuring the continuation of the Black/White achievement gap. What I'm trying to do is highlight the fact that these inequalities are structurally and culturally patterned.' The Professor was passionate about this and his voice grew a little angry. 'Black kids don't just *happen* to be expelled more than every other ethnic group, they don't just *happen* to be over-represented in the lowest ranked teaching groups, and they don't just *happen* to be the kids most likely to be entered for examinations where the highest pass grades are simply not allowed.'[31]

The Professor drew a deep breath, then continued more quietly. 'These patterns reflect *centuries* of White racist domination. They reflect and strengthen assumptions that White people learn from the cradle and are topped up every time they switch on a TV, read a newspaper or watch a movie.[32] It's by no means an accident. But that doesn't mean it's a deliberate plot.'

Steve shifted in his seat. 'I'm sorry but it still feels like we're missing something,' he said. 'It's more of a feeling than a clearly worked out idea. I mean it *looks* like a conspiracy, it *feels* like a conspiracy and it has the *effects* of a conspiracy. Doesn't it?'

'Yes and no,' the Professor replied. 'You see, a conspiracy sounds like a diabolical plot – you know, a group of people meeting secretly in smoke-filled rooms. Whiteness doesn't work like that. You remember the quote from Delgado and Stefancic about critical race theory being concerned with "business-as-usual" forms of racism?[33] The racism that is so accepted and normalized that merely to name it as racism seems nonsensical to most Whites?'

'Yes, I see that.' Steve was still struggling to find the right way to express his disquiet. 'But a conspiracy doesn't *have* to take that form, does it?'

'Doesn't it?' The Professor was genuinely puzzled. 'I'd say that a conspiracy denotes a conscious decision between people to do harm to others, wouldn't you? It means there's a plot.'

'Maybe *plot* is the wrong word,' Steve offered. 'A plot definitely sounds like one of those crazy blogs on the net. You know, *the aliens are among us.*'

'Right,' the Professor agreed.

'But the first part of what you just said, that sounds exactly right.'

'Wha – the first part of what?' The Professor was losing track of the argument as Steve tried to pull his thoughts together. The two men were by now the source of disgruntled looks from several customers resentful at precious seating being taken by people without a drink in hand. Unaware or unconcerned, the two carried on their discussion.

'You said a conspiracy was doing harm,' Steve offered.

'No,' the Professor corrected, 'I said it was a *conscious* decision between people to do harm.'

'Well, that's what the evidence suggests.' Steve was suddenly elated: the idea was coming together. 'We talked earlier about how policymakers use different terms and arguments but, regardless of the superficial changes, decade after decade they keep on generating policies that blame the victims and encourage schools to do things that they *know* will harm Black kids.[34] So they *know* what they are doing.' Steve sounded triumphant. He, at least, was convinced.

'But,' the Professor added, 'they don't *set out* to hurt Black kids. There's no evidence that any of these policies are deliberately designed to sustain or worsen race inequality.'

'Well, no,' Steve countered, 'but you can't prove it *isn't* deliberate and, in any case, that isn't the point. We know for sure that they don't worry about it when they disregard antiracists' warnings. Do you think they'd overlook a threat to middle-class White interests?'

There was silence while the Professor worked through the arguments again in his head. Steve watched him expectantly. He wasn't sure where this was going but he was relieved that the Professor now seemed to share some of his misgiving.

'Alright.' The Professor began thinking out loud. 'So even if policymakers don't set out to create race inequality they don't care if it happens as a result of their policies?'

'Yes, it's a conspiracy of ... of ...' Steve searched for the right word. 'A conspiracy of *omission*.'

'No,' the Professor corrected, 'it's *worse* than that.'

'What?' Now it was Steve's turn to be confused.

'A conspiracy of omission suggests that they forgot to ask the question,' the Professor explained, 'as if they didn't think about race and so they were unprepared for the racist outcomes. But they knew about the likely outcomes – or at least they had plenty of people *warning* them. Activists, parents' groups, academics – I even know of civil servants who made similar warnings behind the scenes at quite senior levels. Policymakers could have taken those warnings seriously and changed the policies before they were announced – no need to lose face with the White public and media.'

Steve sighed as he searched for a better term. 'Errr ... okay, a conspiracy of apathy. They just don't care.'

The Professor looked pained. 'But apathy sounds too passive. Remember Zeus Leonardo's critique of White privilege: don't lose sight of agency. This is harm caused by the actions of policymakers and practitioners.'

'Okay, I guess you were right after all,' Steve offered. 'Maybe conspiracy is the wrong word.'

'I'm not so sure.' The Professor looked Steve square in the eye: he was deadly serious.

Chapter by chapter

As the friends left The Dog and Duck and headed through the last of the rush hour traffic towards the nearest tube station, the Professor suggested a way through their conceptual deadlock.

'Let's think about the conspiracy angle some more and come back to it,' the Professor offered. 'You've got exams to worry about and I've got a book outline to finish. Let's meet up at the Muslim education conference next month? I assume you're planning to attend?'

'Perfect,' Steve agreed. 'Now tell me about this new book of yours: how's it shaping up?'

As the two men picked their way through the crowds, the Professor began to set out his ideas: 'Well, my aim is to write the first thorough analysis of the English education system using Critical Race Theory. I think CRT offers a powerful set of tools that antiracists everywhere should be refining and using.'

'That won't go down well,' Steve laughed. 'The US isn't very popular right now and academics are especially sensitive to accusations of jumping on the latest bandwagon. Work from the States has even been called "cultural imperialism".[35] You know they'd much sooner be citing dead White men.'[36]

'Well, I've never been known for my fashion sense,' the Professor exclaimed with a laugh.

The two men crossed the street to avoid a crowd that had gathered opposite them: a side road had been cordoned off and was now providing entertainment to at least a hundred sightseers, who were jostling to get to the front or craning their necks to catch a glimpse of the parked vehicles and flashing lights further down the road. Most locals just walked by. Steve looked at the crowds. 'I wonder what they think they're looking at: movie set or global terrorism?' [37]

'When you watch TV it's sometimes hard to tell the difference: every one-dimensional bad guy is suddenly from the Middle East,' the Professor observed, then continued to describe how he saw the chapters of his book developing.

Critical Race Theory

'First of all I'll have to explain what Critical Race Theory is. Although it's been around for a few decades, it started in legal studies and has only really been a presence in US education for a decade.'

'And it's still very much seen as a radical minority perspective,' Steve interjected. 'I've yet to see it listed in textbooks along with Marxism or Feminism as a major school of thought – though it deserves the same status.'

'I'll need to explain its origins; discuss the key concepts – especially the central focus on racism,' the Professor continued. 'I don't think there's anything in CRT that a serious antiracist would have a problem with but the central focus on race and racism will be pretty challenging for most readers.'

'You'll need to show that it's still developing,' Steve prompted. 'I hate those theory-by-numbers guides where all the complexity, subtlety and uncertainty is lost.'

'Steady on, I do have a word limit you know,' the Professor joked. 'But yes, I'll try to explain that CRT isn't a closed and finished doctrine, it's very much alive and changing. I'll look at the issue of "intersectionality"; how CRT views the connections between race and other forms of exclusion, especially class.'

'That's vital,' Steve agreed. 'Every time I try to focus a discussion on race and racism, the first thing I hear is, "What about class?"'

'I know what you mean.' The Professor nodded. 'People often misrepresent CRT as if it were saying that racism is the *only* thing we need to worry about. The truth is that the best critical race theorists are passionate about other things too – especially classism and sexism, but they refuse to have race sidelined as a kind of afterthought.'

'You know,' Steve commented, 'it never fails to amaze me how quickly you White folk bridle against being treated as a race group. White people do it all the time to others – they don't flinch when they hear about research on Black kids, or Muslims, but the moment someone says something critical about "Whites" the whole world starts screaming about class and gender and every other kind of division they can think of.'

'Not *all* of us,' the Professor corrected with a smile.

'True,' Steve laughed. 'It sounds like a sensible place to start, but won't most people skip that chapter? *Theory* sounds so boring.'

'They might but I hope they'll look at it. CRT's so much more direct than most approaches. I plan to use the Jean Charles de Menezes case to show racism is a constant presence that can have literally murderous consequences.'

Steve shook his head. 'I still can't believe that an innocent man can be shot dead on a commuter train and no-one – *no-one* – is prosecuted. Instead, there's talk of handing out medals!'

The Professor nodded. 'I'm afraid that the War on Terror highlights Whiteness at its most dangerous. It's a theme that will keep re-emerging throughout the book.'

'Sounds like a powerful start,' Steve smiled. 'What's next?'

Inequality, inequality, inequality

'Do you know that if past trends continue, the Black/White achievement gap will *never* close?' the Professor asked his friend.

Steve stopped in his tracks and narrowly avoided being bumped by strangers hurrying by. '*Never*? That's a pretty big statement, Prof. You got the numbers to back it up?'

'I'm afraid so,' the Professor replied. 'I've been looking at how the Black/White gap has fluctuated over the last 15 years or so. Unless there is a massive and persistent change in the relative improvements of the different groups, unlike anything we've seen before, there will *always* be a significant inequality of achievement. It's a case of what Daria Roithmayr calls *locked-in inequality*: the inequalities are so big that they won't close without serious dedicated action that foregrounds race – and that's not happening anytime soon.'[38]

'But I keep seeing news stories that say the main under-achieving group are White working-class boys and that all minorities are improving,' Steve observed.

'I'll show how the White issue is created by focusing on a small minority of the school population and that the politicians' constant references to minority improvement give a completely unrealistic spin to tiny yearly fluctuations. I call it "Gap Talk" and it's everywhere!'

'Talk of gaps will get people arguing about how you *measure* inequality. I remember that case where two people said the same statistics showed exactly opposite findings,' Steve laughed.[39]

'I'll explain that very carefully,' the Professor sighed. 'Is there any better way to hide injustice than with statistics? On the other hand, I know that many people need to see the numbers before they believe there's a problem. So I'll use a range of official stats to painstakingly lay out the key inequalities between different groups.'

The two men stopped by a fish and chip shop and exchanged knowing glances. Without further discussion they went inside, emerging a few minutes later to continue their discussion between mouthfuls of fatty fried food – oblivious to the damage to their health.

Policy

'Having documented the true extent of race inequality in English education,' the Professor continued, 'the next logical step is to ask what policymakers have been doing about it.'

'Making it worse?' Steve offered.

'Pretty much,' his companion agreed. 'But, of course, they've done it in a variety of ways. The key terms keep changing and there is a succession of small projects and initiatives that they can highlight as evidence of their good-will.'

'Meanwhile, the interests of White people are always central?' Steve asked.

The Professor nodded. 'And the so-called War on Terror has provided a powerful spur to even more regressive moves. Despite ten years of a Labour government supposedly committed to social justice, we now have the head of the main equality body pronouncing that "multiculturalism" isn't a useful term and government ministers attacking Muslim women for choosing to wear the veil.'

'That's especially disgusting,' Steve snapped – almost dropping his chips. 'Tony Blair pouring out his heart about the importance of fighting sex discrimination while he supports new immigration rules that will make it harder for women to enter the country to be with their husbands. And if they ever do get in, Gordon Brown wants them to do community service!'

'Gregg Beratan calls it *transposition*,' the Professor replied. 'You re-code racism by presenting it as a concern for class- or gender equality.[40] It's a very effective technique because it splits the opposition and allows policymakers to present themselves as liberal and concerned while they actually propose measures that are more and more regressive.'

'There's a lot of it about.' Steve laughed sarcastically as he threw his empty chip wrapper in a bin. 'But it's sometimes hard to see through the official rhetoric. Despite all the attacks on the idea of multiculturalism, Labour still claim to champion diversity.'

'Yeah,' the Professor agreed. 'But there was a real change after 9/11. Policymakers retained the rhetoric but it was a kind of *cynical multiculturalism* that put a liberal veneer over moves that were really a return to the assimilationism of the past.'

'And the gloves really came off after the London bombings in 2005,' Steve added.

The Professor winced at the thought. 'That's when *aggressive majoritarianism* took hold. Terms like "integration" and "cohesion" are now used to give licence to whatever White people think is necessary.'

'How did Tony Blair put it?' Steve tried to recall the words. '"Tolerance ... makes Britain, Britain. So conform to it; or don't come here." *Very tolerant!*'

Assessment

'The next chapter asks whether educational assessments merely report inequality, in a neutral scientific fashion, or do they actually create it. It covers a lot of the things we discussed earlier: selection, setting, tiered exams, tracking and "gifted and talented" schemes.'

'That's important,' Steve noted, 'but I hope you mention the Foundation Stage Profile – you know, the new assessment for five-year-olds that took Black kids from "above average" to "below average" almost overnight. That was a national disgrace. I still can't believe that a new system can be introduced with such devastating effects and no-one in authority thinks there's a problem.'

'Don't forget that under the new system White kids suddenly became the highest achievers,' the Professor reminded his friend. 'Why would the education department question a system that confirms what they've always believed?'

'I remember when you first publicized what was happening,' Steve recalled. 'You made it the focus for a keynote lecture at a national conference[41] and someone in the audience – a man with an international reputation in the field – said that he'd never really believed the earlier data showing Black kids as the highest achievers.'

'I remember.' The older man sighed. 'Black success is literally inconceivable for some people.'

Steve shook his head in disgust.

'And what's even worse,' the Professor continued, 'is that schools are using these results more and more as if they indicate natural limits to kids' capabilities. Those results could condemn a generation of Black kids to even lower teacher expectations, justified by reference to their supposedly lower *ability*.'

'You should say something about IQ too,' Steve suggested. 'I know it sounds old fashioned but I can't believe how many people at my law school talk about ability as if it's printed on people's genes.'

'I hear the same thing in school staffrooms,' the Professor nodded. 'And you can see the same assumptions written through education policy. It's as if politicians and teachers have simply substituted the word "ability" for how people used to talk about "intelligence" in the 1940s and 1950s.'

'I remember you called it "the new eugenics"', Steve noted.

'Yes,' the Professor recalled. 'Several people have used the phrase and it accurately points to the dangers.'

The two men stopped. Having reached their tube station, neither wanted to end the conversation. 'You going home?' Steve asked.

'I thought I'd go back to the office, answer a few emails,' the Professor said with a sigh. 'I wonder what people did with themselves before there was email to worry about?'

Steve laughed and made his friend an offer: 'Tell you what. I'll walk you back on two conditions: first, you make me a cup of that disgusting instant coffee you're addicted to; and second, you let me tell you about some chapters *I* think should be in the book.'

The Stephen Lawrence case

The crowds became thinner as the two men left Soho and headed towards the university. Their conversation remained no less animated, and their words echoed off the now empty buildings that they passed.

'First,' Steve explained, 'you have to talk about the Stephen Lawrence case. I don't mean just describing it, I mean *analysing* it – focusing on the details of how the Lawrence family were fought at every turn and how, even after a public inquiry had vindicated them, Doreen Lawrence is still having to fight for justice.'

'You're right,' the Professor agreed. 'I was talking with some colleagues in the States and they'd heard about the Lawrence case and the legal changes that followed it; they assumed things were a lot better now. I had to explain that although official inquiries had agreed that institutional racism saturates the system – in schools, prisons, police stations, hospitals – very little has really changed as a result.'

Steve shook his head. 'I have White friends at law school who tell me that the Stephen Lawrence case shows how *well* the system works. They think it has removed racism in the police force and the David Bennett Inquiry has solved racism in the health service!'

'What do you tell them?' the Professor asked.

'I try to explain that those inquiries only came about because Black men were killed by White people in such disgusting circumstances that the state was forced to acknowledge it; I tell them that the bereaved families fought for years to get the inquiries; and I tell them that the reports *highlighted* the problem but that the system has dragged its feet about actually *doing* anything.' Steve took a deep breath and sounded more optimistic as he said, 'At least the Lawrence Inquiry prompted changes in the law – I think there is still hope.'

The Professor looked at his friend and broke some terrible news: 'There's always hope but even landmark victories aren't secure. I just received details of new Government proposals for a Single Equality Act,' he said. 'They want to "modernize" equality legislation: all the Lawrence gains could be swept away.'

'Send me the details,' Steve said, suddenly energized. 'We'll need to protest against this.'

'I will,' the Professor agreed as the two men entered the university lobby and headed for the elevator. 'But I'm afraid it's following a familiar pattern. Derrick Bell has written about "contradiction-closing cases": individual cases where the façade of a colour-blind world is ripped to sheds and so policymakers are forced to take action. On the surface things appear to be changing but actually the changes are slow, piecemeal and sometimes non-existent.'

Steve nodded. 'We know that the education system has been among the least active of all the public institutions covered by the post-Lawrence laws.'[42]

'Yes,' the Professor continued, 'and once the heat has died down, the changes that have been won come under fire. The new proposals would let schools decide which equality measures are relevant to their circumstances and how much effort it's worth expending on them.'

Steve looked at him in disbelief.

Model minorities

As the two friends exited the elevator and headed down the darkened corridor the younger man smiled at his mentor. 'I know you'll hate this, but you should write about model minority stereotypes.' The Professor rolled his eyes but Steve continued, 'Every single time I'm involved in a protest against racism the first question I'm asked by the media is, "How come Indians and Chinese do so well if racism is as common as you say?"'

As he unlocked his door the Professor agreed. 'I get the same thing at conference after conference.' He threw his bag across the room, where it landed perfectly against his desk in its usual place, and he moved to turn on the kettle. 'I try to point out that White people have always had different stereotypes about different minoritized groups and that those stereotypes work in different ways in different contexts. Racism isn't as simple as White people think.'

Steve gave a look that seemed to say 'Tell me about it'.

The Professor stared at the kettle, willing it to boil. 'I just get so tired of the same question over and over again.'

'That's why you should address it directly,' Steve said as he sat on one of the two chairs next to a small coffee table entirely covered in papers and computer disks. 'You should look at the research evidence about Indian and Chinese kids. Point out the complexity of their situation. They do well in tests but there's a growing amount of research that shows they have a very difficult position in terms of urban youth culture and the school playground.'

'Sorry about the mess,' the Professor said as he poured the promised cup of coffee. 'I think you're right: there are serious problems if we look beneath the model minority façade – the image works for Whites, they get to say "Look, we're not racist" – but I'm not sure who else benefits in the long run.'

'It's a fact that Indian and Chinese students face a great deal of racism but the system assumes everything is fine because they tend to do well in exams,' Steve added.

'I'm afraid that model minorities might be a *disposable* asset,' the Professor suggested and, seeing Steve's puzzled expression, he explained. 'I remember when Montserratian kids were evacuated to the UK after a volcanic eruption in the 1990s. The news media were full of stories about how these kids from a Caribbean island were years ahead of their English classmates. The stories were very patronizing – as if it were strange that a Caribbean island could educate its children so well – and they also served as ammunition for attacks on the state-system in England. But once the kids entered the system all the usual negative stereotypes about Black kids were attached to them. They were treated disgracefully and their attainment fell through the floor. It's a tragic story and, of course, the media lost all interest them.'

Steve nodded and sipped his coffee. He looked the Professor in the eye and announced, 'This is the worst cup of coffee I've ever tasted!'

White World

Steve rose from his chair. 'I'd better be getting back. I assume you'll have a chapter on Whiteness – exploring some of the issues we discussed earlier?'

'CRT has a very rich vein of work on Whiteness,' the Professor agreed. 'It'll be useful to explore how the War on Terror reveals some deeper truths about Whiteness: how "normality" is defined by and for White people; how the terrorist threat is used to justify violence – both symbolic and real – against minoritized groups; and how the notion of "free speech" is used to silence minority voices while giving free reign to White racists.'

'Free speech?' Steve queried. 'At law school we're drilled in how free speech is essential to guarantee minority rights and expression.'

'Are you also drilled in copyright, libel and laws against incitement to commit murder? Those are all restrictions on free speech but it's only when minoritized people call for control of hate speech that suddenly we start hearing about principles and rights of expression. I'm building up a picture of how different everyday acts contribute to hate speech – say on national radio phone-ins that proclaim their democratic function on the basis of audience interaction.'

'That'll upset a lot of people,' Steve warned.

'Exposing how Whiteness operates is one of the most important aspects of the book,' the Professor explained. 'Cheryl Harris's work on Whiteness as a property right is very useful. She shows how one of the key aspects of Whiteness is the *absolute right to exclude*.[43] And you can see it on a day-to-day basis in how White people act: from policymakers to phone-in contributors, White people feel free to define minoritized people as untrustworthy, emotional and irrational.'

'Whereas Whites are assumed to have no axe to grind,' Steve added. 'It sounds like you have it all planned out. How on earth will you conclude such a wide-ranging book?'

The Professor smiled. 'Let's discuss it after the Muslim education conference next month?'

'Great,' Steve said as he pulled the door closed behind him. 'See you there.'

Conclusion

Steve and the Professor will return in Chapter 9, where they review the main arguments that I set out in the rest of this book and consider the nature of the racism that patterns the education system. By beginning the book with a chronicle discussion between two invented characters I have already introduced one of the features of Critical Race Theory that is most strange to readers who are unfamiliar with the approach. There is more to CRT, however, than adopting novel narrative styles. In the following chapter I set out the key elements that form critical race theory in education and explore some of the areas of controversy that set it apart from other approaches.

2 Critical Race Theory
A new approach to an old problem

> As I see it, critical race theory recognizes that revolutionizing a culture begins with the radical assessment of it.
>
> John O. Calmore[1]

Introduction

Critical Race Theory was first introduced into the field of education in the mid-1990s.[2] Interest in the approach has grown rapidly and CRT has been enthusiastically embraced by many educators, especially (but not exclusively) people of color. Predictably, CRT has attracted critical comment on both sides of the Atlantic, especially from those who feel that it gives undue attention to racism rather than class divisions.[3]

In this chapter I set out the basic elements of CRT and explore its complex and changing character. Having described its central theoretical tenets, I look at some of the key conceptual tools that CRT scholars use (including storytelling, the notion of interest convergence and the role assigned to understanding 'Whiteness' and White Supremacy). Finally, I consider areas where CRT is yet to arrive at an agreed position, including questions of intersectionality (where racism cuts across and interacts with other axes of oppression) and the vexed question of the relative importance of race and class. One of the most attractive aspects of CRT is the immediacy of its analysis, offering powerful insights into everyday issues and conflicts. I begin, therefore, by reviewing an (in)famous case in recent British history where CRT provides important ways of understanding the complex operation of race-thinking and its consequences.

'Maybe things just happen that way'

The story of Jean Charles de Menezes

At around 9.30am on 22 July 2005 Jean Charles de Menezes, a 27-year-old Brazilian national working as an electrician in London, left his apartment.[4] The son of a bricklayer, Jean Charles had previously hoped to move to the US but failed to obtain the necessary visa. Like thousands of migrants before him, he chose the UK as the next best option.[5] He had quickly picked up a working understanding of the language and was sending money home to his family. Ultimately, he planned to return to Brazil and use his savings to settle in his home state of Minas Gerais.[6]

As he left for work Jean Charles was unaware that his apartment block was being watched by police who believed that Hussain Osman was there. Mr Osman was wanted in connection with one of four failed suicide bombings that had been attempted in the city the day before.

As Jean Charles turned the corner towards his bus stop, a series of events was already underway that, within the hour, would culminate in his death at the hands of armed police and army officers.

The surveillance team watching the block was using photographs of Osman as a means of identifying the suspect if he left the building. One officer who saw Jean Charles leave reportedly said that he 'thought it would be worth someone else having a look', but there are no video tapes of the scene because at the time, the officer claims, he was busy 'relieving' himself and could not switch on the camera.[7] A leaked report later threw more light on the events and the officers' thinking: 'One of the clinching factors in the mistaken identification appears to have been the fact that some of the officers agreed Mr de Menezes [*sic*] had the "same Mongolian eyes" as one of the terror suspects.'[8]

A few streets from home Jean Charles caught the number 2 bus for a 15-minute journey to the underground train ('tube') station at Stockwell. Despite the length of the journey, no officers intercepted him and the Metropolitan Police have since refused to explain the chain of command in operation nor have they revealed what instructions, if any, were given during this time.[9] Just over a year later the officer in command of the operation was promoted to one of the most senior roles in the force.[10]

At around 10am Jean Charles left the bus and made the short walk to the train station. As he entered the station his movements were watched silently by a series of closed circuit TV cameras (common to all underground stations).

Later that day the chief of the Metropolitan Police, Britain's highest ranking police officer, would tell the news media that Jean Charles 'was challenged and refused to obey police instructions'.[11] A police press briefing also spoke of Jean Charles running from officers and wearing suspiciously heavy clothing; a possible sign of carrying hidden explosives. This story remained unchallenged in public for weeks. But the truth was quite different. A worker at the Independent Police Complaints Commission (IPCC) later recalled her horror when she learned what had actually happened inside the station:

> I thought that Jean Charles de Menezes' suspicious behaviour was the reason he was shot. Then we were given a bombshell briefing at work. We were told he hadn't vaulted over a ticket barrier and run down an escalator to escape firearms officers, and that he hadn't been wearing a bulky coat that could have concealed explosives. In fact, he had strolled into Stockwell tube wearing a denim jacket, picked up a free newspaper, then made his way down the escalator to catch his train.[12]

Carrying his free newspaper, Jean Charles boarded a train. The carriage was unusually quiet for a weekday morning. Many commuters had chosen to avoid the tube: just over two weeks ago more than 50 people had died when suicide bombers struck three tube trains and a London bus during the morning rush hour. Then, just the previous day, four identical attacks had been attempted but none of the devices had detonated properly.

As he took his seat, Jean Charles was unaware that at least three surveillance officers (all White men in plain clothes: codenamed Hotel 1, Hotel 3 and Hotel 9) were on the train with him: Hotel 3 was seated just a couple of places along from him; Hotel 9 stood by the open carriage door. According to leaked statements from the officers, between 10 and 15 seconds after Jean Charles entered the train, a group of firearms officers was seen on the platform outside. One of the officers on board the train jammed the doors open with his foot and shouted 'He's here!' and pointed at the suspect. Startled, Jean Charles stood up. Almost immediately he was knocked back onto his seat as Hotel 3 threw himself onto him, wrapping his arms around the innocent man so as to pin his arms by his sides. The officer reported hearing shots close to his left ear and then being dragged away by a colleague.[13] In less than 30 seconds a total of 11 shots were fired: Jean Charles was shot in the head seven times; another bullet passed through his shoulder; three shots missed him entirely.[14]

Almost a year later the IPCC announced that no individual officers would face a criminal prosecution. In fact, no firearms officer in Britain has *ever* been prosecuted for murder or manslaughter while on duty.[15] The officers who killed Jean Charles returned to their duties. Sir Ian Blair clung to his job as Britain's most senior police officer and responded to calls for his resignation as follows:

> I think there is a tendency in Britain at the moment to say that if something goes wrong, somebody somewhere has to be to blame. Well actually, maybe not. Maybe things just happen that way. Dreadful as they are, but things happen with good intentions.[16]

Racism, identities and theory

Critical Race Theory is a relatively new, extremely challenging perspective on the role of racism in contemporary 'Western' capitalist societies. It is not a Grand Theory in the tradition of Marxism: CRT does not seek to explain all past social history (though it does have some particular views on it) and it does not predict the future (though it warns of some possible futures if we do not act quickly enough or with sufficient energy). In this chapter I outline what CRT is and consider some of the key tools and concerns that currently occupy critical race theorists. This is not meant to be an exhaustive account; think of it as a kind of 'primer' – a conceptual map that will help lay the groundwork for the rest of this book.

CRT often uses stories and other unusual approaches as a way of throwing issues into relief and helping people think Otherwise; hence, the earlier account of Jean Charles de Menezes's death. In relating the events my purpose is not to shock

– though the murderous outcome is truly shocking; rather, I want to raise some issues that are central to CRT but which usually remain hidden from public gaze. The events show how quickly understandings of race can be turned on their head; how high the stakes are; who makes the decisions; and how quickly racist violence is normalized.

People tend to think of race as relatively fixed but the Menezes case shows how fluid race can be. Crucially, we see that these decisions are about *power*. I have discussed the shooting with people from Central and South America who are clear that Jean Charles was 'White' according to the dominant racialized perspectives in their homelands. Contemporary social theory has a lot to say about how complex and shifting people's social identities can be, but here is a case that shows just how quickly, and with what costs, identity can become fixed in the eye of aggressors: in this instance White officers who saw Jean Charles as Other, as having 'Mongolian eyes'. But equally shocking as the killing itself is how quickly powerful voices (in government, the police and the media) came to the rescue of the officers concerned.

The day after leaked documents had begun to reveal the full background to the shooting the *Daily Express*, a prominent conservative national newspaper, published a front page dominated by two photographs that depict the faces of Hussain Osman and Jean Charles de Menezes, labelled 'SUSPECT' and 'VICTIM' respectively (see Exhibit 2.1). The pictures were printed beneath the headline 'IT WAS JUST A TRAGIC MISTAKE' and separated by a subheading in underlined type: 'Why the police should NEVER face murder charges over shot Brazilian'.[17] The juxtaposition of the two photographs is highly significant. By placing the victim's picture alongside that of the suspected bomber, the images implicitly call upon the White racist stereotype that all non-Whites look alike. Indeed, one of the country's leading columnists, Richard Littlejohn, told his readers (in Britain's biggest selling daily newspaper *The Sun*) that Menezes 'bore an uncanny, unfortunate resemblance to the suspected suicide bomber'.[18] Once again the article used the same pictures of Menezes and Osman, this time placing the images together over a background picture of the wrecked train in which the majority of the '7/7' victims died.

Much of the press followed a similarly strident line, arguing that although the police had killed an innocent man, they had actually performed appropriately. A former chief of the Metropolitan Police, now a member of the House of Lords and adviser on international security to Gordon Brown (Tony Blair's successor as prime minister), described their actions as heroic and argued that far from facing possible legal action, the officers 'should get medals'.[19] Melanie Phillips, another leading columnist,[20] went still further: not only defending the actions of the police but insisting on the continued *necessity* of such a response:

> It is crucial, however, that the correct conclusions are drawn from this appalling tragedy. The first and most important point is that the police response to the threat they believed was posed at Stockwell station was correct, and indeed was the *only* action they could responsibly have taken.[21]

Source: Twomey and Pilditch (2005). Reproduced with permission.

Exhibit 2.1

The killing on the tube train was the tip of a much larger iceberg of intimidation and hate crime happening at the time. There was a 600 per cent increase in reported 'religious hate crime' in the weeks following the first London bombs and this is likely to be a significant under-estimate of the true level of harassment and violence.[22] Shekhar Bhatia, a respected South Asian journalist, has written of the widespread unexpected but deep impact on almost every 'Asian' he knows:

Even a BNP [British National Party] member spitting in my face as I interviewed him did not hurt like this. At least that is what I expected of him. My story is not unique. Friends ranging from some of Britain's biggest Asian show-business names to the bearded Muslim who runs the newspaper kiosk outside Leytonstone station tell me they have been abused, accused and shunned. The newspaper seller, who often bores me in his cockney accent about the achievements of Arsenal, cannot understand why customers who used to greet him, now choose to humiliate him, simply because he wears a religious cap and has a beard. It is a commonly known fact that none of the bombers wore religious clothing and some even tried to deflect their plans by wearing an England shirt and a New York shirt. Another Asian friend, who works for a national newspaper, has been stopped by police outside a tube station merely for looking at them.

He protested that he was not a Muslim, but they still searched his bag and made no apologies for holding him up. 'Good job, I wasn't late for work and running from the tube. I was in a state of shock all morning' he told me. Nearly every Asian I come into contact with, has a story to tell of how life has changed since 7/7 and July 21st.[23]

As you will see, these events – although shocking – are not only *intelligible* within a CRT framework, in some ways they are actually *predictable*.

Critical Race Theory: its origins and promise

> Critical Race Theorists put forward novel readings of a hidden past that disclose the flagrant shortcomings of the treacherous present in the light of unrealized – though not unrealizable – possibilities for human freedom and equality.
>
> Cornel West[24]

CRT has its roots in US legal scholarship where it began as a radical alternative to dominant perspectives, not only the conservative 'mainstream' but also the ostensibly radical tradition of *critical legal studies* which, in the words of Cornel West, '"deconstructed" liberalism, yet seldom addressed the role of deep-seated racism in American life'.[25] Frustration with the silence on racism prompted CRT scholars to foreground race and to challenge not only the foci of existing analyses, but also the methods and forms of argumentation that were considered legitimate.[26] Derrick Bell is usually credited for coining the term 'Critical Race Theory' and his writings continue to shape the field. Other foundational legal CRT scholars include Kimberlé Crenshaw, Richard Delgado, Alan Freeman, Angela Harris, Charles Lawrence, Mari Matsuda and Patricia Williams.[27] As Kimberlé Crenshaw and her colleagues observe:

> Critical Race Theory embraces a movement of left scholars, most of them scholars of color, situated in law schools, whose work challenges the ways in

which race and racial power are constructed and represented in American legal culture and, more generally, in American society as a whole.[28]

Although CRT's detractors, on both left and right, often portray it as a monolithic and dogmatic approach, the truth is very different. Not only is CRT constantly developing but it has already spawned a number of important off-shoots, each with a core of influential writers developing a distinctive approach. Examples include Latino/a Critical Race Theory (LatCrit), Queer-Crit and Critical Race Feminism.[29] These 'spin off movements' retain a constructive relationship to legal CRT and there is a mutual benefit from the dialogue that occurs.[30]

In 1995 an article by Gloria Ladson-Billings and William F. Tate, in the *Teachers College Record*, set out the first steps towards applying CRT to the field of education.[31] Both authors have subsequently developed their views[32] and a new wave of radical educators has begun to take the perspective forward in novel ways, in relation to different issues and focusing on an increasing range of minoritized groups.[33]

CRT does not offer a finished set of propositions that claim to explain all current situations and predict what will occur under a certain set of conditions; rather, it is a set of interrelated observations about the significance of racism and how it operates in contemporary Western society, especially the US. In fact, the vast majority of CRT focuses exclusively on the US. There is no reason, however, why its underlying assumptions and insights cannot be transferred usefully to other (post-) industrial societies such as the UK, Europe and Australasia. Indeed, every chapter of this book is shaped and informed by CRT. It is important, however, to recognize that CRT is very much a work in progress: CRT is neither dogmatic, exclusionary nor inflexible: 'there is no canonical set of doctrines or methodologies to which we all subscribe'.[34]

As with British antiracism, there is no single, unchanging statement of what CRT believes or suggests. William Tate captures the dynamic of CRT when he describes it as 'an iterative project of scholarship and social justice': hence, CRT is constantly developing and involves a reciprocal dialogue between scholarship and activism.[35] David Stovall argues that activism is an *essential* component of CRT that 'challenges scholars to "spend less time on abstract theorizing and more time on actual community based anti-subordination practice"'.[36]

CRT complements much of the work that critical antiracists have pursued in places like Britain and Australia but also offers an *advance* on current antiracist perspectives for a number of reasons, not least its greater clarity about the development and application of key concepts.[37] There is a series of thematic elements (perspectives and insights) that can be taken as largely representative of a distinctive CRT position; in this sense CRT is more systematic than traditional antiracist approaches, which have tended to be reactive and to shy away from systematizing an approach to theory and policy.[38]

CRT has also developed a number of more specific methodological and conceptual tools; these are often used by CRT scholars but their use is neither sufficient nor necessary to identify research as part of the CRT tradition. This distinction, between defining elements and conceptual tools, is used here as a heuristic device – a kind of shorthand – meant to help clarify thinking about the 'shape' of CRT as an approach. I have found this useful in discussions with colleagues and students, but it is by no means a fixed picture.[39] As more writers add to the tradition, and priorities alter, it is likely that certain features may change in status, or disappear, while new aspects might be added. For the time being, however, this is a useful strategy that builds on a wide range of existing approaches. For the sake of clarity, therefore, in this chapter I outline these elements and tools separately, although their use and interpretation in the literature necessarily relies on a great deal of mutual citation and application.

CRT: some defining elements

Racism

The starting point for CRT is a focus on racism; in particular, its central importance in society and its routine (often unrecognized) character. Delgado and Stefancic state:

> CRT begins with a number of basic insights. One is that racism is normal, not aberrant, in American society. Because racism is an ingrained feature of our landscape, it looks ordinary and natural to persons in the culture. Formal equal opportunity – rules and laws that insist on treating blacks and whites (for example) alike – can thus remedy only the more extreme and shocking forms of injustice, the ones that do stand out. It can do little about the business-as-usual forms of racism that people of color confront every day and that account for much misery, alienation, and despair.[40]

CRT argues that racism is 'endemic in US society, deeply ingrained legally, culturally, and even psychologically'.[41] It is vital to note that the term 'racism' is used not only in relation to crude, obvious acts of race hatred but also in relation to the more subtle and hidden operations of power that have the *effect* of disadvantaging one or more minority ethnic groups. This is a more radical approach than many liberal multiculturalists are comfortable with. Nevertheless, it is an approach that is in keeping with recent developments, not only in the academy, but also in British legal approaches to racism and race inequality.[42] This reflects the long history of antiracist struggle and the attempt to broaden the approach to examine *institutional racism* that operates through subtle, sometimes unintended processes, expectations, assumptions and practices. As Stokely Carmichael and Charles Hamilton observed decades ago, in what is widely credited as the first attempt to define the term:

> institutional racism … is less overt, far more subtle, less identifiable in terms of *specific* individuals committing the acts. But it is no less destructive of human life. [It] originates in the operation of established and respected forces in the society, and thus receives far less public condemnation.[43]

The last part of this quotation is highly significant: institutional racism 'originates in the operation of *established* and *respected* forces in the society' (emphasis added). This is vital because CRT amounts to more than a perspective on institutional racism: it involves a critical perspective on the nature of politics and society in general.

CRT's focus on racism as a central feature of contemporary society has been widely misrepresented and misunderstood, and so it is worth taking a moment to clarify a couple of points in relation to the notion of 'race'. Delgado and Stefancic argue:

> The 'social construction' thesis holds that race and races are products of social thought and relations. Not objective, inherent, or fixed, they correspond to no biological or genetic reality; rather, races are categories that society invents, manipulates, or retires when convenient.[44]

This perspective echoes the dominant position within the social sciences where most writers agree that 'race' has no objective biological meaning.[45] Nevertheless, the continued influence of race-thinking means that critics need to engage with the notion of 'social race', i.e. race as a shifting and complex social construct. Indeed, as David Mason argues, the social relationships and structural positions that explain the continued use of the term 'race' in everyday society in fact presume the existence of racism.[46] There is an extensive literature on how the meaning and use of 'race' shifts over time, including studies of how particular groups have been defined differently according to their location at certain historical and political moments, the Whitening of the Irish being the best known example.[47] Any suggestion that CRT necessarily essentializes 'race' or engages in mere 'identity politics' is, therefore, both crude and over-stated.[48]

Critique of liberalism

Although CRT uses the language of 'race', it is a thoroughly critical perspective that seeks relentlessly to get beneath the rhetoric of legal and public policy debates to expose the material racist inequities that are created and sustained behind an inclusive and progressive façade. For example, among further defining features that William Tate identifies are:

> CRT reinterprets civil rights law in light of its limitations, illustrating that laws to remedy racial inequality are often undermined before they can be fully implemented.[49]

> CRT portrays dominant legal claims of neutrality, objectivity, color blindness, and meritocracy as camouflages for the self-interest of powerful entities of society.[50]

Both of these positions are examined in subsequent parts of this book: in particular, Chapter 6 shows how the seemingly radical moves that followed the

Stephen Lawrence Inquiry have been gradually undermined and redefined in the years that followed. Chapters 4 and 5 show how policies that are presented as 'best practice' for all students, or as purely technical matters, actually serve the interests of particular groups and are predicated on an assumption that, as a group, the welfare of White students must always be assured.

These perspectives, of course, are not unique to those identifying with CRT. Indeed, as Tate notes, CRT 'borrows' from numerous traditions and is frequently characterized by a readiness to cross epistemological boundaries. This theoretical eclecticism is so strong that Tate includes it as one of his key characteristics of the approach.[51] Similarly Tara Yosso and her colleagues describe CRT as a 'transdisciplinary perspective'.[52] As Delgado and Stefancic note, the most important thing is how these various insights are brought together in new and challenging ways.[53]

Revisionist critique of civil rights laws

CRT analyses raise deeply troubling questions. Indeed, CRT is frequently misinterpreted as taking a dismissive stance on the advances achieved by the civil rights movement in the US, advances achieved at enormous human cost. This criticism, however, misreads CRT. As Kimberlé Crenshaw and her colleagues argue:

> Our opposition to traditional civil rights discourse is neither a criticism of the civil rights movement nor an attempt to diminish its significance … we draw much of our inspiration and sense of direction from that courageous, brilliantly conceived, spiritually inspired, and ultimately transformative mass action.[54]

CRT's critique of liberalism springs from its understanding of racism (as wide ranging, often hidden and commonplace) and its frustration with the inability of traditional legal discourse to address anything except the most obvious and crude versions of racism. As already noted, CRT's principal concern is with 'the business-as-usual forms of racism' that are 'normal' and ingrained in the fabric of US society.[55] CRT not only criticizes the inability of traditional legal doctrine to deal with such complex and comprehensive racism, it goes further, by viewing mainstream legal assumptions as one of the prime means by which such a critical perspective is denied legitimacy and the status quo is defended as illustrated by Crenshaw *et al.*:

> Racial justice was embraced in the American mainstream in terms that excluded radical or fundamental challenges to status quo institutional practices in American society by treating the exercise of racial power as rare and aberrational rather than as systemic and ingrained. … [This perspective] conceived racism as an intentional, albeit irrational, deviation by a conscious wrongdoer from otherwise neutral, rational, and just ways of distributing jobs, power, prestige, and wealth. … [L]iberal race reform thus served to legitimize the basic myths of American meritocracy.[56]

CRT's criticisms of meritocracy, and related notions such as objectivity and colour-blindness, are not a rejection of them in principle but a criticism of their raced effects *in practice*. It is simply and demonstrably the case that these notions, despite their apparent concern for equity and justice, currently operate as a mechanism by which particular groups are excluded from the mainstream (in relation to legal redress, employment and educational opportunities). For example, arguments about the possibility of neutrality and objectivity in social research are well rehearsed. There is neither space, nor need, to go over that ground again here; suffice it to say that debates about the standard of 'proof' required of antiracist research in the UK echo precisely the same kinds of attack that have focused on critical race scholarship in the US, where deeply conservative and regressive perspectives masquerade as a concern for 'objectivity' and 'standards of evidence'.[57] By claiming their own position as the only respectable scientific and/or rational stance, for example, traditionalists close down the possibility for critical analyses because the very terms of debate are stacked against all but the most limited and conservative viewpoints.[58]

Call to context: the importance of experiential knowledge

William Tate concludes his review of the 'defining elements' of CRT by noting that the approach 'challenges ahistoricism and insists on a contextual/historical examination of the law and a recognition of the experiential knowledge of people of color'.[59] This relates to what Richard Delgado terms the 'call to context'; an insistence on the importance of context and the detail of the lived experience of minoritized people as a defence against the colour-blind and sanitized analyses generated by universalistic discourses. In relation to the legal roots of CRT, the call to context is essential to understand the full background to any major dispute or issue. For example, even something as seemingly simple and obvious as a speeding violation might be rethought if the contextual information revealed that the speeding vehicle was an ambulance. Sociologically, of course, ethnographic and other forms of qualitative research already take for granted the need to understand the viewpoints and experiences of multiple actors as an essential step in making sense of the social world. Not because of any sentimental attachment to the 'under-dog' position (as Howard Becker is frequently assumed to have argued) but actually as a recognition that people in different social locations have different perspectives and understandings. In interview Becker explained:

> [E]very analysis of a hierarchical situation must contain explicitly or implicitly some proposition, some empirical proposition about how the subordinates view things ... they, after all, know more about certain things than the people above them. ... I systematically question as a routine matter whether the people who run any organization know anything about it. I don't say they don't, I just say it's a question ... it's not that you do that for political motives you do it for scientific ones. But it has political consequence and the political consequence is almost invariably in the direction of anti-establishment.[60]

Antiracism (in Britain and elsewhere) has long emphasized the need to build upon and respect the viewpoints and experiences of minoritized groups.[61] This approach not only adds essential data and perspective, it can offer a fundamental challenge to the 'common sense' assumptions through which so much racism operates and the mechanisms by which it is legitimized. Several scholars have written, for example, of the heated, and sometimes emotional, exchanges that occur when the silence about White racism is challenged in university classrooms.[62] The exchanges by no means guarantee an equitable outcome, but they dramatically highlight the ways in which notions of 'validity' and 'objectivity' operate in racialized ways. They also draw attention to the human scale of issues that are too often reduced to an apparently *technical* level in academic discussion. In a recent class, for example, I was exploring institutional racism and criticisms of 'Whiteness' with a large and diverse group of adult learners, most of them experienced school-teachers. After a long exchange with a White teacher, who vehemently disagreed with my interpretation of some particularly damning statistics on race inequality, a Black woman intervened to draw attention to the consequences of her White peer's apparently technical argument:

> I'm really sick and tired of sitting in class and listening to people tell me that it's not about race. My children get it. I get it every day – at school, here, in the supermarket, everywhere. How dare you sit there and tell me that I'm wrong and that *you* don't believe the statistics. Don't you believe *me*?

CRT: some conceptual and methodological tools

It is highly significant that CRT scholars have been reluctant to identify a rigid set of unchanging theoretical tenets and would rather talk of 'basic insights'[63] or 'defining elements'.[64] This reflects CRT's recognition of the changing and complex character of race/racism and its opposition in contemporary society. Nevertheless, as CRT grows, so the range and sophistication of its conceptual toolbox becomes clearer. In particular, concepts which have, in the past, been seen as definitively 'CRT' in nature, may now be viewed as tools rather than defining tenets. These are lines of analysis that often appear centrally in CRT treatments but whose presence does not necessarily signify a conscious appeal to CRT.

Storytelling and counter-storytelling

A particularly striking aspect of some CRT is the use of storytelling and counter-storytelling. Here myths, assumptions and received wisdoms can be questioned by shifting the grounds of debate or presenting analyses in ways that turn dominant assumptions on their head. Of course, auto/biography and the use of narrative have long characterized many minoritized cultures. In addition, in the European academy such approaches are already well established in feminist work, perhaps seen at its most powerful in *écriture féminine*.[65]

CRT storytelling takes many different forms, from imagined episodes, conversations and debates – often called 'chronicles' – through to fully fledged stories and book-length exercises, that develop numerous critical analyses as the characters move through both mundane and extraordinary events.[66] As Gloria Ladson-Billings has argued, these narratives are neither frivolous nor fanciful. Most CRT stories are heavily referenced, making clear the real-world truths behind the accessible style:

> CRT scholars are not making up stories – they are constructing narratives out of the historical, socio-cultural and political realities of their lives and those of people of color. The job of the chronicle is to give readers a context for understanding the way inequity manifests in policy, practice, and people's experiences.[67]

I return to the issue of storytelling and its analytic force later in this chapter in relation to Derrick Bell's story of the *Space Traders* and the current 'War on Terror'.

Interest convergence and contradiction-closing cases

Derrick Bell is generally credited with coining the concept of 'interest convergence' in a paper in the *Harvard Law Review*.[68] This notion proposes that 'white elites will tolerate or encourage racial advances for blacks only when such advances also promote white self-interest'.[69] It is a concept that has been especially important, for example, in understanding the history of Affirmative Action in the US; a policy that superficially privileges Black interests but whose principal beneficiaries (in terms of numbers benefiting from Affirmative Action hiring policies) have been White women.[70] Similarly, it has been argued that the famous *Brown* decision on the de-segregation of US public schooling – when the Supreme Court ruled against the 'separate but equal' doctrine – owed a great deal to Cold War politics and the need to protect the US's image overseas, especially as it competed with the Soviet Union for influence in Africa.[71] More recently, for example, a Supreme Court decision on Affirmative Action is widely thought to have been swayed by representations that linked the policy to national security by arguing that without Black officers (promoted via Affirmative Action) the US forces could become unmanageable.[72]

It has been argued that interest convergence offers a strategy for making further equity gains in the future, if such strides can be viewed as necessary for the long term interests of Whites. It is important to note, however, that interest convergence is not simply about a bargaining process – as if minoritized groups are in a position to negotiate with Whites on an equal footing. When changes like the *Brown* decision occur they are not gifted by a benign power; rather, they happen as the very *least* that White interests view as necessary to safeguard their position.

A related concept, which is less well known but equally powerful, is the idea of the contradiction-closing case. Again, initially coined by Derrick Bell, a contradiction-closing case is identified in those situations where an inequity becomes so visible and/or so large that the present situation threatens to become unsustainable. Bell argues that such cases 'serve as a shield against excesses in the exercise of white power, yet they bring no real change in the status of blacks'.[73]

Herein lies one of the dangers of relying on interest convergence alone as a change strategy. While landmark cases may appear to advance the cause of justice, in reality there is often foot-dragging at every stage. Meanwhile, conservative opponents re-double their efforts and overall little or nothing changes; except, as Richard Delgado notes, that the landmark case becomes a rhetorical weapon to be used against further claims in the future:

> Contradiction-closing cases ... allow business as usual to go on even more smoothly than before, because now we can point to the exceptional case and say, 'See, our system is really fair and just. See what we just did for minorities or the poor.'[74]

Once again, the *Brown* desegregation case offers a powerful example of this concept. More than half a century has passed since the *Brown* decision and yet '[t]oday more African Americans attend segregated schools than they did when *Brown v. Board of Education* was decided'.[75]

Interest convergence and the related notion of contradiction-closing cases, therefore, offer a critical perspective on those apparently exceptional instances where major advances occur in race equity nationally. These concepts help explain how such instances occur and highlight the need for vigilance in ensuring that apparent victories are not recolonized by racist forces. For an application of this idea to the UK see Chapter 6.

Critical White studies and White Supremacy

> A poor rural Mississippi 'white' man was asked by a New Orleans newspaper reporter, 'What is white?' After musing for a little while, the man responded, 'Well, I don't know a lot about that. But, I'll tell you one thing ... it's not black!'
>
> Bruce R. Hare[76]

As Rosa Hernandez Sheets has argued, focusing on White people (their sense of self, their interests and concerns) has become such a fashionable pastime within parts of the US academy that there is a danger of *Whiteness studies* colonizing and further de-radicalizing multicultural education.[77] However, the field is extremely wide and increasingly includes important scholarship that exposes the shifting and exploitative bases upon which 'Whiteness' is constructed and legitimized.[78]

Whiteness and White people

> 'Whiteness' is a racial discourse, whereas the category 'white people' represents a socially constructed identity, usually based on skin colour.
>
> Zeus Leonardo[79]

Critical scholarship on Whiteness is not an assault on White people per se; it is an assault on the socially constructed and constantly reinforced power of White iden-tifications and interests.[80] What Alastair Bonnett names *'so-called "White" people'*[81] do not necessarily reinforce Whiteness any more than heterosexual people are *necessarily* homophobic, or men are *necessarily* sexist. However, these analogies are useful because they highlight the social forces that recreate and extend the kinds of unthinking assumptions and actions which mean that most heterosexuals *are* homophobic and most men *are* sexist. It is possible for White people to take a real and active role in deconstructing Whiteness but such 'race traitors'[82] are relatively uncommon and the power of White identifications and interests is such that White antiracists must constantly interrogate their actions and locations. As Derrick Bell notes, White authors tend to receive greater rewards and recognition, even when they are repeating analyses made elsewhere by scholars of color.[83] Nevertheless, as David Stovall argues, if CRT takes seriously the importance of experiential knowledge, then White-identified people have a responsibility not only to reject their own raced privilege but to help inform critical interventions, making use of their 'insider' knowledge:

> Whites should be included in the focus on White privilege in that the respon-sibility in educating other Whites rests heavily with them. Their experiential knowledge of the construct enables them to unpack the intricate and subtle functions of White privilege and its various rationales.[84]

This focus on Whiteness is a frequent cause of alarm. In particular, it is interesting that academics – especially White ones – who are happy to talk in broad terms about other social groups become especially concerned about the dangers of homogenizing White people. Indeed, even within the ranks of those scholars who focus on race/racism, there are many who argue that it is too simplistic to use a single category of White to capture such complex relations and actions. But this misreads both the intent and practice of CRT. The emphasis in CRT is on the shared power and dominance of White interests. *All White-identified people are implicated in these relations but they are* not *all active in identical ways and they do* not *all draw similar benefits – but they* do *all benefit, whether they like it or not.*

For example, it has been argued that the existence of categories such as 'White trash' demonstrates that racialized exclusion can operate against White-identified people, especially through class cultural mechanisms.[85] But as Philip Howard notes: 'The presence of the adjective "white" serves to distinguish the people it targets from other kinds of "trash" who are implicitly assumed to be non-white.'[86]

And so, even with the most extreme forms of poverty and exclusion, Whiteness matters. CRT does not assume that all White people are the same – that would be ludicrous; but CRT does argue that all White people are implicated in White Supremacy.

White Supremacy

> Although Critical Race scholarship differs in object, argument, accent, and emphasis, it is nevertheless unified by two common interests. The first is to understand how a regime of white supremacy and its subordination of people

of color have been created and maintained … The second is a desire not merely to understand the vexed bond between law and racial power but to change it.

Kimberlé Crenshaw, Neil Gotanda, Gary Peller and Kendall Thomas [87]

Whiteness studies is a growing area but, in relation to CRT, it is the nature of the questions and analyses that are important. It is insufficient merely to state a concern with how Whiteness is organized and understood. What matters for CRT is the deeply critical and radical nature of the questioning. A popular element in a great deal of writing on Whiteness concerns the notion of 'White *privilege*' which frequently equates to an understanding of the multitude of ways in which White-identified people enjoy countless, often unrecognized, advantages in their daily lives. Peggy McIntosh states:

> I have come to see white privilege as an invisible package of unearned assets that I can count on cashing in each day, but about which I was 'meant' to remain oblivious. White privilege is like an invisible weightless knapsack of special provisions, assurances, tools, maps, guides, codebooks, passports, visas, clothes, compass, emergency gear, and blank checks.[88]

McIntosh famously listed 50 privileges that accrue from being identified as White, ranging from the ability to shop without the threat of being followed by security personnel, to the possibility of living free from harassment and the option to act however you choose without being seen as emblematic of an entire racial group. This important work has proved useful to many critical educators trying to raise the consciousness of their students but, as Zeus Leonardo argues, there has been a tendency for talk of 'privilege' to mask the structures and actions of domination that make possible, and sustain, White racial hegemony:

> [T]he theme of privilege obscures the subject of domination, or the agent of actions, because the situation is described as happening almost without the knowledge of whites. It conjures up images of domination happening behind the backs of whites, rather than on the backs of people of color. The study of white privilege begins to take on an image of domination without agents.[89]

In addition, work on Whiteness has not always retained a critical sense of reflexivity and, as Michael Apple has argued, can 'become one more excuse to recenter dominant voices' by subverting a critical analysis and substituting an argument along the lines of 'but enough about you, let me tell you about me'.[90]

It is in this sense that many critics, especially those working within CRT, talk of White *Supremacy*. In these analyses, White Supremacy is not only, nor indeed primarily, associated with relatively small and extreme political movements that openly mobilize on the basis of race hatred (important and dangerous though such groups are); rather, supremacy is seen to relate to the operation of forces that saturate the everyday mundane actions and policies that shape the world in the interests of White people. Frances Lee Ansley states:

> [By] 'white supremacy' I do not mean to allude only to the self-conscious racism of white supremacist hate groups. I refer instead to a political, economic, and cultural system in which whites overwhelmingly control power and material resources, conscious and unconscious ideas of white superiority and entitlement are widespread, and relations of white dominance and non-white subordination are daily reenacted across a broad array of institutions and social settings.[91]

Some critical race scholars argue that White Supremacy, understood in this way, is as central to CRT as the notion of capitalism is to Marxist theory and patriarchy to Feminism.[92]

The question of White power – of racial domination by White people – is central to this book: indeed, every chapter adds to the analysis of how educational inequities are shaped and legitimated by the assumptions, interests and actions of White people. It is a question that takes centre stage in Chapter 8 and, of course, offers the core focus for the question of racism operating as a conspiracy across the educational system.

CRT: continuing debates and unresolved issues

I have noted repeatedly that CRT is very much a perspective in its formative stages. Each of the key elements and concepts noted previously continues to evolve as it is applied in new situations by an array of writers who bring different experiences and preoccupations to bear. Not surprisingly, this makes for a good deal of internal debate within CRT which, for the most part, has so far escaped the kinds of self-referential and patronizing theory-wars that have distorted social science scholarship in many parts of the academy. In this section, therefore, I wish to briefly highlight some of the continuing areas of dispute and development, where CRT has yet to establish a unified position but where further analysis and work continue to advance our understanding of the creation and defence of race inequity in society.

Intersectionality

Although the word 'race' is in its title, CRT involves more than an unswerving focus on race and racism. Detractors frequently misrepresent CRT as arguing that race and racism must always be *the* key issue in any analysis but this is simply untrue. Critical race theorists often focus on how racism works with, against and through additional axes of differentiation including class, gender, sexuality and disability. This concern with 'intersectionality' is especially strong in Critical Race Feminism.[93] Indeed, Avtar Brah and Ann Phoenix argue that intersectionality itself can provide a useful focus that offers numerous advances on current single-issue thinking.[94]

The multiple and changing interactions between racism and other axes of oppression is a complex area. Hopefully, as more researchers add to the body of CRT scholarship, new aspects of intersectionality will emerge. There is a danger, however, that some writers might simply use the *idea* of intersectionality as an alternative to seriously considering some of these issues; as a kind of 'mantra' that signposts a need for further work but does not actually engage the issues.[95] The mantra-like citation of intersectionality as an excuse to dodge difficult questions is something that many scholars will recognize from conference presentations and it is a serious issue that needs to be addressed. However, it is by no means limited to CRT: several years ago, the late Barry Troyna complained of 'commatization', that is, the tendency among writers merely to list a series of issues as if, once cited, they could be ignored (disability – *comma* – gender – *comma* – age – *comma* – sexuality).[96] Indeed, CRT began as a response to the constant commatization of racism.

Race, class and Marxism

Although the engagement between CRT and Feminism has been especially productive, the relationship between CRT and class-based analyses has been somewhat more strained. Indeed, some of the most pronounced attacks on CRT in education arise from writers working from a Marxist perspective who feel that CRT pays insufficient attention to the role of class as *the* central organizing principle in capitalist societies. Antonia Darder and Rodolfo D. Torres, for example, explicitly 'acknowledge and commend' the efforts of CRT scholars.[97] However, on the very same page that they state 'Our aim is not to dismiss this important body of work' they go on to assert:

> [T]o employ alternative constructs derived from legal theory to shape arguments related to educational policy and institutional practices, although well meaning and eloquent, is like beating a dead horse. No matter how much is said, it is impossible to enliven or extend the debate on educational policy with its inherent inequalities by using the language of 'race'.[98]

In response David Stovall notes that many of the criticisms of CRT arise from over-blown descriptions that do not fairly represent the object of their criticism:

> Vital to this misinterpretation is the semantics of referencing CRT as a critique solely of 'race'. In no CRT literature is there a claim to the unanimity of race. The critique has and continues to be one of the functions of White supremacy and the complexities of race.[99]

The best CRT scholarship tries to work through the interrelations between racism and other forms of structural and ideological exclusion, including class, but a conceptual debate with Marxist orthodoxy may simply be redundant because by definition Marxists place class in a position that supersedes all other forms of exclusion.[100] Indeed, Ricky Lee Allen views contemporary academic Marxism as an exercise of White power and celebrates the growth of CRT as a long overdue advance:

Across all disciplines, white Marxists and their supporters have had a history of scrutinizing the contradictions of Blacks much more harshly than those of non-Blacks … I don't think that our focus should be on merely bridging the emergent rift between CRT- and Marxist-oriented critical pedagogists by concocting some sort of synthesis. I won't do this because I believe that this rift marks a historic and much needed shift in the racialized plate tectonics of critical pedagogy.[101]

Charles W. Mills has written extensively on the relationship between 'White Marxism and Black Radicalism':

[C]ritical race theory is far from being an adjunct to, or outgrowth of, critical class theory; in fact, it long predates it, at least in its modern Marxist form. Long before Marx was born, Africans forcibly transported to the New World were struggling desperately to understand their situation; they were raising the issues of social critique and transformation as radically as – indeed more radically than – the white European working class, who were after all beneficiaries of and accessories to the same system oppressing blacks.[102]

Mills' point is extremely powerful. Marx moved to London, the centre of the British slave trade, in 1849, just a decade after slavery was finally abolished throughout the British Empire and more than a decade before it would be abolished in US territories.[103] These simple facts make the minimal presence of race in Marx's analyses all the more damning. Rather than perpetuate circular theory-wars, therefore, the best way ahead may simply be to make use of analytical tools as and when they seem most revealing: this will not satisfy people who seek to fetishize a single concept or theory above all else but it is entirely appropriate to the tradition of CRT, which has always stressed the importance of connections to real-world struggles:

Through an awareness of intersectionality, we can better acknowledge and ground the differences among us and negotiate the means by which these differences will find expression in constructing group politics.

Kimberlé Crenshaw[104]

Arguing across conference tables is useless. For those of us who are concerned with the social justice project in education, our work will be done on the frontline with communities committed to change … neither race nor class exists as static phenomena.

David Stovall[105]

The overwhelming desire to stay connected to social action and political struggle is one of CRT's distinctive features and perhaps offers the best way forward. CRT does not claim to have all the answers but we each make choices faced with what Mills describes as 'the absence of that chimerical entity, a unifying theory of race, class, and gender oppression'.[106]

Essentialism and anti-essentialism

A question related to the issue of intersectionality concerns the appropriate level of analysis and action when it comes to group identification: to what extent should differences between and within minoritized communities be ignored for the sake of a united front? I have already commented on the development of new forms of CRT, such as Latino/a CRT and Critical Race Feminism: a key element in this process has been a rejection of the Black/White binary as sufficient basis for a general analysis of racism. Much has been written about the political struggles and experiences of African Americans but this does not necessarily provide a blueprint for those seeking to advance the position of other minoritized groups. In particular, Latino/a CRT is already a large and growing field of study, reflecting the changing demographic and political landscape in the US, where the Latino population is already larger than the total population of Canada and, by 2020, will have surpassed African Americans as the largest minoritized group.[107] Similarly 'American Indian' scholars note that a history of literally genocidal policies and a succession of separate political settlements means that American Indian/Native American and First Nation groups in Canada occupy a unique cultural, political and legal status.[108]

Similar arguments have also raged in the UK. Tariq Modood, for example, has been especially prominent in arguing against a 'racial dualism' that sees the Black/White binary as a model for all forms of race- and/or culture-sensitive research.[109] In fact, racial binary thinking is less common in the wake of 9/11 and the subsequent increase in anti-Muslim racism that has characterized national and international political responses. Nevertheless, it remains true that a great deal of social science research on race and education in the UK focuses explicitly on Black (African Caribbean) groups. This partly reflects their history of higher profile political mobilization in the twentieth century and the background of many prominent writers. This book, for instance, focuses primarily on the educational experiences, resistances and exclusions of Black students, their parents and communities: this reflects the bulk of research to date and my own biography as both an antiracist scholar and activist involved in campaigns that especially focus on Black educational attainment.

There is no doubt that the coming years will witness a much more diverse range of research foci, not least because of the rapidly changing nature of migration into the UK. As a result of European Union expansion, for example, reciprocal arrangements exist between the UK and 26 other member states including several Eastern- and Southern European nations such as Poland, Slovakia, Slovenia, Romania and Bulgaria. Official statistics suggest that Britain is the most popular destination among migrants from recently joined states and a spate of scare stories in the media has followed, including government pronouncements that have fuelled growing xenophobia.[110]

Action, optimism and despair

Is Critical Race Theory pessimistic? Consider that it holds that racism is ordinary, normal, and embedded in society, and, moreover, that changes in relationships among the races (which include both improvements and turns for the worse) reflect the interest of dominant groups, rather than idealism, altruism, or the rule of law.

... And if CRT does have a dark side, what follows from that? Is medicine pessimistic because it focuses on diseases and traumas?

Richard Delgado and Jean Stefancic[111]

Exhibit 2.2: Critical Race Theory: a conceptual map

Key themes

- *Racism as endemic*: racism as so extensive that it is normal, not aberrant nor rare; 'race' is viewed as socially constructed and constantly changing;
- *Critique of liberalism*: views claims of neutrality, objectivity, colour-blindness and meritocracy as camouflages; formal equal opportunities laws as too limited in scope;
- *Revisionist critique of civil rights laws*: identifying the limits of progress to date and the means by which apparent advances have been clawed back;
- *Call to context*: challenges ahistoricism and emphasizes the importance of experiential knowledge.

Conceptual tools

- Storytelling and counter-stories
- Interest convergence
- Critical White studies

Continuing debates and unresolved issues

- *Intersectionality*: CRT recognizes the importance of other axes of oppression (such as class, gender, sexuality, disability) but scholars are still working through possible ways of incorporating each successfully.
- *Essentialism and anti-essentialism*: there is on-going debate about the level of group-identification/abstraction that is appropriate for different analytic and political purposes.
- *Action, optimism and despair*: detractors misread CRT as lacking hope. In fact, a central feature of CRT is a dedication to social action to bring about change, but CRT sees this as hard won and victories as insecure.

CRT's detractors often accuse it of lacking hopefulness. For example, Derrick Bell argues that racism in the US is so deep rooted, and so comprehensively written into the structures of society, that there is no realistic possibility of it being removed entirely in the foreseeable future.[112] Many people have responded angrily, asserting that such a position denies the possibility of progress and amounts to having 'given up, or surrendered, or, worse, sold out'.[113] These responses, however, betray a form of zero-sum thinking (as if racism were either simply present or absent in a uniform fashion) and, most revealingly, indicate little or no serious engagement with the work of Derrick Bell or other critical race theorists.

Bell argues passionately that action against racism is not only necessary but carries its own rewards and is required of any serious race scholar. Similarly, many critical race theorists now argue that an element of direct action, especially involving work with oppressed community groups, is a *defining characteristic* of CRT.[114] Whether racism is permanent is a moot point, in many ways an irrelevant question: none of us will live forever but we oppose racism regardless of whether we anticipate its defeat in our lifetime. Critical race theorists have never argued that racism cannot be disrupted, nor that its opposition is in any way futile. Indeed, critically informed social activism becomes a requirement for serious critical race scholars because one of the clearest lessons of their work is that *nothing* is gifted to the oppressed by their oppressors and, if left unchecked, things can certainly get a whole lot worse. CRT does not deny the possibility of improvement, therefore, but it does argue strongly against any comforting belief in the essential goodness of the human spirit or a myth of automatic incremental improvement. I return to this issue later (see Chapters 4 and 6).

Exhibit 2.2 offers a simple conceptual map of CRT, recapping the key features that I have outlined in this chapter and which are pursued in various forms as the analysis unfolds with each successive chapter of this book. Before moving on, however, I want to take a moment to consider a story that is one of the most famous parts of the CRT canon: a story once dismissed as outrageously pessimistic and over-stated, but now revealed as not only historically accurate but also remarkably prescient. If even this most extreme element of CRT has come to pass, how valuable is the rest of the CRT toolkit?

Conclusion: fantasy and reality – from *Space Traders* to the War on Terror

> CRT's usefulness will be limited not by the weakness of its constructs but by the degree that many whites will not accept its assumptions; I anticipate critique from both left and right.
>
> Edward Taylor[115]

One of the most famous of all CRT stories is Derrick Bell's *Chronicle of the Space Traders*.[116] In 1994 the story was adapted as part of a trilogy for HBO TV; it was shown once and then refused distribution by every major national video retailer.[117] The chronicle has attracted a great deal of controversy and is often cited as representing a fatalism bordering on despair.

The *Chronicle of the Space Traders* is a short story that describes what happens when the US is visited by aliens who offer a simple trade: all the gold and technology necessary to solve the country's economic and environmental crises, but in return the 'traders' want every African American for themselves – to be taken away to an unknown fate. The chronicle tells of the events surrounding the trade offer: the frantic discussions across the media; the internal debates within the political administration; and even secret meetings between politicians and capitalists where the latter warn of the dangers of losing such a significant market and a handy scapegoat. Resistance is organized, legal challenges are made and some seek sanctuary elsewhere but, ultimately, laws are passed to ensure that African Americans fulfil their 'patriotic duty' as defined by a new Amendment to the Constitution that subjects 'every United States citizen ... to selection for special service for periods necessary to protect domestic interests and international needs'. The story ends with millions of African Americans entering the holds of the Trader ships, leaving 'the New World as their forebears had arrived'; in chains.

Bell summarizes the message of the story like this:

> Everpresent, always lurking in the shadow of current events, is the real possibility that an unexpected coincidence of events at some point in the future – like those that occurred in the past – will persuade whites to reach a consensus that a major benefit to the nation justifies an ultimate sacrifice of black rights – or lives.[118]

The everpresent threat that Bell divines has become more explicit as we adjust to life as part of the so-called 'War on Terror'. I have already shown, in relation to Jean Charles de Menezes, how a human life can be sacrificed to the fears of White powerholders so long as certain conditions are met: the man was defined as non-White and the White police's fears were assumed to be genuine. Consequently, the bullets in his head were later defined by the country's most senior police officer as 'dreadful' but nothing that anyone should be *blamed* for. Meanwhile, the conservative press hailed the shooters' actions as reasonable and even heroic. But in case you are still in any doubt about the level of racialized threat, the role of White racism and the incisive power of serious Critical Race Theory, let me offer one final piece of evidence on the matter of the Space Traders.

The evidence comes from a radio programme broadcast on one of the BBC's major national stations (also available on the net). The programme in question is a prime-time phone-in. The transcript that follows occurred at around 9.40am. This is not, therefore, some extremist 'shock-jock' nor an obscure late-night show catering to a handful of listeners. On the day in question, almost a year after the London bombs of 2005, the discussion focused on a high-profile police raid in the Forest Gate area of London. Around 250 police had been involved in the raid; two Muslim men were taken into custody; one was shot (not fatally) at close range; both were later released without charge. The phone-in invited listeners to offer their views on the events. The programme generated some violent and highly offensive contributions.[119] But more worrying even than the sentiments of some listeners was the banality of the programme and the way the presenter read out views without comment. It appears that the Space Traders have landed and their offer has been accepted:

Victoria Derbyshire (Presenter):

Five Live, welcome to the programme, do join the conversation, you're very welcome.

The station's phone number is 0 500 909 693.

Are you prepared for the police to make mistakes sometimes?

Here's a text from John in Gloucestershire: 'If there were no Muslim terrorists, there would be no police raids on Muslims. It's simple.'

Another listener says, 'It's *good* that these Muslims, Arabs and Asians are having it rough here. I'd rather the odd one got shot than a relative of mine got blown up.'[120]

In this chapter I have set out the key characteristics of Critical Race Theory and discussed some of the conceptual tools that will be applied in subsequent parts of this book. Having outlined my theoretical perspective, the next step is to focus on the material scale of inequality by exploring the shape and nature of differences in educational achievement. The following chapter, therefore, discusses both the statistics and the politics of race inequity.

3 Inequality, inequality, inequality

The material reality of racial injustice in education

One of the most common phrases in today's education literature is 'the achievement gap'. The term produces more than 11 million citations on Google. 'Achievement gap', much like certain popular culture music stars, has become a crossover hit. It has made its way into common parlance and everyday usage. The term is invoked by people on both ends of the political spectrum, and few argue over its meaning or its import.

Gloria Ladson-Billings[1]

Introduction

In her 2006 presidential address to the American Educational Research Association (AERA), Gloria Ladson-Billings remarked on how commonplace talk of the 'achievement gap' has become. Adopting an approach influenced by Critical Race Theory, Ladson-Billings insists on an historically contextualized perspective that calls attention to the centuries of racism and exclusion that have shaped the present situation; creating an educational *debt* rather than a simple gap. In this chapter I set out a critical race perspective on the inequalities of achievement that characterize the English system.

Speaking at the Labour Party's national conference in 1996, shortly before he was first elected prime minister (PM), Tony Blair famously stated that his government's three priorities would be 'education, education, education'. The years that followed witnessed a succession of significant education reforms; averaging at least one new Education Act every year during his term as PM. But how, if at all, did these affect the inequitable distribution of educational rewards?

This chapter examines the main contours of educational inequality as measured at the end of compulsory schooling.[2] Before looking at the statistics themselves, however, the first section considers the most appropriate way of *measuring* achievement 'gaps'. This might appear obvious – a gap is a gap – but, as with almost everything to do with race inequality, nothing is straightforward: depending on their approach, two different commentators may describe *identical* statistics as showing exactly *opposite* trends.

The chapter then describes the relative importance of, and intersections between, inequalities based on race, class and gender. An exploration of the current data highlights the complexity of the interactions and reveals that, contrary to popular belief, economic background is not equally important for all students: an exclusive focus on class, therefore, has particular racialized consequences.

Finally, the chapter draws on official statistics to document how patterns of achievement have changed during a period of intense political pressure on schools to 'raise standards'. The data suggest that race inequalities of achievement are more persistent than is imagined by most policymakers and commentators. Indeed, the chapter ends with a discussion of how popular discourse on annual fluctuations in attainment has created a form of 'Gap Talk' that gives the impression that things are getting better (and that White students may now be the new race victims). These views are interrogated and the data analysed for signs of when (if at all) the current gaps might close. I conclude that, contrary to the comforting stories of policy-makers, educational race inequality in England is a form of 'locked-in inequality'[3] that is inevitable and permanent under current circumstances.

Measuring educational inequalities

When is a gap not a gap?

> Dear Drs Gillborn and Mirza,
> I have been reading with interest *Educational Inequality*[4] … Needless to say, I recognised [the local authority that I represent] as LEA #3 of the four in your conclusion and you will not be surprised that your remark 'the authorities seem to be planning for greater ethnic inequality in the future' is rejected as both unwarranted by the data and gratuitously insulting.
>
> Personal communication, November 2000

In 2000, with my colleague Heidi Safia Mirza, I co-authored a report on race equality in England. Part of the report drew on extensive data from more than 100 different local education authorities (LEAs) which, at the time, offered the most comprehensive picture ever assembled of differences in attainment around the country. The material had been submitted to the Education Department as part of a bidding round, as each LEA sought to win additional funds from central government.[5] Our analysis of the bids showed that there was no overall agreement about how LEAs should respond to inequalities of achievement. Indeed, we high-lighted the case of some authorities that seemed to be planning for even greater disparities in the future.[6] One LEA, for example, reported that 28.4 per cent of White students achieved at least five higher grade GCSE passes compared with just 8.3 per cent of African Caribbean students.[7] When describing their future plans the LEA declared that in four years time they hoped that White attainment would have risen to 40 per cent and African Caribbean to 17 per cent. We argued, therefore, that the policymakers were actually planning for even greater inequality in the future: the 'Black/White' gap would worsen from 20.1 percentage points to 23 percentage points. The LEA, however, responded that this conclusion was 'gratuitously insulting' and 'methodologically unsound'. They stated that:

Educationally-speaking, to target an improvement of over 100 per cent (the African-Caribbeans) … is, in normal circumstances, fairly heroic … nevertheless, the LEA has to aim for higher rates of improvement, otherwise the minority ethnic groups would never catch up.[8]

This LEA firmly believes that it is planning for a future where minoritized students will 'catch up'. But the LEA is getting its sums wrong: it assumes that a greater proportionate increase for an 'underachieving' group must automatically equate to a narrowing of the achievement gap. To understand why this is incorrect we need to consider competing approaches to the measurement of achievement by different social groups. These are not mere 'technical' concerns: there is no single measure of educational inequality that is without weaknesses or critics. In fact, two researchers have been known to examine the same set of figures and declare exactly the opposite conclusion; one asserting that inequalities are growing, the other that things are getting better. Before looking at the multiple areas of education that are scarred by race inequalities, therefore, it is necessary to explain and justify the approach that I use.

Two approaches: percentage points *versus* proportionate change

The most common way of assessing inequalities in educational outcomes is known as the 'percentage point' method. This compares the proportion of two or more groups that attain a certain level of achievement (such as graduating or attaining a pass grade in a test). So, if 60 per cent of Group A reach a particular threshold but only 45 per cent of Group B, then the inequality between them is 15 *percentage points*.

This method is used extensively to compare the achievement of students in different social groups, including those based on social class background, gender and ethnic origin. The percentage point approach is used in both academic and public policy research and has been especially important in establishing the need to take seriously the ethnic diversity of the school population.[9] Eventually, as new surveys added to the available data on race and achievement, it became common for researchers to compare percentage point differences over time, as a way of judging whether inequalities were worsening or improving. This remains the dominant approach to judging such inequalities, or 'achievement gaps', on both sides of the Atlantic.

Despite its relative dominance in public discussions of education, however, the percentage point approach is not without its critics. In the UK the most prolific writer on the subject has been Stephen Gorard, who calls the approach, somewhat disparagingly, 'the politician's error'[10]. He argues that:

It has become commonplace for writers, media commentators and researchers to refer to percentage points as percentages. Therefore if unemployment decreases from 8 per cent to 7 per cent it may be reported as a decrease of 1 per cent, whereas it actually represents a decrease of 1 point or 12.5 per cent of the original.[11]

Gorard's concern is not merely that the wrong term is used ('percentage' rather than 'percentage point') but rather that the percentage point method itself is misleading because it produces incorrect conclusions about inequalities in education. Among his preferred options is to calculate the change as a proportion of each group's original figure: 12.5 per cent rather than 1 percentage point in his example above. Gorard refers to this method as '% change'[12] or the 'proportionate' change.[13] His approach tends to produce results which suggest that class, gender and race inequalities are falling: a rather different picture than that produced by critical research. This leads Gorard to offer a particularly optimistic view of where education is heading. For example, although he says 'this does not mean that there is room for complacency', he explicitly advises policymakers that: 'there is no need to do anything specific to ameliorate these gaps. Things are already getting better.'[14]

When reflecting on why his method is not more popular, Gorard offers the following, less than generous, assessment:

> In most cases the differences cited [using the proportionate method rather than the percentage point approach] are not as great as they appear, and are getting smaller over time, but such a finding does not make such a good news story, and is unlikely to lead to the release of greater funds for the researcher or public body concerned.[15]

This implied attack on his fellow researchers was repeated in 2003 when Gorard presented his arguments to the House of Commons Select Committee on Education, a group of MPs (Members of Parliament) with a particular remit to consider education policy: 'Much public money is being spent on research that cannot produce the answers required of it, and on policies to ameliorate growing gaps in attainment that do not exist.'[16]

Paul Connolly suggests that part of the reason why Gorard's 'proportionate change' method has not been subject to close scrutiny may be that it has offered academics in gender studies a means to counter the media's presentation of a 'crisis' of male underachievement.[17] Connolly goes on to offer an alternative approach to the gender statistics but, for my purposes, it is the relevance of Gorard's work to *race* research that is most pressing. In this respect, Gorard's proportionate method produces an entirely different set of results to those more usually cited. In addition, the proportionate method is the style most often cited to me as the 'correct' way to do the calculations when I am challenged by people who take issue with talk of race inequalities (whether students, local authority officers, MPs, or academics), as in the example at the start of this chapter. The point has been made to me on numerous occasions and so it is necessary to address it explicitly.

Calculating race inequalities

Gorard uses statistics on race inequalities as an explicit part of his early work on the 'politician's error'.[18] In particular, he repeatedly cites an example drawn from my work with Caroline Gipps.[19] He constructs a table based on some local authority data from our study (see Exhibit 3.1). Gorard makes two factual errors in his presentation of the data[20] but these alone are not fatal to the substance of his argument.

Exhibit 3.1: Comparing 'percentage point' and 'proportionate change' calculations: Gorard's 'ethnicity' example

Group	1991	1993	Percentage point	% change	Ratio
Asian	30.0	38.0	8.0	27%	1.27
White	26.9	32.3	5.4	20%	1.20
African Caribbean	19.1	25.6	6.5	34%	1.34

Source: adapted from Gorard (1999): 242.
Note: the original data refer to average exam scores in the London Borough of Brent (Gillborn and Gipps 1996: 21).

In the original report Caroline Gipps and I conclude, using the percentage point approach, that in this case *'the gap grew between the highest and lowest achieving groups* ('Asian' and African Caribbean respectively)'.[21] Gorard draws the opposite conclusion based on his proportionate change method: 'The ethnic group with the highest proportionate improvement are the African Caribbeans, and therefore the gap between the highest and lowest achieving groups is actually getting smaller.'[22]

Gorard repeats this assertion, that ethnic inequalities of achievement are 'getting smaller', in numerous publications; twice he repeats the point *verbatim*[23] and at other times he uses it as the basis for a more generalized dismissal of wider arguments about ethnic inequalities in achievement.[24] When considering these apparently contradictory conclusions, Martyn Hammersley argues that *both* approaches have validity if they are used carefully and we recognize that they are measuring different things:

> Gillborn and Gipps use percentage point difference as a measure of achievement gaps because they are comparing the situation as it is with how it should be, in terms of a particular definition of equity. ... [Gorard] is concerned with whether improvement has taken place, and if so how much. ... [W]hat the two approaches provide are different perspectives on the same situation, perspectives that do not contradict one another, and that are for many purposes complementary.[25]

This contribution helps by clarifying *why* the two approaches produce such differing results but it fails to resolve the contradictory conclusions about what the findings mean in terms of race inequality in education, i.e. whether inequalities/gaps in achievement are worsening or narrowing. These differences cannot be reconciled and the explanation does not require any high level mathematics nor a degree in sociology.

A logical fallacy: greater **progress** *is not the same as a closing* **gap**

When people use the word 'gap' most of them have in mind a spatial judgement. For example, a quick internet search for definitions of the word commonly produces solutions such as:

• a conspicuous disparity or difference as between two figures;
• opening: an open or empty space in or between things.

A good way of resolving the conflict about widening/narrowing 'gaps', therefore, is simply to plot them spatially. In the example in Exhibit 3.2, this shows the space between the highest and lowest groups getting bigger (signalled by the length-ening vertical arrows). But, it could be argued, this does a disservice to the propor-tionate method by failing to take account of the scale of improvement being made by the lower attaining group. If the lower attaining group is improving more than the other groups then surely it must be closing the inequality? This appears to be Gorard's reasoning when he asserts '*therefore* the gap between the highest and lowest achieving groups is actually getting smaller'.[26] But the space (the gap, the inequality) between the groups is *not* getting smaller (as Exhibit 3.2 shows). For the 'gap' even to have remained the same, in this example, African Caribbean attainment would have had to reach an average exam score of 27.1 (remaining 10.9 *points* behind the highest rate): that is a proportionate increase of 41.8 per cent of the original level, not the 34 per cent recorded in Exhibit 3.1. And here lies the simple explanation for why a greater proportionate increase does *not* automat-ically equate to a narrowing 'gap'. When the starting point is significantly lower than other groups, a relatively small change in performance will look impressive according to the proportionate model. But a greater proportionate change would have to be sustained year-on-year to make a dent in the actual inequality of achievement (what most people would reasonably view as the 'gap').

My experience of teaching and presenting these data, to many different kinds of audience over a lengthy period, suggests that readers will largely be divided into three camps by now: one group that is about to skip ahead (if they haven't already) because the point is made; a second group that still thinks a higher proportionate growth *must* logically mean a narrowing of the 'gap'; and a third group that is quickly losing the will to live faced with so many statistics. So, especially for those in the second and third camps, here are a couple of case studies that, I hope, will illuminate the argument.

Case one: let me draw you a(nother) picture

If we take the data upon which Gorard builds his race arguments (Exhibit 3.1) we can extrapolate what would happen to the relative attainments of the top and bottom attaining groups if they continued to improve at a constant rate: i.e. 27 per cent for Asian students and 34 per cent for African Caribbean students (see Exhibit 3.3). As the chart indicates, to sustain the same proportionate increase a

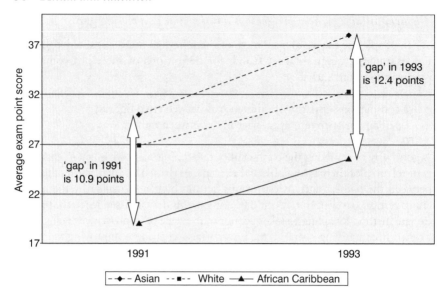

Exhibit 3.2: Measuring inequality with the percentage point method

group must improve its actual (raw) performance more and more each year: signalled by the increasingly steep rises. Even if such year-on-year changes were sustained, in Gorard's example the inequality of achievement between the groups does not disappear until some 14 years have passed. But the assumptions embodied in the model are unsustainable: in order to continue their 34 per cent improvement rate between 2005 and 2007, for example, African Caribbean students would have to raise their average exam score from 147.9 points (equivalent to 18 separate passes at the highest level: A*) to an even more incredible 198.1 average exam score (equivalent to 24 grade A* passes). This, of course, is ludicrous: most students do not even enter half that number of GCSEs. However, this is precisely the kind of situation that would have to occur if we use the proportionate method as a guide to trends in achievement inequality.

Case two: Show me the money

Data published in 2007 showed that the top fifth of households in Britain received an annual income of at least £66,300 and the bottom fifth received an income of £4,300 or less.[27] Let's imagine that a worker in the bottom group is offered an apparently huge rise of 30 per cent while a peer in the top group accepts a miserly rise of just 5 per cent. These figures, using the proportionate method, make it appear as if the low paid worker is getting a great deal more than the other and, in Gorard's terms, the lower paid worker *must* be narrowing the pay gap. But because the bottom fifth start at such a low level the 30 per cent rise for a low paid

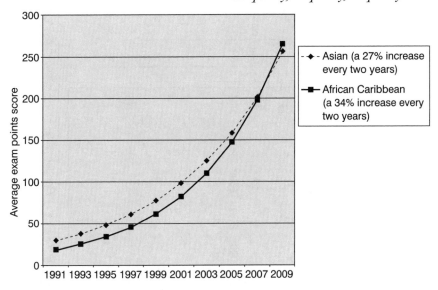

Note: data for the years 1991 and 1993 are based on Gillborn and Gipps (1996): 21 and cited extensively by Gorard (1999, 2000a, 2000b); all other years are projections based on the percentage change model.

Exhibit 3.3: Visualizing progress: the proportionate change method

worker equates to an extra £1,290 per annum at most. The already better-off person's 5 per cent delivers them at least an extra £3,315 per annum. So, would you prefer £1,290 or £3,315? Whose wage has gone up the most? Has the gap narrowed or grown? The percentage point method is demonstrably the best suited to measuring inequalities.

Race, class and gender

It is well known that, on average, students from economically advantaged backgrounds tend to achieve higher results than their peers from less advantaged homes. This is one of the clearest and longest established findings in the sociology of education: although specialists differ in how they define and measure 'social class'[28] there is agreement that economic background is a hugely significant variable when trying to understand young people's educational experiences and achievements.

One way of conceiving of the importance of social class is presented in Exhibit 3.4, which charts the proportion of students in certain groups gaining at least five higher grade GCSE passes over a 15-year period. The horizontal axis represents the overall proportion of students nationally who attained five or more higher grades in each year; the further above or below that line, the further in advance, or behind, a group is performing. In 2004, for example, that level of success was attained by 54 per cent of students nationally: in relation to gender, 59 per cent of

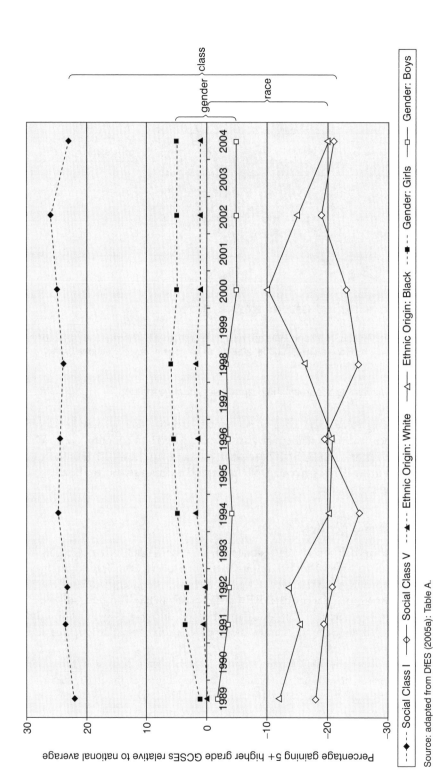

Source: adapted from DfES (2005a): Table A.

Exhibit 3.4: Educational inequality by class, race and gender: England and Wales, 1989–2004

girls and 49 per cent of boys achieved that level. Therefore, the line for girls appears 5 points above the horizontal axis and the boys lie 5 points below the average.

Perhaps the most striking thing about Exhibit 3.4 is how relatively stable the gaps remain over time: there is some fluctuation from survey to survey but significant disparities exist throughout. The brackets on the right signify the size of the gaps in the latest data but the general picture is fairly constant insofar as the social class inequality (comparing groups I and V) is considerably greater than the race gap (comparing Black and White students) and the gender gap. It should be remembered, however, that the class measure is comparing the very highest and the very lowest attaining class categories (groups I and V): there are three additional class categories between these extremes (which include nearly two in every three classified students) that are not shown on the graph.[29] Nevertheless, it is common to hear commentators, and many academics, arguing that the most important inequality is that associated with income. Gorard and White state: 'Most crucially, the attention paid to differences in attainment between ethnic groups obscures much larger differences, such as those between rich and poor.'[30] This view, however, neglects the fact that everyone is classed, raced *and* gendered. It also risks falling into the trap of arguing *between* inequalities, as if each were not a source of injustice or some are too small to concern us. What is rarely appreciated when such arguments are made is that *privileging class inequality has the effect of privileging White interests*: this is because educational inequalities associated with social class do not appear to be equally important for all students regardless of ethnic background.

Class is not equally important for all groups

Exhibit 3.5 shows the proportion of students gaining at least five higher grade GCSEs by race, class and gender. In comparison with the earlier data, these statistics have the advantage of being based on returns for every student in England and use a more sophisticated ethnic breakdown. However, the social class indicator is receipt of free school meals (FSM), which is a common, but very crude, proxy for family poverty. Indeed, some minoritized groups are known to be less likely to apply for benefits of this kind even if they qualify.[31] Nevertheless, the illustration gives the best currently available indication of how these variables interact for ethnic groups nationally.

Exhibit 3.5 combines a great deal of information. Perhaps the most striking feature is the scale of the differences in attainment between groups, ranging from 84.9 per cent of students gaining five higher grades (Chinese non-FSM girls) through to 24 per cent (White FSM boys). Two further patterns are also immediately apparent. First, students who are *not* in receipt of free school meals are more likely to attain the required level than their peers of the same gender and ethnic origin who do receive FSM: the pattern is common to all groups without exception. A second commonality is that girls are relatively more successful than boys of the same ethnic group and FSM-status: again, a pattern common to each ethnic group.

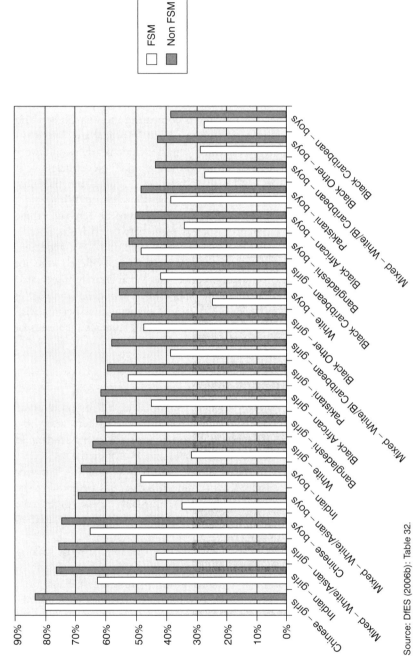

Source: DfES (2006b): Table 32.

Exhibit 3.5: Educational achievement by race, class and gender: England, 2006: 5+ A* to C

Within these broad class- and gender-based trends, however, lie some important variations. It is clear that FSM status is associated with much more dramatic variations in attainment for some groups: in particular, White students and their peers of Dual Heritage (White/Asian) background are the only groups where the FSM/non-FSM gap is 25 percentage points or higher. This suggests that *an exclusive focus on inequalities associated with class profile would be of most benefit to White students – where class inequalities are most pronounced*. This is an important observation because commentators (in the press, politics and the academy) have tended to emphasize the scale of class inequalities as if they were a common factor. In particular, the talk of a 'crisis' of *male* under-achievement[32] combines with this view to support a particular obsession with *White boys*.

White under-achievement and selective reporting: the hidden 86 per cent

White boys falling behind
White, working-class boys have the worst GCSE results … Just 24 per cent of disad-vantaged white boys now leave school with five or more good GCSEs.

This compares with 33.7 per cent for black African boys from similar low-income households.

There were fears last night that the figures could hand votes to the far-Right British National Party because additional funding is available to help children from ethnic minorities.

Daily Mail[33]

Notwithstanding the misleading impression that all minoritized groups benefit from additional funding (they do not – additional funds have to be bid for as part of limited special initiatives), the emphasis on White students in this extract is extremely important. The story accurately quotes the official statistics but its delivery would seem calculated to draw attention to a Black/White gap where *Whites* are the group that lose out. In fact, Black African boys (who are high-lighted in the story) are the highest achieving of all the Black male FSM groups (9.7 percentage points ahead of their White counterparts).[34] The gap between Whites and other FSM Black boys is considerably smaller: those categorized as 'Black Other' were 4.4 points ahead, Black Caribbean 3.1 points, and Dual Heritage (White/Black Caribbean) 2.8 points ahead.

In addition, the newspaper account fails to mention any of the inequalities of attainment between *non*-FSM students. This is particularly important because non-FSM students form the great majority of the cohort (86.6 per cent of the young people counted in Exhibit 3.5 were *not* in receipt of free school meals).

Just a few months later similar headlines appeared once again, this time generated by an academic study rather than official statistics.[35] As before, the prime focus was on the very lowest achievers and newspapers repeated the image of White failure:

School low achievers are white and British

The Times[36]

White boys 'are being left behind' by education system

Daily Mail[37]

White boys 'let down by education system'

Daily Telegraph[38]

Deprived white boys 'low achievers'

Daily Express[39]

White working-class boys are the worst performers in school

Independent[40]

Half school 'failures' are white working-class boys, says report

Guardian [41]

White non-FSM students enjoy higher success rates than most of their peers of the same gender from different ethnic groups.[42] The largest of these inequalities of achievement are between White students and their Black Caribbean counterparts. This is true for both sexes and gives a rather different picture to the one painted by the sensationalist headlines:

- White non-FSM girls outperform their Black Caribbean counterparts by 9.7 percentage points;
- White non-FSM boys outperform their Black Caribbean counterparts by 17.2 percentage points.

These findings are extremely significant. Remember that the non-FSM category is very broad (accounting for around five in every six students). The data show that, far from the picture of White failure generated by media coverage of the statistics,[43] *White non-FSM students – of both sexes – are more likely to succeed than their peers from Pakistani, Bangladeshi, Black Caribbean, Black African, Black Other and Dual Heritage (White/Black Caribbean) backgrounds*.

These figures act as a corrective to the distorted view of White failure that is generated by over-emphasis on the FSM numbers alone. It is difficult to over-estimate the significance of this finding because the disproportionate focus on FSM students is not limited to newspaper accounts. The Education Department itself carried the same emphasis when reporting similar data. The government has begun to publish annual reports that pull together a variety of information about ethnicity and educational attainment. When the Education Department first published analyses of FSM-status, ethnicity and gender as cross-tabulations in 2006, *there was no separate analysis of non-FSM students*: this contrasts sharply with the detailed accounts that were offered for FSM boys and girls (who were the subject of *three* different illustrations in the report).[44]

Reform and inequality: changes over time

Since the late 1980s the education system in England has become increasingly dominated by a concern to measure and improve educational 'standards' as judged by
performance in a series of national assessments. This drive is common to many capitalist nations including Australia, New Zealand and the USA.[45] As already noted the
proportion of students achieving at least five higher grades in GCSE examinations
has been the dominant measure of attainment at the end of compulsory schooling.
The Education Department publishes these data on *every* school in the country and
the statistics are frequently re-ordered in the form of league tables by local (and
national) newspapers, which then present lists of 'best' and 'worst' schools. The
overwhelming focus on this criterion, and its importance in official judgements of
schools' success/failure, has led schools to prioritize attempts to improve their
performance on this measure.[46] Not surprisingly, overall rates of success have risen
dramatically from 30 per cent of students achieving five or more higher grades in
1988 to around 57 per cent in 2006.[47] This raises a further vital question: have
minoritized students shared equitably in the improving rates of GCSE success? The
best available data suggest that the answer is no.

All have improved, but not equally

Exhibit 3.6 charts the changing patterns of GCSE attainment from the late 1980s
through to 2004. The data are drawn from the Youth Cohort Study (YCS). A
disadvantage with the YCS is that it reports on a *sample* of 16-year-olds, rather
than the whole cohort. Although the sample is large (more than 14,000 in 2004)
it is considerably smaller than the numbers involved in the Pupil Level Annual
Schools Census (PLASC) which, in 2002, began to gather systematic data on the
ethnicity of *every* child in the state system. Although the ethnic categories in the
YCS are relatively crude, the project is unique in offering a fairly reliable picture of
how different ethnic groups have fared over a 15-year period, since the start of the
major reforms that began with the Education Reform Act 1988.

The data are generated by a questionnaire sent to a representative sample of 16-
to 19-year-olds. Exhibit 3.6 records the proportion in each of the main ethnic
groups who achieved five or more higher grade GCSE passes (or their equivalent).
Alongside the relevant percentage is a calculation of the 'gap' in terms of the
percentage point method.

*Only one of the ethnic groups identified by the YCS has enjoyed an improvement in
every one of the surveys since 1989: White students.* The performance of the other
groups has been less certain, with periods where their attainment in one study
remained static or actually fell below that of the previous survey. These changes
could relate to actual fluctuations nationally, but they might also be a product of
relatively small changes within the sample groups. Consequently, it is advisable to
treat year-on-year changes with caution and focus more on the longer-term trends.
Despite this, it is undoubtedly significant that *only White students* have drawn clear
benefit every year since the main reforms got underway.

Exhibit 3.6: Ethnic origin and GCSE attainment, 1989–2004

Percentage gaining five higher grade GCSEs and percentage point difference with the 'White' group

	1989		1991		1992		1994		1996		1998*		2000		2002		2004	
	%	gap	%	gap	%	gap	%	gap	%	gap	%	gap	%	gap	%	gap	%	gap
White	30	–	35	–	37	–	43	–	45	–	47	–	50	–	52	–	55	–
Black	18	-12	19	-16	23	-14	21	-22	23	-22	29	-18	39	-11	36	-16	34	-21
Indian	n/a	–	n/a	–	38	+1	45	+2	48	+3	54	+7	60	+10	60	+8	72	+17
Pakistani	n/a	–	n/a	–	26	-11	24	-19	23	-22	29	-18	29	-21	40	-12	37	-18
Bangladeshi	n/a	–	n/a	–	14	-23	20	-23	25	-20	33	-14	29	-21	41	-11	45	-10

Source: adapted from DfES (2005a): Table A.

Notes:
n/a = not available: separate calculations were not made for Indian, Pakistani and Bangladeshi students until the 1992 cohort.
Year = the year of the cohort being questioned: the GCSE examinations were taken in the previous calendar year.
* includes equivalent GNVQ qualifications from 1998.
Please note: these are the official statistics and include students attending independent schools.

Black students

Over the entire period represented in Exhibit 3.6 the proportion of Black students attaining at least five higher grades almost doubled (from 18 per cent to 34 per cent). This improvement (of 16 points), however, did not keep pace with White students (whose attainment improved by 25 percentage points over the same period). Despite improvements, therefore, it remains the case that the 'Black/White gap' is significantly larger (at 21 percentage points) than it was more than 15 years ago (12 percentage points in 1989). But this comparison does not tell the whole story.

The data show that the Black/White gap grew considerably during the early to mid-1990s. This was a period of intense emphasis on raising exam performance and improving positions in the newly introduced school performance tables (first published for secondary schools in 1992). In contrast, surveys in 1998 and 2000 showed a narrowing of the Black/White gap. However, it should be noted that since 1998 the data include the results in other forms of assessment that are counted as equivalent to GCSEs, including General National Vocational Qualifications (GNVQs). Evidence shows that Black students are disproportionately entered for these lower status examinations, which do not carry the same weight in competition for jobs or places in academic studies in higher education.[48]

Pakistani students

The pattern of attainment by Pakistani students is even more complex. Since 1992 the achievements of Pakistani young people have varied considerably: falling in two consecutive cohorts before showing some important gains more recently. Overall, between 1992 and 2004 the proportion of Pakistani students attaining five or more higher grade passes improved by 11 percentage points (from 26 per cent to 37 per cent). This is a significant increase but it should be noted that the gap between Pakistani students and their White peers, while fluctuating considerably, was actually smallest in 1992 when data were first gathered separately for this group.

Bangladeshi students

From a very low starting point in 1992 the Bangladeshi group showed quite dramatic improvements until the 2000 survey, when their attainment fell below the level of the previous cohort. However, the upward trend resumed in subsequent surveys and, overall, Bangladeshi students are now three times more likely to attain five higher grades than they were in the early 1990s. Nevertheless, Bangladeshi students remain less likely to achieve these higher grades than their White counterparts.

Indian students

The picture for Indian students is markedly different from the other minority ethnic groups counted in the YCS. From a position of virtual equity in 1992, when the YCS first disaggregated the composite 'South Asian' category, Indian students have improved *more* than their White peers. Although the proportion attaining five or more higher grades remained static between 2000 and 2002, overall Indian students have improved from 38 per cent in 1992 to 72 per cent, an increase of 34 percentage points: almost double the White improvement (of 18 percentage points) over the same period.[49]

Data on ethnic origin and achievement for approximately the last 15 years, therefore, show that none of the existing inequalities are fixed. Each of the attainment inequalities have varied over time, with the early and mid-1990s being a period of especially pronounced inequality. All groups have enjoyed some improvement over the period but significant problems persist. The Black/White gap is almost as great as ever and both Bangladeshi and Pakistani students have experienced periods of *growing* inequality.

Exclusions from school

The patterns of unequal achievement are worrying but even these statistics do not reveal the full story of how certain minoritized groups face a harsher and less rewarding education. By the time the high-stakes tests come around a disproportionate number of Black students are no longer in school; and unlike North America (where the notion of 'dropping out' superficially presents the issue as driven by the students),[50] in England the figures are unequivocally about 'exclusion': where a school decides it will no longer accept a student on its roll.

The most serious sanction that an English school can take against a student is to permanently expel them ('exclusion' in the official lexicon). The local state has a duty to ensure that such students receive a basic education elsewhere, usually through placement in some form of special unit or limited separate tuition. Official statistics suggest that exclusion is strongly associated with highly negative outcomes in education and in longer-term life chances:

> Young people excluded from school are much less likely to achieve 5 GCSEs at grade A*-C than other groups – just one in five young people compared to more than half overall. More than four times as many young people excluded from school fail to gain any qualifications at 16 compared with those not excluded. Being out of school is a major risk factor for juvenile offending. Research has found an almost direct correlation between youth crime rates in an area and the 'out of school' population. Young people excluded from school are more than twice as likely to report having committed a crime as young people in mainstream school.[51]

In view of these experiences the persistent and significant over-exclusion of Black students is a major area of controversy and concern. They have tended to be over-represented in permanent exclusions whenever relevant data have been broken down by ethnicity. In the mid-1980s, for example, 'Afro-Caribbean' students accounted for 14 per cent of London school children but made up more than 30 per cent of all exclusions in the capital.[52] This problem became even more pressing during the 1990s when the total number of exclusions increased dramatically: the figure for 1995–6 was 12,476: four times the number recorded at the start of the decade.[53] In the mid-1990s new data, based on official school inspections, suggested that nationally Black Caribbean children were excluded from secondary schools at almost *six times* the rate for White students and it was calculated that this meant around 1,000 additional and potentially unjust Black expulsions every year.[54]

In 1998 the first report of the newly created Social Exclusion Unit focused on exclusions and truancy from school. The unit's recommendations were taken up by Government and committed it to drastically reduce the number of permanent exclusions by a third from 12,700 in 1996–7 to 8,400 by 2002.[55] The Government abandoned this target in 2001, arguing that the reduction had all but been achieved (at 8,600 in 1999–2000) and that no new targets were necessary. Perhaps predictably, the following years saw a rise in the number of students being permanently excluded.[56]

However, the official statistics on permanent exclusions are only part of the story. Indeed, there are indications that 'unofficial exclusions', which evade official recording, are becoming increasingly common.[57] In addition, a growth in alternative provision, including the use of referrals to support units, will have helped reduce the official numbers but do not guarantee students access to the mainstream curriculum. Black parents' groups have also raised concerns about 'internal exclusion', where students may be repeatedly removed from class: a form of exclusion from equal access to schooling but not a form of exclusion that shows up in official data.[58] With these warnings in mind, the official statistics on ethnicity and exclusion are summarized in Exhibit 3.7.

Exhibit 3.7 shows the recorded levels of permanent exclusion since the overall peak in 1996–7. The columns show the number of students in each ethnic group formally recorded as having been permanently excluded. The percentage column shows that number as a percentage of their ethnic group in school; hence, the figure of 0.06 Bangladeshis in 2004–5 represents 6 students in every 10,000, and 0.39 for Black Caribbean students represents 39 in every 10,000.

The first thing to note is the complexity of the statistics. The number of White students recorded as permanently excluded declined each year between 1996–7 and the overall low of 1999–2000, but then rose in each of the next two years. In contrast, the number of Black Caribbean students excluded barely changed in the first year of the overall decline, but (having begun to fall more rapidly) then continued to decline even in 2000–1, when overall numbers began to rise once again. Indian students had the least chance of being excluded (as a percentage of their numbers in the school population) throughout the entire period in question, but the number (and proportion) of Indians excluded actually rose in 1997–8, just as overall rates began to fall. The exclusion rate for Bangladeshi students has been volatile throughout the period; including a rise in 1999–2000 (the third successive year of overall reductions), a fall in 2000–1 (when the overall rate started to rise) and a steep increase in 2001–2. In view of the limitations of the official statistics,

Exhibit 3.7: Ethnic origin and permanent exclusions from school: England, 1996–7 to 2004–5

Ethnic origin	1996–7 N	%	1997–8 N	%	1998–9 N	%	1999–00 N	%	2000–1 N	%	2001–2 N	%	2002–3 N	%	2003–4 N	%	2004–5 N	%
White	10,555	0.18	10,303	0.18	8,801	0.15	6,890	0.12	7,574	0.13	7,820	0.13	6,800	0.12	7,860	0.14	7,470	0.13
Bl. Caribbean	770	0.78	765	0.77	589	0.60	455	0.46	385	0.38	410	0.41	360	0.37	400	0.41	380	0.39
Bl. African	200	0.31	203	0.30	157	0.21	145	0.17	156	0.17	160	0.15	130	0.12	200	0.16	190	0.14
Bl. Other	334	0.71	287	0.58	268	0.50	218	0.37	236	0.39	220	0.35	90	0.32	120	0.42	100	0.36
Indian	91	0.06	116	0.07	71	0.04	54	0.03	47	0.03	60	0.03	50	0.03	40	0.02	70	0.04
Pakistani	286	0.18	218	0.13	165	0.10	129	0.07	113	0.06	170	0.09	130	0.08	130	0.07	160	0.08
Bangladeshi	60	0.10	60	0.10	42	0.07	53	0.08	44	0.07	80	0.11	40	0.06	70	0.09	50	0.06
W/Bl. Caribbean	n/a	n/a	n/a	n/a	n/a	n/a	n/a	n/a	n/a	n/a	n/a	n/a	180	0.29	240	0.37	280	0.41
W/Bl. African	n/a	n/a	n/a	n/a	n/a	n/a	n/a	n/a	n/a	n/a	n/a	n/a	40	0.26	40	0.23	50	0.24
W/Asian	n/a	n/a	n/a	n/a	n/a	n/a	n/a	n/a	n/a	n/a	n/a	n/a	40	0.11	40	0.12	30	0.09
TOTAL*	12,668		12,298		10,424		8,314		9,122		9,519		9,270		9,860		9,380	

Sources: for 1996–7 to 2000–1 DfES (2002); thereafter DfES (2003): Table 2; DfES (2004a): Table 4; DfES (2005b): Table 7; DfES (2006c): Table 7.

Notes:

N = number of pupils permanently excluded.

% = number of pupils excluded in that ethnic group expressed as a percentage of that ethnic group in compulsory schooling.

n/a = data not available for that period.

*includes some groups not shown separately above.

and the volatility of figures for minoritized groups, we should be cautious when interpreting these data. Overall, it appears that *students in each of the principal ethnic groups shared to some degree in the overall reduction that occurred in the late 1990s* (between 1996–7 and 1999–2000 inclusive).

When we focus on the likelihood of exclusion within each ethnic group some consistent patterns begin to emerge. Students of 'South Asian' ethnic heritage, for example, have almost always been *less* likely to be excluded (as a percentage of their ethnic group) than their White and Black counterparts.[59] In contrast, Black students (those categorized as Black Caribbean, Black African or Black Other) have almost always been *more* likely to be excluded than their White peers: a pattern that is true in every year and for each of the Black groups.[60]

Dual Heritage students (classified 'mixed' in the official terminology) have only featured in official statistics since 2002–3. Dual Heritage (White/Asian) students experience the lowest exclusion rate, marked by a 25 per cent proportionate decrease between 2003–4 and 2004–5 compared to a 25 per cent increase for Dual Heritage (White/Black African) students for the same period. Data for Dual Heritage (White/Black Caribbean) students reveal a particularly high rate of exclusion, similar to students of Black Caribbean heritage, with a 55 per cent increase since data on this group were first collected.

Exclusions have become one of the most controversial areas of inequality so far as race and education are concerned. The over-exclusion of Black students frequently emerges as one of the most important issues in the eyes of Black teachers, parents and students.[61] It is also an area where public debate seems entirely immune to evidence: despite academic research and community-based initiatives that highlight the inequitable treatment of Black students in schools,[62] the popular media continue to repeat crude stereotypes that reinforce powerful deficit images of Black communities in general and Black young men in particular.[63] Nevertheless, there is compelling evidence that the over-representation of African Caribbean students in exclusions is the result of harsher treatment by schools, rather than simple differences in behaviour by students.[64]

False hopes and the illusion of 'closing gaps': is the Black/White gap permanently 'locked-in'?

> There are three kinds of lies: lies, damned lies and statistics.
>
> Benjamin Disraeli [65]

Black students' achievement relative to their White peers has been a central part of debates about race and education since the 1960s. As I have shown, the debate continues to be hotly contested: depending on the methods used – and the data that are consulted – academics, policymakers and commentators argue about whether the gap is worsening or narrowing. If we take a slightly different approach to the issue, however, an even more worrying diagnosis suggests itself. Drawing inspiration from Critical Race Theory and analyses of the persistence of race inequality in the US, it is possible to conceive of the Black/White gap in education as an example of 'locked-in inequality', that is, an inequality so deep rooted and so large that, under current circumstances, it is a practically inevitable feature of the education system.[66] In this section I examine the evidence for this perspective and conclude that the current talk of 'gaps' in educational attainment hides the true scale and nature of race inequality in the English system.

Locked-in inequality

In a succession of articles in US law journals Daria Roithmayr has developed the notion of 'locked-in inequality'.[67] Drawing on work in economics and legal antitrust theory, Roithmayr defines inequality as locked-in when historical advantages built through conscious discrimination in the past become institutionalized to such a degree that even the removal of all existing barriers cannot create a level playing field:

> Market monopolies can become self-reinforcing, locked in, and ultimated under certain circumstances. For example, in markets characterized by positive feedback, an early competitive advantage can feed on itself to produce a perpetually increasing lead that ultimately becomes impossible to overcome … When that occurs, we say that the product has become 'locked in' to its monopoly or market leader position.[68]

Roithmayr has applied this model to several examples of race inequality including admissions to US law schools and public education in South Africa. In each case, she argues, the focus of contemporary equality legislation is inadequate to deal with the locked-in nature of the inequalities. In such cases the scale of the historical discrimination is so large that there no longer needs to be any conscious intent to discriminate; the historical legacy of inequality (in housing, education, wealth etc.) is so large that the inequalities become self-perpetuating:

> In contrast to the individual intent model, the lock-in model suggests that the definition of discrimination be expanded, to include persistent racial inequality that can be traced historically to earlier 'anti-competitive' conduct. This definition, and the lock-in model itself, bring to light the historical, institutional and collective dimensions of racial inequality that the individual intent model suppresses.[69]

I am not arguing that 'anti-competitive' practices have been eliminated from the English system: indeed, much of this book is concerned with exploring such contemporary practices. Nevertheless, there may be utility in the idea that inequality can become so large and so firmly entrenched that it 'can feed on itself'.[70] In particular, the concept appears especially useful as a means of shedding further light on the persistence of race inequality in educational achievement: the approach provides a viewpoint that is in marked contrast to the optimistic, even misleading, nature of official pronouncements. Before examining the statistical data, therefore, it is useful to consider how policymakers deploy yearly fluctuations as a means of suggesting that things are improving: I call this 'Gap Talk'.

Gap Talk

The proportion of students attaining the chosen measure of educational 'standards' varies from year to year (see Exhibits 3.4 and 3.6). These fluctuations are often cited by policymakers as a sign that inequalities are narrowing and social justice is being advanced across the system. These occasions represent more than the mere *reporting* of the latest statistics: the news of the changing rates is conveyed with a particular tone and emphasis that encourages positive interpretations. Talk of 'closing' and/or 'narrowing' gaps operates as a discursive strategy whereby statistical data are deployed to construct the view that things are improving and the system is moving in the right direction. Exhibit 3.8 includes examples of Gap Talk from 2001 to 2007.

This Gap Talk serves a particular strategic and political purpose. The continual statements that gaps are being 'narrowed', 'reduced' and are 'closing' deliberately feed the impression that incremental progress is removing inequality from the system. As Louise Archer and Becky Francis have noted, the Education Department has a habit of headlining rises in minority attainment in a 'self-congratulatory' manner that belies the 'persistent enormity of the ethnicity gap between some groups'.[71] The repeated assertion that the inequalities are being reduced fails to recognize the scale of the present inequality and how relatively insignificant the fluctuations really are. In order to gauge the scale of the issues it is useful to return to the longitudinal data presented earlier in this chapter.

Closing the gap or locked-in inequality?

Data from the Youth Cohort Study (see Exhibit 3.6) offer a unique glimpse of Black/White inequalities over a longer time span than is usual in educational statistics. By looking at how the gap has fluctuated in the past it is possible to consider what similar patterns would mean in the long term. A quick glance at the raw data shows that changes in one time period tell us little about what may happen in subsequent surveys. In addition, it is likely that any measure of 'standards' used for accountability purposes would be abandoned once the majority of students achieve that level of success.[72] By its nature, an assessment of educational 'standards' must produce both winners and losers. It follows that if the large majority of candidates succeed, the measure becomes less effective as a selection device. This response has already begun in England where the proportion of students achieving five higher grade passes – once an elite measure – has now risen above 50 per cent. Consequently, the government recently introduced a new 'Gold Standard' benchmark, i.e. the proportion of students attaining five higher grade GCSEs *including* passes in English and mathematics. The stipulation that these so-called 'core' subjects be present had the desired effect: whereas 56.9 per cent of students achieved five higher grade passes in any subject (and its equivalent), only 43.8 per cent could boast that their passes included English and maths.[73]

Exhibit 3.8: Gap Talk

2001: 'long established achievement gaps begin to be narrowed'

Last year, even the lowest scoring local education authority (LEA) in the English and mathematics tests achieved better than the national average of four years ago. *And the fastest improving areas in the country are among the most disadvantaged as long established achievement gaps begin to be narrowed*.

DfES (2001b): 9, emphasis added.

2003: 'major programmes … help to reduce the gap'

[T]here has been a clear expectation that policies aimed at raising attainment levels amongst pupils from disadvantaged backgrounds will disproportionately benefit ethnic minorities. Indeed, major programmes such as the National Strategies for Numeracy and Literacy, Beacon Schools, Specialist Schools and Excellence in Cities are all *expected to have disproportionate benefits in low social class areas and should consequently help to reduce the gap. Indeed, some evaluations report that these programmes are already having positive impacts on ethnic minority groups*.

Cabinet Office (2003): 58, emphasis added.

2005: 'evidence showing that the gap was closing'

Asian and Black pupils made the greatest rate of improvement in 2004 examinations according to figures released today. The proportion of Pakistani, Bangladeshi, Black Caribbean, Black African and other Black pupils achieving 5 or more A* to C grades at GCSE and equivalent in 2004 has improved by more than 2.5 percentage points in each group. … Schools Minister Derek Twigg welcomed the figures, saying that minority ethnic groups were making great progress and that *evidence showing that the gap was closing between Black, Pakistani and Bangladeshi pupils and other pupils at GCSE and equivalent was also encouraging*.

DfES (2005c), emphasis added.

2006: 'closing the gap'

Pakistani, Bangladeshi and Black pupils have made the greatest improvement in this year's GCSE results according to figures released today. The biggest improvers are Bangladeshi and Black Caribbean pupils with the proportion getting five good GCSEs jumping by 3.5 percentage points from 52.7 per cent to 56.2 per cent, and 2.7 percentage points from 41.7 per cent to 44.4 per cent respectively. The increases are well above the national increase of 2 percentage points … Schools Minister Andrew Adonis welcomed *this continuing upward trend and the sustained progress that the Government is making in closing the gap between Black, Pakistani and Bangladeshi pupils and other pupils at GCSE and equivalent* … The proportion of both Black Caribbean and Bangladeshi pupils achieving 5+ A*- C at GCSE and equivalent is up 10 percentage points since 2003, compared to a national increase of 6 percentage points.

DfES (2006d), emphasis added.

2007: 'significant progress in tackling educational attainment gaps'

We are *already making significant progress in tackling educational attainment gaps* but recognise we need to go much further. As a result of work in schools, the proportion of Black Caribbean boys achieving five good GCSEs is up 11 per cent points since 2003, compared to the national increase of 7 per cent points.

Department for Communities and Local Government (2007a), emphasis added.

Exhibit 3.9: When will the Black/White gap close?

Six-year Trend Percentage gaining 5+ A* to C grade GCSEs

	1998	*gap*	*2004*	*gap*
White	47%	–	55%	–
Black	29%	18 points	34%	21 points

The overall trend: Over this six-year period (1998 to 2004) the achievement gap widened and so, on this basis, Black students would not begin to catch up until Whites hit 100 per cent.

Whites hit 100 per cent: Whites improved 8 percentage points in six years (an average of 1.3 per annum): at that rate the remaining 45 per cent would reach saturation in about 34 years, i.e. 2038.

The gap finally closes: Black students improved 5 percentage points in six years (an average of 0.8 per annum): at that rate the remaining 66 per cent reach saturation (and close the gap) in about 83 years, i.e. 2087.

Ten-year Trend Percentage gaining 5+ A* to C grade GCSEs

	1994	*gap*	*2004*	*gap*
White	43%	–	55%	–
Black	21%	22 points	34%	21 points

The overall trend: Over this ten-year period (1994 to 2004) the achievement gap narrowed by 1 percentage point. At this rate (0.1 percentage points per annum) the 21 point gap would take 210 years to close. However, Whites would hit 100 per cent before that date and, at that point, the gap would begin to close more quickly.

Whites hit 100 per cent: Whites improved 12 percentage points in 10 years (an average of 1.2 per annum): at that rate the remaining 45 per cent would reach saturation in about 38 years, i.e. 2042.

The gap finally closes: Black students improved 13 percentage points in 10 years (an average of 1.3 per annum): at that rate the remaining 66 per cent reach saturation (and close the gap) in just over 50 years, i.e. 2054.

15-year Trend Percentage gaining 5+ A* to C grade GCSEs

	1989	*gap*	*2004*	*gap*
White	30%	–	55%	–
Black	18%	12 points	34%	21 points

The overall trend: Over this 15-year period (1989 to 2004) the achievement gap widened and so, on this basis, Black students would not begin to catch up until Whites hit 100 per cent.

Whites hit 100 per cent: Whites improved 25 percentage points in 15 years (an average of 1.66 per annum): at that rate the remaining 45 per cent would reach saturation in just over 27 years, i.e. 2031.

The gap finally closes: Black students improved 16 percentage points in 15 years (an average of 1.1 per annum): at that rate the remaining 66 per cent reach saturation (and close the gap) in 60 years, i.e. 2064.

Source: calculations based on data from DfES (2005a): Table A.

Notwithstanding these caveats, the data suggest a shocking conclusion. Exhibit 3.9 presents some simple calculations, based on official data, comparing the average improvements made by Black and White students over periods of 6, 10 and 15 years.[74] The findings suggest that if these trends were continued then practically speaking the Black/White inequality of achievement is permanent:

- In each case White students hit 100 per cent before the Black/White inequality closes: this happens between 2031 (based on the 15-year trend) and 2042 (on the 10-year averages).
- The soonest that Black students would hit 100 per cent, and finally close the gap, is 2054 (based on 10-year trends).

Despite the favourable spin that political Gap Talk places on yearly fluctuations, therefore, unless we see change on a totally unprecedented scale then past experience suggests that the Black/White inequality of achievement is a permanent feature of the education system. Even the most optimistic trends still have White students reaching 100 per cent well before their Black peers close the existing achievement gaps. As already noted, in the real world this would not happen because any measure of 'standards' eventually becomes meaningless as more people attain it. Consequently, *the present incremental changes in attainment, accompanied by self-congratulatory Gap Talk, disguise a situation where pronounced racial inequalities of attainment are effectively locked-in as a permanent feature of the system.*

Conclusion

> While some gaps have narrowed, for example, for black and minority ethnic pupils, others have proved to be extremely persistent nationally. This is despite overall improvement in the attainment of all groups of pupils. For example, the difference in the proportion of boys and girls achieving the expected levels in English at the end of primary school has remained fairly static since 1999.
>
> 2020 Vision Group Report[75]

This quotation is taken from an official document announcing a major change in education policy, asserting the importance of 'personalized learning'.[76] The review group was asked to consider a new vision for education by 2020. Its final report runs to more than 50 pages and, although it does not once use the words 'racism', 'prejudice' or 'discrimination', the review claims a deep commitment to changing the shape of achievement across the country. Indeed, the report includes a chapter entitled 'Closing the gap – a system-wide focus on achievement for all'. The report provides one of the clearest and most disturbing examples of what I have termed Gap Talk: that is, the assertion that minor fluctuations in rates of attainment between ethnic groups is evidence that the system is making incremental progress towards a point where race inequalities in achievement are banished. Incredibly, the report positions race inequality as a 'gap' that has proven amenable to change, unlike the 'extremely persistent' gender gap. I have shown that this is not merely over-optimistic, it is simply incorrect: it is a deception that hides the true scale and locked-in nature of race inequality.

Throughout this chapter I have used official statistics as a means of charting the major race inequalities that characterize compulsory schooling in England. I have shown how apparently technical matters of measurement are actually political decisions because different methods produce diametrically opposed conclusions from identical data. Hence, changes in attainment that look significant using the proportionate change model hide inequalities that might be widening when measured using the percentage point approach. The approaches suggest very different understandings of policy and, in at least one case, have been used by a local authority that proclaims its commitment to social justice while setting targets that will exacerbate an already inequitable situation.

A complex but disturbing picture emerges when examining what contemporary data can tell us about the scale and interaction of different inequalities. Policymakers, commentators and some academics are keen to stress the supreme importance of economic status and the data certainly confirm that social class background is associated with gross inequalities of achievement at the extremes of the class spectrum. However, class does not appear to be equally significant for all groups: White attainment is much more closely associated with these differences. The growing emphasis on students in receipt of free school meals (FSM), therefore, projects a view of failing Whites that ignores the five out of every six students who do not receive FSM. Contrary to the popular image created by media scare stories and official Gap Talk, particular minoritized groups (Black students and their peers of Pakistani and Bangladeshi heritage) continue to be significantly less likely to achieve the key benchmarks when compared with White peers of the same gender.

Educational targets have become a staple of policy making and each year brings a raft of new statistical data. Beneath the annual fluctuations, however, certain key inequalities remain largely unchanged. Each of the principal ethnic groups is much more likely to achieve five higher grade GCSEs than they were when the main education reforms got underway. Unfortunately, groups have not shared equally in the overall improvements. White students are the *only* group to show an increase in every survey since the late 1980s and, despite concerted moves to reduce the number of students who are expelled from school, it remains the case that young people in each of the 'Black' monitoring categories are more likely to be permanently excluded: a school decision that is strongly associated with the most devastating effects on subsequent life chances. The Black/White inequality of achievement remains significant and shows no sign of closing in any meaningful way.

In view of these findings it is necessary to ask what role education policy has played in creating and sustaining these inequalities. How did we get here and what are the prospects for change in the near future? These are the questions that shape the next chapter.

4 Policy
Changing language, constant inequality

Critical analysis in education … must 'bear witness to negativity.' That is, one of its primary functions is to illuminate the ways in which educational policy and practice are connected to the relations of exploitation and domination in the larger society.

Michael W. Apple[1]

Introduction

In recent years there has been an explosion of academic writing about 'policy'. This includes a huge range of material, from narrow organizational/managerialist studies through to international comparisons of policy developments. As Michael Apple reminds us, however, policy is fundamentally a political issue: it is one of the means by which power operates. This chapter maps the main contours of recent British social and educational policy in relation to race: the aim being to understand how exclusions and oppressions have been made, remade and legitimized.

The following extract is from a 400-year-old Royal Proclamation that licensed a Dutch trader to literally round up and deport any 'Negroes and blackamoors' found on the streets of London. I have used the extract several times in my teaching and students are frequently shocked, not only by the fact that forced racist expulsions were practised so openly, but also by the simple fact that a Black presence was so public an issue in Shakespeare's England.

> Whereas the Queen's majesty, tendering the good and welfare of her own natural subjects, greatly distressed in these hard times of dearth, is highly discontented to understand the great number of Negroes and blackamoors which (as she is informed) are crept into this realm … who are fostered and relieved here, to the great annoyance of her own liege people who want the relief which these people consume … hath given especial commandment that the said kind of people shall be with all speed avoided and discharged out of this her majesty's dominions.[2]

There is a common assumption that Britain was ethnically homogeneous before the major post-war migrations from the Caribbean and Indian sub-continent in

the mid-twentieth century. In fact, Britain has *always* been ethnically
very name Britain derives from an invading European (Roman) force .
first century AD. The British Empire was established through colonial
including the systematic exploitation, murder and human trafficking
transatlantic slave trade and so, in a fundamental sense, the history of Brita
inextricably bound up with racism.³

As the Royal Proclamation of 1601 demonstrates, state sponsored racism .
neither new nor alien to Britain: contemporary politicians (of all major parties)
like to claim 'tolerance' as a core British value but a glimpse beneath the surface
reveals that the state has always preferred particular groups. What is most striking
about the Elizabethan proclamation is the familiarity of the sentiments: a 'great
number' of people with no natural right to be present are seen as consuming scarce
resources 'to the great annoyance' of British people. These are essentially the same
arguments that feature in newspaper articles and radio phone-ins about immigration and asylum issues in twenty-first century Britain. And here lies one of the
major aspects involved in any analysis of contemporary policy, i.e. that *policy
embodies strong continuities with the past while it simultaneously reshapes contemporary
priorities, actions and beliefs.* The combination of old and new is always complex and
always changing. It is simply wrong to imagine that nothing changes but it is naive
to think that each new policy statement represents a fresh start or a new chapter
untouched by centuries of prior actions and assumptions.

In this chapter I review the wider policy context for race and education debates over
the last 50 years or so, with a particular focus on the years of Labour Government
(from 1997). Much has changed during this time but the continuities are shocking:
indeed, it can be argued that, despite some superficial differences in rhetoric, *in relation
to race and ethnic diversity the current policy agenda is more narrowly focused, more mean-
spirited and more obsessed with social control than at any time in the last half century.*

Power, policy and discourse

The significance of social policy in general, and education policy in particular, is a
highly complex matter. Policy changes do not automatically lead to any particular
outcome in the daily realities of schooling. Stephen Ball, for example, has argued
that 'policy' is made and remade continually in a number of different contexts, each
inter-related, including the context of wider debates that influence basic assumptions
about a field of social policy; the arena of policy production itself; and, of course, the
context of practice where policies can be dramatically reshaped at the chalk face.⁴

The language and symbols that are used to describe policy are hugely important.
In this sense policy *discourse* relates not only to specific documents and discussions
about the next round of legislation, it also addresses the wider arena of social action
and controversy, where particular ideas are promoted as 'necessary' or 'common sense'
while others are dismissed as unworkable or even unthinkable. Stuart Hall says:

> A discourse is a group of statements which provide a language for talking
> about – i.e. a way of representing – a particular kind of knowledge about a

topic. When statements about a topic are made within a particular discourse, the discourse makes it possible to construct the topic in a certain way. It also limits the other ways in which the topic can be constructed.[5]

Discourse, therefore, is never merely descriptive; it is *constitutive*. Discourse involves power. Deborah Youdell states:

> We can also identify discourses of race or gender that set out what it means to be a gender or a race, but do it *as if* these were natural and/or self evident … While the terms of discourses may well be taken as reflecting 'truth', the way things are, for Foucault these are not reflections but the very moment and means of the *production* of these truths.[6]

In this Foucauldian sense, therefore, the wider debates are at least as important as the actual policy directives that emanate from sources such as the national Education Department and local education authorities (LEAs). As we shall see, debate about race and education is frequently controversial and highly contested. These debates, however, are vital in shaping the possibilities for greater race equality in the education system.

Charting race and education policy

Sally Tomlinson produced the first serious attempt to chart the position of 'race' issues in British education policy in the late 1970s.[7] Since then numerous writers have produced their own versions, almost all borrowing terms from Tomlinson's original.[8] This approach typically categorizes changing perspectives and actions via a series of 'models' or 'phases'. This has its dangers, not least the temptation to gloss over contradictions and resistance in an attempt to describe (create?) neat categories. The problem is visible in the wide variety of terms used by authors. As with previous attempts, my policy map is necessarily incomplete: the start/end dates for each phase are rarely precise and there are points of opposition and counter-developments, e.g. where national trends contrast dramatically with local practice in some areas. Indeed, as Peter Figueroa highlights, the entire post-war period can be viewed as a succession of developments where contrasting aims ('pluralist, antiracist, equitable' on one hand, 'antipluralist, racist, anti-immigrant' on the other hand) have been an ever-present source of contradiction, struggle and conflict.[9] Nevertheless, it is possible to identify certain key turning points and developments that, in hindsight, appear to have dramatically closed down certain possibilities and made other priorities seem not only acceptable, but even inevitable.

From neglect to colour-blind via 'swamping' (1945–97)

In previous studies I have presented detailed accounts of the different policy phases between 1945 and 1997.[10] It is not possible to reproduce those analyses in full here because of the limits of space. It is useful, however, to briefly identify some of the key historical trends because so much of contemporary policy is shaped, and given particular meaning, by what has gone before. Exhibit 4.1, therefore, presents a brief overview of the main policy directions during that period. As we will see, many of the key ideas have a disturbing resilience despite the changing rhetoric at a superficial level.

Exhibit 4.1: Phases and themes 1945–97

Ignorance and neglect (1945 to the late 1950s)

- Race and ethnic diversity are largely ignored by policy;
- Blatant popular racism is widespread, including in the public services.

This was a period when the 'signs in windows: "No Dogs, No Coloureds, No Irish" … were almost iconic in their depiction of London in the 1950s.' (McKenley 2005: 16)

'We didn't expect prejudice at all. We thought England was the home of justice – so we got quite a shock.' (Lawrence 1974: 39)

Assimilation (late 1950s to the late 1960s)

- Nottingham and London witness sustained outbursts of violence against minoritized people, including attacks coordinated by fascist groups;
- Despite the aggressors being White, the issues come to define 'the colour problem' as arising from the destabilizing presence of too many minoritized people;
- Major immigration controls are introduced;
- Policy assumes the goal of assimilation: the attempt to eradicate (or at least reduce to an absolute minimum) signs of racial and cultural difference;
- 'English for Immigrants' and dispersal policies characterize the educational response: emphasizing the teaching of the English language and moves to limit minoritized student numbers at the school and classroom level;
- The concerns of White parents/voters are paramount.

'The trouble makers … were shouting what others were whispering.' (Ramdin 1987: 210)

'A national system cannot be expected to perpetuate the different values of immigrant groups.' Commonwealth Immigrants Advisory Council, 1964 (Tomlinson 1977: 3)

Integration (1966 to late 1970s): Assimilation by a new name

- A change in rhetoric: 'cultural pluralism' and 'integration' become the aims;
- Dispersal ends;
- Race Relations Act 1976 establishes the Commission for Racial Equality (CRE) to work towards better race relations and advise on changes to the law;
- Curricular materials are produced that focus on *lifestyles*: minoritized groups portrayed as strange, exotic and Other;
- Education policy continues to view minorities as a problem needing to adapt to a largely unchanged system.

'… not a flattening process of assimilation but equal opportunity, accompanied by cultural diversity, in an atmosphere of mutual tolerance …' Roy Jenkins, home secretary, 1966 (Swann 1985: 196)

'[T]o enable integration to take place, it was argued that the majority society needed to be more aware of historical and cultural factors … [However] [t]he emphasis was still upon integrating the minorities with the majority society and culture … This meant that it was up to the minorities to change and adapt, and there was little or no pressure upon the majority society to modify or change its prevailing attitudes or practices.' Eric Bolton (former Chief Inspector of Schools) (Swann 1985: 196)

Cultural pluralism and multiculturalism (late 1970s to mid-1980s)

- Following community protests, an inquiry is established into race and education. Its interim findings (the Rampton Report) provide the first official acknowledgement that racism (in schools and society) is a factor in Black children's achievement. Teacher unions are outraged and the inquiry chairman is replaced;
- 'Multicultural education' becomes an accepted part of public policy rhetoric but remains synonymous with 'lifestyles' and celebratory approaches: criticized by antiracists as *the 3S's* – saris, samosas and steel bands (Troyna and Carrington 1990: 20);
- Antiracist movements gather strength in parts of the country but remain mostly a radical outsider perspective;
- The Swann Report recommends 'Education for all': a perspective that includes a range of approaches. The role of racism is downplayed and the education secretary effectively rejects the report on the day of publication.

'… under-achievement is not confined to the ethnic minorities … [Our] policies apply to all pupils irrespective of ethnic origin. As they bear fruit, ethnic minority pupils will share in the benefit.' Keith Joseph, Secretary of State for Education, March 1985 (Hansard 1985)

Thatcherism (mid-1980s to 1997): The New Racism and colour-blind policy

- Thatcherism personifies 'The New Racism': a discourse that promotes White interests by emphasizing supposed cultural differences and fear of swamping (Barker 1981);
- The implied threat of White reaction to perceived 'bias' rules out any policy attention to diversity;
- Colour-blind policies, ignoring/denying racial diversity, are defined as the only 'fair' way;
- A National Curriculum with no meaningful acknowledgement of race/ethnic diversity is imposed.

'[There is] no such thing as society.' Margaret Thatcher (Thatcher 1993: 626)

'Few things would inflame racial tension more than trying to bias systems in favour of one colour – a reverse discrimination that fuels resentment. An artificial bias would damage the harmony we treasure. Equality under the law – yes; equality of opportunity and reward – yes. These promote harmony. Policy must be colour-blind – it must just tackle disadvantage. Faced by British citizens, whatever their background might be.' John Major, Conservative prime minister (Major 1997)

Naive multiculturalism (1997–2001): New Labour and the Blairite project

Goodbye Xenophobia

Front page headline, *The Observer*[11]

It is difficult to over-state the sense of widespread relief with which progressive commentators welcomed the election of Tony Blair's 'New' Labour Party in May 1997.[12] Unfortunately, the promise was short-lived. Initially, at least, there were signs that equity would be taken seriously but, overall, Blair's first term in office can reasonably be described as a period of 'naive multiculturalism'. Naive because, although there is evidence of a limited commitment to equity, that commitment was largely superficial: it consisted of rhetorical flourishes that left mainstream policy untouched except for the area of separate faith schools, where the action indicated acceptance of a weak notion of equality of *access* and diversity of *provision* with no deeper analysis of the consequences nor a genuine understanding of the scale of race inequality in the system.[13]

Rhetoric but no serious action on race inequality

In a break with the state mandated colour-blind approach of the previous years, Labour's first policy documents involved a new emphasis on 'equal opportunities' and an explicit concern with race inequalities. Just 67 days after taking office the new Government published a statement of its policy intentions, 'Excellence in Schools', proclaiming 'the Government's core commitment to equality of opportunity and high standards for all'.[14] The ritual citation of 'standards' (measured in a crude form through national tests) was a clear legacy from the previous Thatcherite policy phase, but the focus on equality of opportunity contrasted sharply with the Conservatives' open hostility to equity issues.[15]

A further important break with Tory education discourse was Labour's readiness to openly acknowledge *race* inequalities. 'Excellence in Schools' included a section entitled 'Ethnic minority pupils' that referred to inequalities in achievement and offered modest commitments to consult on ethnic monitoring and 'best practice' in multi-ethnic schools.[16] A year later another major policy intervention repeated the same pattern: the first report of the new Social Exclusion Unit (SEU) took education as its theme and, once again, the scale of race inequities was noted.[17] Unfortunately, the symbolic break with Conservative colour-blind approaches did not translate into meaningful action. Both documents discussed ethnic inequalities separately from the rest of the analysis and left the main thrust of policy untouched by any sense of ethnic diversity. Consequently, an understanding of racism and racial inequality remained almost completely absent from how the principal policy issues were conceived. As a result, policy continued to pursue colour-blind targets.

Superficial equality and state-funded religious schools

One area where multicultural policy *did* change decisively involved the provision of state funding for Islamic schools. Labour's commitment to 'equality of opportunity' was important, in view of the Conservatives' open disdain for the notion, but their actions on race and education remained firmly locked into a superficial and weak understanding of equity.[18] After a decade of refusals by successive Conservative Governments, within a year of its election Labour had granted state funding to a handful of Islamic schools. In granting the applications the Secretary of State reportedly emphasized their technical merit rather than any ideological points, stating that the schools 'will comply with the statutory provisions governing all maintained schools, such as delivering the national curriculum and offering equal access to boys and girls'.[19] It is significant that equal opportunities, in terms of *gender* and *access*, were mentioned but not, apparently, any of the related issues that the decision raised concerning religious segregation: as I note later, the strategic citation of *gender* equity has become an important feature of Labour's policy pronouncements on *ethnic* diversity.

An especially serious oversight was the total failure to engage with the controversy over 'separate' or 'segregated' provision which had, until then, dogged these debates. When the Swann Committee addressed the issue more than a decade earlier, for example, it could not agree on a unanimous position: the majority argued that the existing support, e.g. for Church of England and Catholic schools, was an anomaly that should be reconsidered; in contrast, a minority of the committee argued that so long as the anomaly existed, natural justice demanded that it should be extended to other religious groups.[20] At the time Labour's decision went almost completely unremarked but it was an issue that would come back to haunt them later, not least because their own perspective on issues of race and education changed from one of naivety to cynicism.

Cynical multiculturalism (2001–5): from 9/11 to 7/7

> Doublethink … to hold simultaneously two opinions which cancelled out, knowing them to be contradictory and believing in both of them.
>
> George Orwell, *Nineteen Eighty-Four*[21]

The period following the attacks of 11 September 2001 saw a marked change in public discourses around multiculturalism. In the UK the wider context was characterized by a growing sense of anger and a desire for retribution. The public mood seemed to fuel, and was in turn heightened by, politicians' readiness to challenge elements of public multiculturalism that would previously have seemed uncontroversial.[22] These trends crystallized into an all-out attack on multiculturalism when one of the country's leading Black politicians – the man heading the public body charged with promoting race equality – declared that the term was no longer 'useful'. Any subsequent discussion of race and education suddenly had to combat a policy context where notions of multiculturalism and diversity were assumed to have *failed*. The government, however, did not abandon its *rhetorical* commitment to ethnic diversity and race equality: rather than a spirited defence of equity, these moves can be seen as a cynical attempt to retain the appearance of enlightened race politics while simultaneously pursuing a policy agenda that increasingly resembled the earlier assimilationist/integrationist phases (see Exhibit

4.1) where the voices and concerns of White people were openly accorded a position of dominance.

Tremendous anger and retaliatory confidence: policy after 9/11

The impact of the 9/11 attacks in the USA, both domestically and in terms of foreign policy, is well documented but their effect in the UK is less frequently remarked. As Matt Adams and Penny Jane Burke note in their work with people in three English villages, however, 9/11 had a powerful emotional impact even in areas where there are few minoritized people and the issue of multiculturalism would ordinarily have been a distant concern. In the following extract Jan (a White middle-aged administrator) has just been asked about her feelings concerning 9/11:

JAN: Tremendous anger.
INTERVIEWER: OK, and is the anger directed, do you have a particular direction of the anger…?
JAN: Well, the perpetrators. And, it isn't actually a racist thing … but because it was that race that did it, obviously your anger is focused towards them. Whichever race did it, I would have been focused, even if it had been white, or, uh, whatever the group responsible. It is not – some reports since say that people are anti- um, anybody from that area. Umm, but I've always taken people as I find them, and the only reason I am … is because of what they've done.[23]

Adams and Burke note that despite Jan's protestations that 'it isn't actually a racist thing', her 'constant slippages and elisions, qualifications and hesitations' betray a deeper struggle as she tries to convey her reactions without adopting what she would define as a racist position. They argue, contrary to Jan's rationalizations, that the fact that the perpetrators were *not* White is fundamental to White people's reactions: *the racialization of the event and the resulting demonization of entire minoritized communities simply could not have happened had the attackers been part of the White racial majority*.[24] The anti-fascist campaigning magazine *Searchlight* accurately captured the deadly combination of genuine horror, strategic fascist mobilization and racist news coverage that fed the poisonous atmosphere in the immediate aftermath of the attacks:

> There has been a terrible racist backlash in the United States and Europe following the attack. People have been shot, mosques bombed and young children attacked. A backlash was always likely … but it has unquestionably been made worse by the actions of far-right groups such as the British National Party [BNP], which has sought to brand all followers of Islam as potential terrorists. The language of the media and political leaders has also contributed to the racist backlash. The talk of a battle between 'civilization' and 'barbarism' invokes racial stereotyping … The press reporting on asylum seekers has done more to stigmatise black and Asian people in this country than anything the BNP could possibly achieve.[25]

The hostility to asylum seekers showed politicians, media and public opinion at their worst. Following 9/11, as plans were drawn up for an invasion of Afghanistan, the Taliban authorities were quickly presented as one of the world's most brutal and anti-democratic regimes. This was in sharp contrast to the response that would-be asylum seekers from Afghanistan received just the previous year when the then home secretary, Jack Straw, stated he wished to see them 'removed from this country … as soon as reasonably practicable'.[26]

As Shabna Begum has argued,[27] the aftermath of 9/11 saw a kind of 'retaliatory confidence' on the part of politicians who took the opportunity to position themselves as plain-speaking honest folk unafraid to voice 'common sense' opinions despite the supposed threat of censure from the forces of 'political correctness'. Straw's successor as home secretary, David Blunkett, argued that minority communities must do more to foster a 'sense of belonging'.[28] He subsequently introduced a policy of 'Integration with Diversity' that included proposals to discourage marriage outside the so-called 'settled community'; to speed up deportation; and to test the English language skills of new migrants.[29] The proposals had an unmistakably assimilationist/integrationist tone: not only was the language the same ('integration' into mainstream society once again became the supreme policy objective) but so too were many of the policy prescriptions including a renewed focus on English language teaching and an attack on so-called mono-cultural schools (which seem predominantly to be interpreted as those with a disproportionate number of minoritized, rather than a majority of White, students).[30]

The temperature of the debate was raised further when Blunkett – who has stated that 'Trust, plain-speaking and straight talking is something which matters so much to me as a politician'[31] – voiced his fears that 'Asylum seekers are swamping some British schools'.[32] The use of the word 'swamping' was incendiary because it directly echoed Margaret Thatcher's warning, 25 years earlier, that 'people are really rather afraid that this country might be swamped by people with a different culture': [33] a statement that is often seen as iconic of the Thatcherite New Racism (see Exhibit 4.1).

The popular press took this claim to new heights when it covered the 2003 report by the official schools inspectorate for England. Although the chief inspector was quoted as saying that only around 3 per cent of schools in England have more than one in ten asylum seeker students (hardly 'swamped' by any definition of the word), this detail was lost amid the sensationalist headlines: those below are from England's two top-selling daily newspapers *The Sun* and the *Daily Mail*:

Official: asylum rush causes crisis for schools
BRITISH kids are suffering as schools struggle to cope with a flood of asylum seekers' children, an official report warned yesterday.[34]

'Threat' of asylum pupils
The huge influx of asylum seeker children is threatening the education of tens of thousands of pupils, a report warned yesterday.[35]

The following year the whole question of multiculturalism and public policy was thrown into further doubt.

Trevor Phillips and the end of multiculturalism

As one of the most prominent Black figures in the country and head of the Commission for Racial Equality (CRE) – the public body with a legal duty to encourage better race relations and powers to prosecute offenders – Trevor Phillips caused a media storm in April 2004 when he told *The Times* newspaper that: 'Multiculturalism does not mean anybody can do anything they like in the name of their culture ... The word is not useful, it means the wrong things ... Multiculturalism suggests separateness. We are in a different world from the Seventies.'[36]

Phillips's interview focused mainly on the need to address the separation of different communities and work towards greater 'integration'. He also warned that politicians and the media share a responsibility to engage in serious debate rather than pander to the lowest common denominator in their pronouncements on immigration:

> The media must deal with facts, rather than some comic-book crusade ... The Government also has to keep its nerve. It must make sure it acts on the basis of real evidence rather than reacting to some of the fears in some of the newspapers or some of the focus groups.[37]

These points, however, were lost amid a political and media scramble to portray Phillips's words as a condemnation of everything associated with the concept of multiculturalism and race equality per se. *The Times* itself gave the interview top billing with the headline (alongside a photograph of an Asian man burning a Union flag):

Britain 'must scrap multiculturalism';

Race chief calls for change after 40 years.[38]

The Conservative Party's spokesperson described Phillips's comments as 'a seminal revision of the conventional wisdom which has dominated this debate for perhaps 30 years'[39] and the leading columnist Melanie Phillips (no relation) wrote an article entitled: 'For years anyone who said multiculturalism didn't work was branded a racist. Guess what? Now the Left admit they got it all wrong'.[40] The *Daily Mail* headlined its news coverage of the story, 'Multiculturalism is dead says race relations chief'.[41] The *Daily Mail*'s reaction is especially noteworthy, not only because it is the second-highest selling daily in the UK, but also because the paper has become emblematic of the middle-class sensibilities that New Labour judges to be crucial to its electoral hopes.[42]

A few days later the same paper published an essay by Ray Honeyford, an ex-headteacher who had been at the centre of a *cause célèbre* in the 1980s concerning his views on race and education.[43] Honeyford's piece was called 'Is the multicultural madness over? You must be joking…'.[44] Throughout these discussions the term 'multiculturalism' was rarely if ever defined. The word came to represent virtually any form of argument that White people should not be free to do and say whatever they please. Any discussion of race and education was now placed in a context where the dominant theme of public debate was an assertion that all such attempts had been pronounced failures by the very body entrusted with pushing forward race reforms.

Simultaneously, several key strands of argument emerged; all of them direct echoes of the earlier assimilationism/integrationism. First, 'diversity' was once again labelled a destabilizing element. Second, commentators drew renewed licence to argue for the supremacy of 'indigenous British' assumptions and sensitivities (a coded reference to the desires of White people). Third, grossly stereotyped arguments were once again paraded under the banner of common sense and plain speaking. Melanie Phillips wrote:

> Those of us who have consistently argued that multiculturalism would … dissolve social bonds, set minorities against each other and, above all, rob the indigenous British of their right to their own culture and identity have been mocked and vilified as bigots. … The phrase 'multicultural society' is a contradiction in terms because multiculturalism is a recipe for social disintegration. Mr Phillips's words are therefore very welcome, and in the current climate also brave.[45]

Robert Kilroy-Silk, an ex-Labour MP and former TV talk-show host, added his voice to those welcoming Trevor Phillips's statement and taking the opportunity to drive forward a crude assimilationist agenda. The following quotation is especially important because of the particular examples that Kilroy-Silk uses to highlight the supposed gulf between cultures:

> Trevor Phillips has pronounced that it is acceptable for us to take pride in our own culture. Thank you very much, sir. … There will be a host of uncomfortable opinions and unpalatable facts for you to deal with.
> We won't be called racist, will we, when we say that genital mutilation is evil?
> We won't be labelled as fascists when we assert that forced marriages are wrong? … Right. So let us be clear about some things. First, we must insist that all those who wish to make their home here must learn to speak English, earn their own living and accept our culture and political values[46]

The mocking tone gives a sense of how far to the right the atmosphere had shifted but Kilroy-Silk's arguments are far from comic: his examples – stressing an apparent concern for women's rights – and his policy recommendations (including an insistence on learning English) were soon to become the staple of official Labour Government pronouncements.

Aggressive majoritarianism (2005–present)

> Our tolerance is part of what makes Britain, Britain.
> So conform to it; or don't come here.
>
> Tony Blair[47]

On 7 July 2005 a coordinated series of explosions was triggered as part of an attack on London that killed 52 members of the public and injured more than 700 people.[48] The day quickly became known in the media as 7/7 in a deliberate echo of the 9/11 nomenclature. The attacks served to heighten still further the retaliatory confidence of politicians and media: indeed, it is fair to say that the mood changed from one of retaliation (hitting back) to one of 'aggressive majoritarianism' where Whites now took the initiative in promoting ever more disciplinary agendas. The rights and perspectives of the White majority were now asserted, sometimes in the name of 'integration' and 'cohesion' (the code words for contemporary assimilationism) but also simply on the basis that the majority disliked certain things (such as Muslim veils) and now felt able to enforce those prejudices in the name of common sense, integration and even security.

'Integration', 'cohesion' and social control: Trevor Phillips and British ghettos

A few months after the London bombings an intervention by Trevor Phillips once again pushed public debate in a new direction. In September 2005 he gave a speech warning against the separation of minority and majority communities. In many ways his speech continued elements of the analysis offered in *The Times* interview the previous year, which had been hyped as signalling the end of multiculturalism. Phillips's latest speech went further, however, by explicitly cementing the spectre of radicalized enclaves divorced from the White mainstream. The speech's title neatly captured its central message: 'After 7/7: sleepwalking to segregation':

> The fact is that we are a society which, almost without noticing it, is becoming more divided by race and religion. We are becoming more unequal by ethnicity. ... Residentially, some districts are on their way to becoming fully fledged ghettos – black holes into which no-one goes without fear and trepidation, and from which no-one ever escapes undamaged.[49]

Once again media and political reaction was immediate and powerful. Even before the speech was made, the *Sunday Times* ran coverage of a leaked version under the front-page headline: 'Race chief warns of ghetto crisis'.[50] Inside, a two-page spread quoted Ted Cantle – a government adviser on 'community cohesion': '[s]chools tend to reach a tipping point when about 45 per cent of the pupils come from ethnic minorities. "The evidence is anecdotal", he said, "but it seems you then get all the white families leaving."'[51]

There are striking parallels here with the arguments that supported the discredited dispersal policy (see Exhibit 4.1). A 1965 Education Department circular read: 'If the proportion [of immigrant children] goes over about one third either in the school as a whole or in any one class, serious strains arise.'[52] In 1965 the upper limit was set at 33 per cent; 40 years later the 'tipping point' was identified just 12 percentage points higher.

Trevor Phillips's comments were, as before, applauded by conservative commentators. In contrast, more progressive writers, especially Black intellectuals, offered a stark warning on how the arguments were turning reality on its head by repeating the historical trick of projecting minoritized communities, rather than White racism, as the problem:

> [T]he value of integration is contingent on whom you are asking to integrate, what you are asking them to integrate into and on what basis you are asking them to do so. The framing of the current debate is flawed on all three fronts. It treats integration as a one-way street – not a subtle process of cultural negotiation but full-scale assimilation of a religious group that is regarded, by many liberals and conservatives, as backward and reactionary. It is hardly surprising that many Muslims would not want to sign up to that.
>
> Gary Younge[53]

> Integration is a two-way process. How do you integrate with boardrooms that only want you to make the tea?
>
> Lord Herman Ouseley[54]

These sane, wise voices, however, were insufficient to quell the tide of aggressive assimilationist sentiments. Indeed, Jack Straw MP (former home secretary, later made Secretary of State for Justice by PM Gordon Brown) made a statement about the veiling of some Muslim women that added yet more vitriol to the debates.

'Open season on Islam': transposition and gender equality

Building on Critical Race Theory Gregg Beratan has developed the concept of 'transposition' to describe situations where one form of injustice is legitimized by reference to a different, more readily acceptable form of argument. When a musical piece is transposed into a different key, Beratan observes, the sound changes but fundamentally the song remains the same.[55] An example of racist transposition can be seen at work in the strategic deployment of gender equity issues as an acceptable trope for otherwise aggressively racist attacks on Muslim communities. One of the most dangerous and frequently repeated examples concerns the veiling of some Muslim women: an issue that has prompted racist harassment of women, including physical attacks.[56]

In October 2006 Jack Straw MP (a very senior Labour figure) declared that he would prefer Muslim women not to be veiled and that he routinely asks them to remove the veil when they come to see him for assistance.[57] He subsequently went further, describing the veil as 'a visible statement of separation and of difference' which, in the new context of policymakers' attacks on anything that delays 'integration', means that it is a problem in need of a solution.[58] A wholly predictable firestorm erupted: many commentators applauded Straw for breaking with 'political correctness'. Melanie Phillips went further, arguing that: 'This is not about prejudice or discrimination. It is about cultural survival.'[59] Politicians from both main parties joined in: the shadow home secretary, David Davis, asked in a Sunday newspaper whether Muslims were engaging in 'voluntary apartheid', while in a different paper a columnist noted that it was now 'open season on Islam'.[60]

These debates were not restricted to the pages of newspapers and the radio/TV news. They translated into changed attitudes and racist physical violence on the street. A BBC (ICM) poll claimed that a third of respondents supported an outright ban on the veil while over half supported a ban in certain places (such as airports and schools).[61] Although no official figures on the violent reaction were ever published, a series of sources documented an increase in racist attacks. The *Evening Standard*, for example, reported a 26 per cent increase in 'racist incidents' in London schools and drew particular attention to 7/7 and the veil row.[62] Similarly, the head of the Metropolitan Police, Sir Ian Blair, was quoted as being in 'no doubt' that 'Muslim women had been subjected to verbal intimidation or victimisation as a result of the debate'.[63] In view of these violent reactions, the response of some Muslim women was all the more courageous: no official figures are available but following the controversy there were reports that an increasing number of young women were adopting the veil in protest. The BBC reported that one trader, in Straw's constituency, had doubled his sales.[64]

The veiling controversy set the scene for a major policy speech by the then prime minister, Tony Blair, which set out the formal government position on integration, multiculturalism and contemporary assimilationism.

The duty to integrate: conform or else

As 2006 drew to a close Prime Minister Blair, who had already stated his intention to step down the following year, made a series of keynote statements intended to cement his legacy and ensure policy continuity (regardless of whoever succeeded him). His statement on 'the duty to integrate' made headline news and seemed designed to project a tough, no-nonsense image. TV news broadcasts repeatedly showed the same soundbite from the end of the speech: 'Our tolerance is part of what makes Britain, Britain. So conform to it; or don't come here.'[65]

'In other words,' as Karen Chouhan noted, 'Britain's tolerance is based on intolerance.'[66] The soundbite was typical of the disciplinary nature of the entire speech. The tone was established early on when Blair described the current tensions as the worst 'in a generation' and, via direct reference to 7/7, made an extraordinary statement ('we're not going to be taken for a ride') that could only be interpreted as a barely coded threat – aggressive majoritarianism and retaliatory confidence personified:

> For the first time in a generation there is an unease, an anxiety, even at points a resentment that our very openness, our willingness to welcome difference, our pride in being home to many cultures, is being used against us; abused, indeed, in order to harm us.

> I always thought after 7/7 our first reaction would be very British: we stick together; but that our second reaction, in time, would also be very British: we're not going to be taken for a ride.[67]

The word 'duty/duties' appeared ten times in the body of the speech and was used in a cavalier fashion that belied both the complexity of the issues and the very real fear and intimidation that had grown up around immigration in general, and the veil in particular. On the latter, Blair acknowledged how 'very hot and sensitive' the issue had become but immediately proceeded to claim support from an Arab source[68] and then assert 'plain common sense' as the overwhelming reason why White prejudice should win the day:

> In Tunisia and Malaysia, the veil is barred in certain public places. Now I know it is not sensible to conduct this debate as if the only issue is the very hot and sensitive one of the veil. For one thing, and let's be clear, the extremism we face is usually from men not women. But it is interesting to note that when Jack Straw made his comments, no less a person than the Mufti of the Arab Republic of Egypt made a strong approving statement; and it really is a matter of plain common sense that when it is an essential part of someone's work to communicate directly with people, being able to see their face is important.[69]

As had become customary, however, Blair was keen to emphasize his (rhetorical) commitment to equity and, once again, the act of transposition was in evidence as the attacks on Islam were presented as a concern for women's rights:

> [W]e stand emphatically at all times for equality of respect and treatment for all citizens. Sometimes the cultural practice of one group contradicts this … A good example is forced marriage … We have also changed immigration rules raising the age at which a person can obtain marriage entry clearance …

> One of the most common concerns that has been raised with me, and most specifically here at a meeting with women from the Muslim community, is their frustration at being debarred even from entering certain mosques. Those that exclude the voice of women need to look again at their practices.[70]

And the speech did not stop at vague threats and innuendo. It announced a new restriction on would-be migrants that echoed the decades-old obsession with the English language but actually went further than any previous policy phase by insisting that the language now become a *prerequisite* for citizenship. Typically, however, the measure was presented not as a restriction, but as a requirement of 'equal opportunity' and 'cohesion':

> [W]e should share a common language. Equal opportunity for all groups requires that they be conversant in that common language. It is a matter both of cohesion and of justice that we should set the use of English as a condition

of citizenship. In addition, for those who wish to take up residence permanently in the UK, we will include a requirement to pass an English test before
such permanent residency is granted.[71]

This policy is even more restrictive and regressive (likely to disproportionately hit
non-White applicants) than anything enacted in the original decades of assimilationism in the 1950s and 1960s. Indeed, it even meets the strident tabloid
demands voiced by Robert Kilroy-Silk in the aftermath of Trevor Phillips's
pronouncement on multiculturalism.

Incredibly, Blair's successor as prime minister, the then-chancellor Gordon
Brown, entered the same territory a few months later and, not to be out-done by
Blair, announced yet another means of disciplining would-be migrants:

> [I]n any national debate on citizenship, it is right to consider asking men and
> women seeking citizenship to undertake community work in our country – or
> something akin to that – that introduces them to a wider range of institutions
> and people.[72]

The openly disciplinary nature of this new requirement is made clear by Habib
Rahman (chief executive of the Joint Council for the Welfare of Immigrants) who
notes: 'Compulsory community service is usually imposed as a non-custodial
penalty for a criminal offence.'[73] Put simply, Blair's successor as prime minister – a
man who prides himself on his socialist background – is recommending that new
migrants be expected to undertake precisely the same activities usually required of
people as part of their punishment within the criminal justice system.

In education this same disciplinary trope combines with the attack on the veil in
the form of new guidance on school uniform codes. Officially entitled 'Getting
Dressed for Success', the guidance was published with the following advice:

> Schools should consult parents and the wider community when setting
> uniform policy. And while they should make every effort to accommodate
> social, religious or medical requirements of individual pupils, *the needs of
> safety, security and effective learning in the school must always take precedence.*[74]

The guidance goes on to stipulate the criteria that should inform schools' decisions. Echoing the key motifs of the era, 'security', 'integration' and 'cohesion'
feature alongside the anticipated focus on teaching and learning which, perhaps
predictably, support Blair's earlier assertion that it is 'plain common sense' that
'being able to see [someone's] face is important':

> security: schools need to be able to identify individual pupils in order to
> maintain good order and identify intruders easily;
> teaching and learning: if a pupil's face is obscured for any reason, the teacher
> may not be able to judge their engagement with learning, and to secure their
> participation in discussions and practical activities …

promoting a strong, cohesive, school identity that supports high standards and a sense of identity among pupils: if some children look very different to their peers, this can inhibit integration, equality and cohesion.[75]

It is revealing that although the guidance did not once mention the veil explicitly, it was precisely that issue which received most news coverage. The BBC ran the story under the headline, 'Schools allowed to ban face veils',[76] and the nation's best selling newspaper, *The Sun*, made the story its front-page lead under the headline, 'Veil ban on kids: schools' health and safety blitz'.[77] As had become usual, the anti-Muslim sentiment continued to be transposed into the more acceptable language of gender equity but the façade was not always well disguised; on its inside pages *The Sun* ran a longer version of the story under the headline 'School minister's verdict: face veils stop girls learning'. The opposite page, however, was dominated by a colour photograph of 'Nikkala 24, from Middlesex' posing topless.[78]

Conclusion: policy for white people

In 2004 I was teaching at a 'multicultural' summer school for graduate students from across Europe. The Danish students argued that their country was pursuing a positive form of integration and they could not understand why British contributors kept arguing that 'integration' was a code word for assimilation. In Denmark, they argued, integration would be an equitable process involving all parties in a fair dialogue.

'Ok,' I said, 'if that's true, then don't call it "integration": call it "the cultural transformation of Danish society" – because that's what you're describing.'

'Oh,' they said, 'we couldn't call it *that*!'

In Chapter 3 I showed that, for as long as relevant statistics have been available, certain minoritized groups have experienced pronounced educational inequalities. In view of the scale and resilience of these inequalities it seemed reasonable to ask what policymakers had been doing all this time. How had the situation been allowed to continue unchecked? In this chapter I have analysed the main thrust of social and educational policy in relation to race equality and ethnic diversity. The picture that emerges is both shocking and revealing. Essentially, race equality in education has continued to persist because social and educational policy has never seriously prioritized its eradication. Rather, policymakers have paid most attention to social control, assimilation and pandering to the feelings and fears of White people. *Most shocking of all, in key respects the contemporary situation is as bad, and in some cases worse, than anything that has gone before.*

Social Control

It is hardly surprising that the state should prioritize its own survival and, more specifically, that ruling parties should seek to maintain popularity with a majority of the electorate. Nevertheless, it is striking that in relation to race and ethnic diversity, policy has had an especially disciplinary edge throughout recent history. From the earliest days of formal assimilationism, in the 1950s, policymakers have displayed a particular desire to control the size, composition and education of minoritized groups. This was clearest in the dispersal policy of the 1960s, a policy that Labour later resurrected as part of its approach to asylum seekers in the twenty-first century[79] and echoed, albeit less formally, in its insistence that 'cohesion' and 'integration' could not be achieved where minorities were allowed to dominate individual schools. This view became most strident in the aggressive majoritarianism that has come to dominate public discourse following the terrorist attacks on the US and London in 2001 and 2005 respectively.

The events of 9/11 and 7/7 are highly significant in sustaining this disciplinary edge through the trope of 'security' and 'cohesion' but it would be a mistake to imagine that this approach was somehow *created* by the attacks. Rather, the attacks provided a new language and the spectre of an iconic threatening racialized Other that served to *justify* further disciplinary policies. Hence, policy has become systematically more assertive of the supremacy of the English language and the need for minorities to conform to the expectations of the majority (regardless of whether they are new migrants or those with a population presence dating back centuries).

Assimilation/integration

It has been argued that policymakers and their advisers often suffer from a form of 'policy amnesia' operating in a sort of historical vacuum where they are unaware, or dismissive, of what has gone before.[80] But it may be too simplistic to see today's politicians simply as unknowingly repeating the errors of the past: as this chapter has shown, key themes are constant and their latest forms build upon their previous incarnations. Nowhere is this clearer than in the fact that 'integration' – a word once dismissed as an historical relic – has been resurrected as one of the most important contemporary policy terms.

Like the previous assimilationist/integrationist era of the 1950s and 1960s, the contemporary period maintains the familiar obsessions of the past, especially the focus on the English language:

> English literature and language [are] 'the central expression of English life and culture and ... the central subject in the education of every English child'.
>
> Ministry of Education 1954[81]

> It is a matter both of cohesion and of justice that we should set the use of English as a condition of citizenship.
>
> Tony Blair 2006[82]

These quotations are separated by more than half a century (made in 1954 and 2006 respectively) but they share an absolute certainty in the supreme importance of the English language. Indeed, the most recent statement goes further than the earlier one by establishing English language competence as a basic requirement for citizenship: something that has never been the case previously and would have barred entry to thousands of South Asian migrants (especially wives and dependent children) in the years that separated the statements.

Buoyed by the retaliatory confidence of the post 9/11 and 7/7 popular back-lashes, and egged on by a conservative press jubilant at the supposed death of multiculturalism, contemporary assimilationism does not end at language use: anything that meets with White disapproval now faces the possibility of being defined as a barrier to integration and cohesion – hence a threat to public order – and therefore deemed illegitimate. Long-standing and complex arguments about the status of the veil, for example, have given way to a simplistic majoritarianism that invokes 'plain common sense' and, in the words of official guidance, renders everything outside mainstream expectations as a potential threat: 'if some children look very different to their peers, this can inhibit integration, equality and cohesion'.[83]

What Whites want

An unspoken but fundamental aspect of social policy in relation to race and ethnic diversity is the apparent assumption that, so far as possible, the status quo must be protected. From the earliest assertions of the supremacy of the 'host' society in the 1950s, including the need to demonstrate to White parents that minoritized students were not damaging *their* children's education, through the Thatcherite 'New Racism' that talked of difference (rather than superiority) and into New Labour's aggressive majoritarian 'common sense' assimilationism – *the constant assumption has been that the interests, feelings and fears of White people must always be kept centre stage.*

Throughout the entire period from the 1950s onwards – when policy has at least *acknowledged* race and ethnic diversity – two things have remained stable. First, there has been a refusal to put race equality at the centre of policy. Sometimes this was easy to detect, such as during the Thatcher–Major years of the 1980s and 1990s when colour-blindness was official policy and talk of equity was seen as antithetical to high 'standards'. At other times there has at least been a rhetorical commitment to recognizing diversity but this has never involved anything more than a few 'specialist' initiatives that left the mainstream thrust of policy unaltered.[84]

A second common element in British social and educational policy has been *the strategic deployment of White racial violence as a limit to policy and a threat against those who would challenge the chosen orthodoxy*. This may sound extreme but the evidence is clear. In the late 1950s, for example, when White mobs terrorized Black and Asian people on the streets of Nottingham and London the political reaction was to impose new restrictions on minoritized groups in general and immigration in particular. In this shameful episode the White mobs, including those organized by fascists, exerted an influence on policy that was wildly disproportionate to their number and set a precedent that subsequent prime ministers have been happy to follow, using the possibility of White violence as a more or less overt threat:

People are really rather afraid that this country might be swamped by people with a different culture … if there is a fear that it might be swamped, people are going to react and be rather hostile to those coming in.

Margaret Thatcher 1978[85]

Few things would inflame racial tension more than trying to bias systems in favour of one colour – a reverse discrimination that fuels resentment.

John Major 1997[86]

[T]here is an unease, an anxiety, even at points a resentment that our very openness, our willingness to welcome difference, our pride in being home to many cultures, is being used against us … we're not going to be taken for a ride.

Tony Blair 2006[87]

The overwhelming weight of social and educational policy, therefore, has failed to address race inequality: it has pandered to White racist sentiment and left the principal race inequalities untouched. In view of this failure to interrogate policy for its racist impact, it becomes even more important that assessment systems within education are fair and transparent, since these are the means by which students are graded and sorted: this provides the focus for the next chapter.

5 Assessment
Measuring injustice or creating it?

Imagine a world where a group of people is continually placed at the bottom of the social pile; in schools, in the labour market, in housing. Imagine that this group is blamed for its own misfortune: its members are seen as lazy, their families 'dysfunctional'; they're just not smart enough. But what would happen if this group started to pass tests more frequently than the dominant group? Would its fortunes change? Or would the test itself change? What would happen if the test was altered and, once again, the group returned to its more familiar lowly status? Outrageous? Impossible? *Think again.*

Introduction

Countless people use the results of educational assessments – politicians, journalists, teachers, students, parents, employers, academics and so on – but how many stop to consider the nature of the assessments themselves? There is a tendency to assume that assessments measure something worthwhile and that they are basically 'fair'. Indeed, assessment is often viewed as a relatively 'technical' area of expertise, much more likely to be viewed as a neutral 'scientific' concern than, say, arguments over teaching styles or curriculum content. But this view is both incorrect and dangerous. It is incorrect because assessments are no less a construction than any other aspect of education and it is dangerous because powerful groups tend to stamp their own imprint on the assessment system. As David Hursh observes, using New York as an example:

> Critics argue that an exam's degree of difficulty has varied depending on whether the State Education Department (SED) wants to increase the graduation rate and therefore makes the exam easier or wants to appear rigorous and tough and therefore makes the exam more difficult. The passing rate for the exam can be increased or decreased simply by adjusting the cut score, turning a low percentage of correct answers into a pass and a high percentage of correct answers into a failure.[1]

Manipulating pass/fail boundaries is a relatively simple and obvious way of influencing assessment outcomes. But what if certain *forms* of assessment were shown to disadvantage particular groups? It is well known that, on average, boys and girls tend to perform differently in different kinds of test. For example, girls appear to do especially well in verbal reasoning tests[2] whereas 'boys perform significantly better than girls on multiple-choice tests'.[3] This points to the fact that even if every student takes the same assessment there is no guarantee of fairness. This, of course, is a familiar point to critical race scholars.

Critical race theorists have long identified assessment as one of the key mechanisms by which current inequalities are reinforced and legitimized. As Gloria Ladson-Billings notes:

> In the classroom, a poor-quality curriculum, coupled with poor-quality instruction, a poorly prepared teacher, and limited resources add up to poor performance on the so-called objective tests. CRT theorists point out that the assessment game is merely a validation of the dominant culture's superiority.[4]

This is a stark and damning conclusion that many critics of CRT would describe as over-blown. Unfortunately, the data that I present in this chapter suggest that the situation is even worse: that the 'assessment game' is rigged to such an extent that if Black children succeed as a group, despite the odds being stacked against them, it is likely that the rules will be changed to re-engineer failure. I am aware that this claim will sound literally incredible to many readers. For this reason, I begin the chapter by reflecting briefly on the difficulty of identifying racism to the satisfaction of those in power. This leads me to adopt an approach that is in keeping with CRT but very much at odds with most self-consciously 'academic' work in the Western philosophical canon: I will tell a short story about assessment. In fact, although the beginning of the story sets out an imaginary scenario, the ending is very real. My purpose is to encourage you, the reader, to think differently about the basic issues raised by the recent history of assessment and Black educational attainment in the UK.

Along the way I will explore the racist impacts of internal selection at the school level (via tracking, setting and tiering) and then step back further to look at a nation-wide change in assessment procedures that appears, based on official data, to inscribe White racial domination from the moment that children enter the compulsory school system. The chapter ends with a brief review of the issues concerning the nature of 'ability' in policy discourse. I show that dated and racist notions of 'intelligence', which have been repeatedly discredited, continually resurface and have been given new impetus in 'Gifted and Talented' reforms that represent an officially sanctioned 'new eugenics'.

Assessment and educational inequality: who counts?

The same phenomenon can look very different depending on the perspective of the viewer; this is especially clear when it comes to identifying racism. It is striking that whenever critics (activists and/or scholars) propose a case where racism is implicated, there is a tendency for others (usually, but not exclusively, White people) to argue that some other factor is *really* to blame. For every Black student who fails an exam or is expelled from school (see Chapter 3) there is almost always an additional or alternate explanation: racism in education is rarely so clear cut that *every* observer will agree on it. One of the clearest cases of this within the academy can be seen in the methodological attacks against antiracist research where, it has been argued, the failure to *prove* the existence of racism to the satisfaction of the White academics in question is sufficient reason alone to assert that such accusations should not be voiced at all.[5] Indeed, even in signature cases like the murder of Stephen Lawrence, a case that ultimately led to the reform of British race equality legislation (see Chapter 6), there are always additional *possible* explanations. For example, as Stephen lay dying on the pavement (having been stabbed by a gang of White youths) a 14-year-old onlooker was astonished that none of the police officers present took action in response to his injuries. The official report notes:

> *She was amazed that no-one was attending to the body on the floor or trying to stem the flow of blood. She saw that there was a lot of blood and her knowledge of First Aid told her that something ought to have been done.*[6]

The attending police officers claimed not to have seen that there was a significant amount of blood and to have thought it best to leave Stephen in the position in which he had collapsed. This claim, essentially one of negligence rather than racism, was accepted by the inquiry team.

Rather than rehearse yet another set of definitions to be queried, clarified and queried again, in this chapter I want to take a somewhat different approach in order to examine how assessment might be intimately related to the racialized patterns of success and failure so familiar in countries such as the UK and the USA. Taking my lead from previous work in CRT, I want to return to the tradition of storytelling as a means of questioning common sense and making the familiar strange.[7] This is not to run from the demands of scientific rigour and conventional forms of academic disputation: readers who see no place for storytelling in science may skip forward to the end of the italicized text at no great loss. My analysis rests on the use of publicly available statistics and draws on a range of empirical studies (both quantitative and qualitative): my story is not an alternative to critique, it is a complement to it; a means of shedding new light on a set of issues whose remarkably damaging consequences might otherwise be lost amid the mundane and routine processes that not only *conceal* race inequality but actually *produce* it.

The 'wrong' result: a story about assessment

Imagine a deeply racist society. In this imaginary society racism saturates all public agencies. I am not describing a place that is generally nice but where the occasional nasty individual spoils things. No, this is a society were racism leaves its imprint on virtually every aspect of life, from birth to death (and everything in between).

    Now, of course, in a society so deeply patterned by racism not everything is plain sailing for the dominant group. People don't simply accept their subjugation no matter how long it has been practised nor how frequently they are assaulted. There are continual points of conflict and resistance but most of the time these are kept in check and barely register on the 'mainstream' consciousness. Consequently, the dominant group is able to sustain its preferred fiction: that the despised people have only themselves to blame for their misfortune. This is possible because – in this imaginary place – racism is present throughout every major part of society. Racism patterns its political system and its public services including the police, the media and the schools.

Until, that is, one day something goes wrong. One day it is discovered that, despite all the odds, the despised group is excelling in school. Totally contrary to the dominant group's view of how things should be, it emerges that the despised group is really good at something. And to make matters worse, this is not something that can be dismissed as frivolous or entertaining, like being good dancers, musicians or athletes.

It emerges that the despised group is excelling in a school test. They are not yet out-performing throughout the entire educational system but it becomes clear that on one particular kind of assessment they are not just holding their own, they are the very highest achievers. The dominant group is stunned: how can this be?

Now, of course, in this imaginary racist society such a thing cannot be permitted. The comforting myths of lazy, dull people who fail because of their own shortcoming will be exposed if they are allowed to display signs of exceptional educational merit.

But what is to be done? An obvious solution is to simply bar the despised group from taking the test. You can't pass what you're not allowed to enter.

Good answer. And, under certain circumstances, that strategy would work. So, let's leave the story for a moment to see what this might look like in practice …

Assessing merit or closing down possibilities? Tracking, setting and tiering

How children perform in school-based assessments frequently leads to systematic differences in treatment within school. These differences can quickly make unequal outcomes *inevitable*.

Tracking

In the US many high schools place students in different 'tracks' that offer academic classes to those who have performed 'appropriately', while less high achieving students find themselves in more general or vocational tracks. It has long been known that minoritized (especially African American and Latino/a) students tend to be over-represented in the lowest tracks.[8] Here, they cover a lower level curriculum, generally receive less stimulating teaching and are more likely to have teachers with low status in the school who see themselves as less effective educators.[9]

Setting

In the UK 'setting by ability' is the most common form of within-school selection; here, students are placed in separate hierarchical teaching groups for one or more subjects.[10] This approach is supported by government as a means of 'raising standards'. For example, the Labour Party's 1997 election manifesto stated explicitly that setting works 'for the benefit of high fliers and slower learners alike',[11] a claim that is directly contradicted by the international research evidence.[12] Nevertheless, setting retains a key place in education policy: in 2007, shortly before taking up his new role as prime minister, for example, Gordon Brown made a commitment to setting a cornerstone of his plans for 'world class' schools.[13]

Research suggests that setting embodies exactly the same kind of racist processes and outcomes seen in US tracking systems. Indeed, one of the most consistent findings in research on school-based selection processes is that when teachers are asked to judge the 'potential', 'attitude' and/or 'motivation' of their students they tend to place disproportionate numbers of Black students in low ranked groups.[14] Exhibit 5.1, for example, shows the proportion of students placed in the top mathematics set in schools that took part in 'Aiming High', a national initiative meant specifically to raise the achievement of Black students.[15] Mathematics is especially important because it is one of two 'core' subjects (along with English) that are required in the new 'Gold Standard' benchmark of achievement (see Chapter 3). Additionally, mathematics is the subject most likely to use setting: in the 'Aiming High' sample, for example, 88 per cent of secondary schools used setting in Key Stage 3 (when students are aged 11–14) rising to 100 per cent for the final two years (Key Stage 4).[16]

Exhibit 5.1 shows that the ethnic groups that tend to achieve well in GCSE exams at age 16 (Indian and White) are generally more likely to feature in the top maths sets earlier in their school careers. Similarly, students in ethnic groups that tend to achieve less well in their GCSEs (Black Caribbean, Black African) are less likely to appear in the top set than their White peers of the same gender.

This association between set placement and final achievement is hardly surprising. Advocates of setting would argue that the relationship simply reflects the 'higher ability' of certain groups over others. However, a more critical perspective suggests that the relationship may reflect a *causal* element, i.e. that certain groups do well *because* they are placed in higher sets. Certainly, it is known that teachers decide set placement on a variety of criteria, not merely test scores, and so set placement does not unproblematically reflect prior attainment earlier in the school. Disciplinary concerns and perception of student 'attitude', in particular, have been documented as factors that teachers take into account and which may exert a disproportionately negative impact on Black students.[17] This is especially worrying because research on the mathematics achievement of almost 1,000 students shows that young people with matched attainment at age 14 achieved systematically different results just two years later depending on which set they had been placed in: on average the higher the set, the higher their final attainment.[18]

The size of the Black/White gap in set placement (see Exhibit 5.1) is surprisingly large in view of the social class composition of the Aiming High schools. The 30 schools had more than twice the national average proportion of students in receipt of free school meals (FSM)[19] and, as I noted in Chapter 3, outcomes for

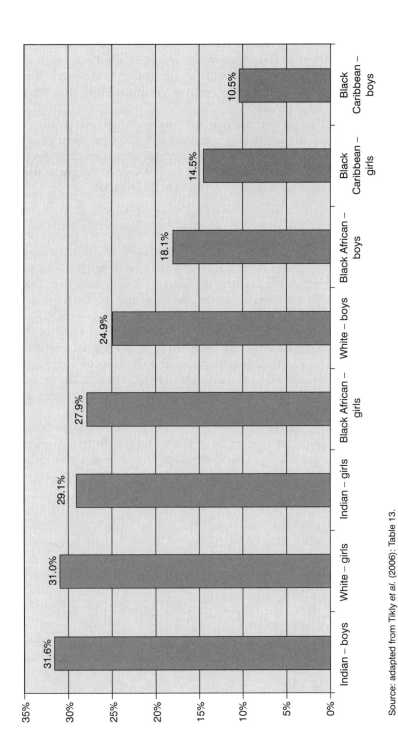

Source: adapted from Tikly et al. (2006): Table 13.

Exhibit 5.1: Top set placement by ethnicity and gender: mathematics, 2004 and 2005

Black and White FSM students tend to be equally low. We might have expected, therefore, that set placements in Aiming High schools would not show significant differences by race. However, comparing White and Black Caribbean students (the largest of the 'Black' groups in the sample) shows that the Whites were more than *twice* as likely to be placed in the top maths sets compared with their Black Caribbean peers of the same gender.

Students' differential set placement is especially important, not only because of its curricular, pedagogical and attainment consequences, but also because it largely determines the *tier* of GCSE examination that young people are entered for at age 16. This is a crucial decision that literally places an upper limit on the grades that can be awarded *regardless of how well students perform in the actual test*.

Tiering

The GCSE was introduced in 1988 and since then most subjects have adopted an approach known as 'tiering' (see Exhibit 5.2). In most subjects teachers allocate students to one of two separate exam tiers (in mathematics there were three tiers until 2006, when it adopted the two-tier model). Students may only enter one tier (there is no dual entry) and the tier places a higher and lower limit on the grades available. Those in the bottom level (called the 'Foundation Tier') cannot do better than a grade C in most subjects; meaning that study at advanced level may be out of the question because the necessary grades A* to B *cannot* be awarded in that tier. In mathematics, under the three-tier system, the Foundation Tier denied even a grade C; usually taken as the *minimum* requirement for entry to higher education and the professions.

In the first study to explore the relationship between race and tiering, Deborah Youdell and I discovered that two-thirds of Black students in two London secondary schools were entered for maths in the lowest tier. No matter how many

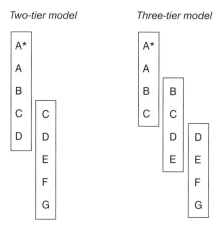

Exhibit 5.2: Tiering and the grades available in GCSE examinations (England)

questions they answered correctly, therefore, two out of three Black children could not possibly achieve the required pass grade in maths because the examination simply did not permit it.[20] The Aiming High sample allows us to explore the same issue in a larger number of schools, from across England, several years after the first research was completed.

As Exhibit 5.3 demonstrates, compared with their peers of the same gender in the main ethnic groups in the Aiming High schools, *Black Caribbean students were the most likely to be placed in the Foundation Tier for GCSEs in both mathematics and English*. As with set placement, the gap between Black Caribbean and White students in the Foundation Tiers was significant: at least 15 percentage points regardless of gender and curricular area.

The research evidence lends support, therefore, to the notion that setting and tiering operate in a cumulative fashion whereby initial decisions about set placement (that disadvantage Black students) compound inequity upon inequity until (because of tiering) success can become literally impossible. It is difficult to think of a clearer example of institutional racism than a test that is disproportionately taken by Black students and in which the highest grades are literally impossible to achieve (the fate of all Foundation Tier students).

And so, if we return to the story of a mythical crude racist society, we can see that denying entry to the test might provide a solution to the dominant group's dilemma. GCSE tiers are not widely understood (by students or parents, let alone the general public). Indeed, the case of GCSE tiering offers a neat example of how the dominant group could respond without even having to compromise its preferred narrative, that the despised group fails because of its own deficiencies rather than because of racism: the dominant group would simply report that the despised group was not good enough to take the test. But in the imaginary racist society of my story, the problem is bigger than that because denying access to the test is not an option. …

Once upon a time, when Black children did best

Despite the evidence of institutional racism throughout in-school selection processes, inequalities of attainment and access (in tracking, setting and tiering) are commonly explained by reference to prior attainment. Hence, it is argued, each decision simply reflects the already lower attainments of Black students at a previous point in their educational careers. But what if Black students started school doing as well, or even better, than their White peers? We can predict the dilemma that such a situation would produce:

Back in our invented racist society, let's imagine that the despised group is excelling at a test that every student must take. You see, in the place I'm asking you to imagine, the state has decreed that all children must be tested throughout their school careers. They are each stamped with a unique code number and a log of their successes – and failures – follows them throughout the system.

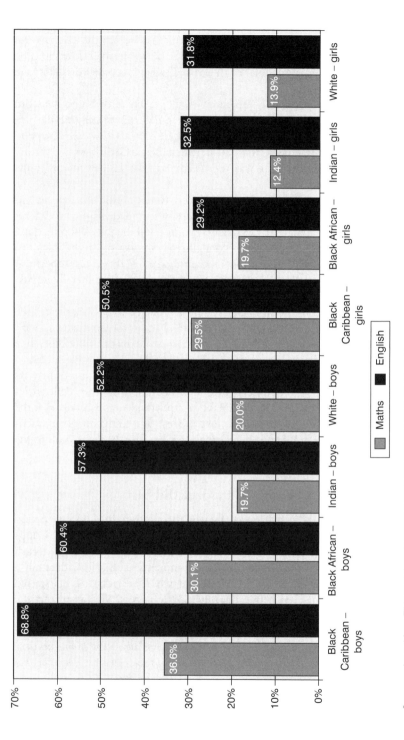

Source: adapted from Tikly et al. (2006): Table 14 (mathematics) and Table 15 (English).

Exhibit 5.3: Foundation Tier GCSE entry by ethnicity and gender: mathematics and English, 2004 and 2005

And so everyone must take the test. But if the dominant group cannot restrict entry to the test it seems that only one course of action remains: it must change the test. The test must be redesigned so that the despised group no longer succeeds. Simple.

But, of course, such a crass and obviously racist set of events would threaten the dominant group's pretence of fairness, wouldn't it? Such actions could never occur in the real world. There would be an outcry. Wouldn't there?

Black children and 'baseline' assessments

In 2000, with my colleague Heidi Safia Mirza, I co-authored a national report on the relationship between race, class and gender inequalities in education. The report was an independent review of evidence commissioned by Ofsted, the official schools inspectorate, as part of its response to the Stephen Lawrence Inquiry.[21] The work was widely reported in the media (including coverage on national TV, radio and newspapers) and certain findings received particular attention. First, in conflict with the dominant stereotypes, we found that there was a great deal of variation in attainment by minority groups in different parts of the country. In 2000 there was no legal obligation to monitor education results by ethnic origin but an increasing number of local education authorities (LEAs) were starting to gather this data, especially where the statistics were needed in order to bid for additional resources from central government. It was precisely this impulse that had led more than 100 LEAs to provide data which, after a somewhat protracted series of negotiations, we were able to access and analyse.[22] Contrary to expectations, we discovered that for each of the principal minoritized groups there was at least one LEA where that group was the most likely to achieve five or more higher grade GCSE passes.[23] This surprised many, including the Education Department, which had previously not realized the scale of variation within (as well as between) different groups.

A second finding that startled many observers arose from the same dataset. Most of the 118 LEAs on which we had data reported ethnic breakdowns from the age of 11 onwards, the point where most students move into secondary school. However, six LEAs also monitored students' achievements at age five, in the so-called 'baseline' assessments carried out when children entered compulsory schooling. The data on all six LEAs indicated that Black attainments fell relative to the LEA average as the children moved through school. The data on one LEA was especially striking: in the largest LEA in our sample (also one of the biggest authorities in the country) we found that Black children were the *highest* achieving of all groups in the baseline assessments (see Exhibit 5.4).

Exhibit 5.4 compares the local average and the proportion of Black children attaining the required level in national assessments at age 5, 11 and 16. At age five Black children were significantly more likely to reach the required levels: 20 percentage points above the local average. At age 11, however, Black children in the same LEA were performing *below* the local average. And at age 16, the end of compulsory schooling, the inequality was so bad that Black children were the *lowest* performing of all the principal groups: 21 percentage points below the average.[24]

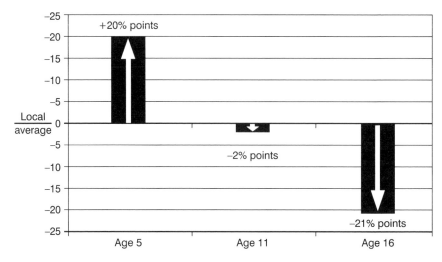

Source: adapted from Gillborn and Mirza (2000): Figure 5.

Exhibit 5.4: Black performance relative to LEA average at selected ages, 1999

In the report we noted that previous work had already begun to document the relative decline in Black attainment at later stages in the education system. A year earlier research for the pressure group Race on the Agenda had shown a similar pattern between the ages of 11 and 16. Its study used data on ten LEAs in and around London and showed that between the end of primary school and the end of secondary school, on average, African Caribbean students dropped more than 20 percentage points relative to the national average (see Exhibit 5.5).[25]

Prior to our Ofsted report, therefore, data were already suggesting that Black/White inequalities might be worsening as children move through the system. What marked out our report for particular attention, however, was the prominence of our funders and the range of our data. Unlike previous analyses the data in Exhibit 5.4 started at age five, much earlier than any other available data. In addition, by showing Black children as the *highest* achievers in the baseline assessments the data fundamentally challenged the assumption that Black children entered the school system poorly prepared (a common argument at the time). This was an important finding that quickly passed into the wider arena of debate on race and achievement. This view of Black children's attainments is now very widely cited; for example, the report is often used as a major source on race and education in textbooks.[26] The finding on five-year-olds has also passed into wider non-academic understandings and is frequently quoted as part of the context for debates on Black achievement:

> According to government figures, black pupils start primary school with some of the highest scores in baseline assessments of initial ability. But after two years they begin to slip behind other pupils.
>
> *The Guardian*[27]

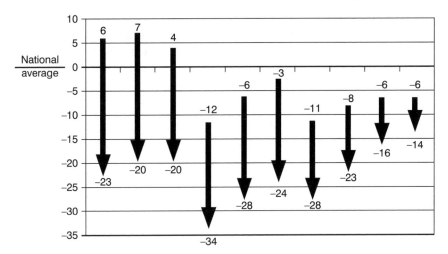

Source: adapted from Richardson and Wood (1999): Table 4.

Exhibit 5.5:   Black performance relative to national average at age 11 and age 16: ten LEAs, 1998

When African and Afro-Caribbean children start school at five they do as well in tests as white and Asian children. By the age of 11 their achievement levels begin to drop off. By 16 there has been a collapse.

Diane Abbott MP[28]

It is remarkable that in such a short time (these statements occurred less than five years after the report's publication) this once startling fact became an accepted part of the educational landscape, frequently used to highlight race inequality in the education system. Unfortunately, there is something even more remarkable, because in that same five-year period the system of assessment on entry to school changed and so did the patterns of attainment: Black children are no longer the highest achieving group, in fact, they are now among the lowest performers.

New assessment, new outcomes but a familiar story?

The Foundation Stage Profile

The term 'Foundation Stage' has been officially applied to the period between a child's third birthday and the end of their reception year in primary school.[29] Simultaneously, the 'Foundation Stage Profile' (FSP) has replaced the baseline assessments used to take place when children entered primary school. The introduction of the FSP completed a system whereby every child is now subject to national systems of assessment at the ages of 5, 7, 11, 14 and 16. Each child's results are individually recorded and forwarded to the Education Department in Whitehall.

There are several important points to note about the FSP. First, it is entirely based on teachers' judgements. The Qualifications and Curriculum Authority (QCA) describes it this way:

> Throughout the foundation stage, as part of the learning and teaching process, practitioners need to assess each child's development … These assessments are made on the basis of the practitioner's accumulating observations and knowledge of the whole child. By the end of the final year of the foundation stage, the Foundation Stage Profile will provide a way of summing up that knowledge.[30]

A second key point about the FSP is that it is a relatively complex assessment in terms of its coverage. Overall there are six 'areas of learning', sub-divided into 13 different 'scales' that are assessed individually in relation to specific 'Early Learning Goals' (see Exhibit 5.6).

Exhibit 5.6: The Foundation Stage Profile

There are six areas of learning in the Foundation Stage Profile (FSP), some are further sub-divided as follows:

1. Personal, social and emotional development:
• Dispositions and attitudes
• Social development
• Emotional development

2. Communication, language and literacy
• Language for communication and thinking
• Linking sounds and letters
• Reading
• Writing

3. Mathematical development
• Numbers as labels for counting
• Calculating
• Shape, space and measures

4. Knowledge and understanding of the world

5. Physical development

6. Creative development

Attainment on each area (and sub-set) is measured using a 9-point scale as follows:

• A score of 1-3 indicates working *towards* the Early Learning Goals;
• A score of 4-7 indicates working *within* Early Learning Goals;
• A score of 8-9 indicates *met* or working *beyond* Early Learning Goals.

Source: adapted from DfES (2006a): 31.

A final significant point in relation to the FSP is that the system was only introduced recently and is still surrounded in some uncertainty. The Department for Education and Skills states:

> *The results should be treated with caution as this is the first year that such data have been collected.* The data result from a new statutory assessment for which teachers have received limited and variable training and the moderation of results within and between local education authorities (LEAs) has been patchy.[31]

In fact, the Education Department was so worried about the quality of the assessments that when the results were first published (in June 2004) the document was entitled 'experimental statistics' and the National Statistics logo was deliberately not used.[32] This first analysis of data from the FSP made no reference to ethnicity at all. About six months later, however, the department made use of the same material in an overview of data on ethnicity and education. This time there was a partial breakdown of results in relation to the principal minority ethnic groups.[33] This is highly significant because it was the first time that any FSP data had been published with an ethnic component.

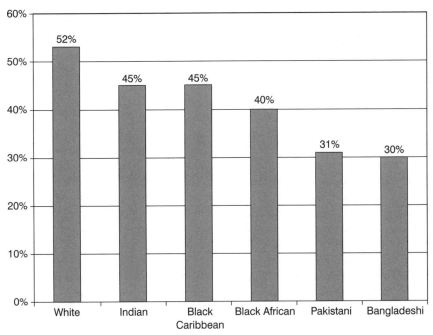

Source: adapted from DfES (2005d): Figure 3.

Exhibit 5.7: Foundation Stage Profile 2003: pupils meeting or exceeding the expected level, 'Language for communication and thinking', by ethnic origin

The DfES presentation included a brief explanation about the Foundation Stage and a note of caution about the level of teacher training involved and the moderation of results. The document then presented a breakdown of results in relation to one of the 13 scales (see Exhibit 5.7) and a summary of key findings. The discussion begins with the following statement: 'Patterns of achievement for minority ethnic groups in Early Learning Goals would appear to broadly mirror attainment gaps at older ages.'[34] This is a surprising summary because Indian students dramatically out-perform other groups at older ages (see Chapter 3) and yet White students emerge as the highest performers in the FSP. In addition, there is no reference to how this finding sits alongside previous work in the field such as the earlier baseline test results. Nevertheless, the document notes that this pattern is common across *all* of the 13 scales that make up the FSP: 'Pakistani and Bangladeshi children … perform less well, followed by Black African and Black Caribbean children (with all groups scoring less well than the average on all 13 of the scales)'.[35]

The DfES document makes no further mention of the Foundation Stage and there is no comment at all about previous research on minority children's assessed levels on entry to compulsory schooling. Consequently, the reader is left with a sense of continuity, not change. But these findings run contrary to the now widely held belief that Black children do relatively *well* on entry to compulsory schooling. As I have already noted, this belief is widely stated and re-stated: it appears in text-books, in the media and even in political discourse. And yet the Department for Education and Skills published the first ever ethnic analysis of results from the new assessments and the pattern was reversed *without comment*.

It is difficult to over-estimate the significance of these events: the received wisdom has been turned on its head; Black children have moved from being *over*-achievers to *under*-achievers; and the new assessment system that produced these outcomes is acknowledged to be based on training and moderation that is described officially as 'patchy'. And yet the results stand. The new pattern of attainment for five-year-olds is reported without further comment and one of the key issues that had raised critical questions about Black children's treatment in schools has been erased, almost over-night.

But what about attainment in the local authority that Heidi Safia Mirza and I had highlighted? The DfES data in the Exhibits are based on national returns and, as already noted, results can differ substantially from one LEA to another. With the co-operation of that LEA, we can judge how far the national picture is reflected at a local level. The result is far from encouraging.

The table reproduced in Exhibit 5.8 shows attainment in all six areas of learning in the FSP broken down by ethnicity and gender. The table relates to the same LEA that featured in the Ofsted report of 2000 (Exhibit 5.4). In order to retain the anonymity of the local authority I have removed the original data and inserted a figure (positive or negative) to show how each cell's value relates to the respective White performance (using the percentage point approach described in Chapter 3).

In total there are 180 different cells relating to minority attainment in the table: 159 of the cells (almost 90 per cent) show minoritized children being ranked

Exhibit 5.8: FSP assessments by ethnicity and gender in one LEA, 2004

Foundation Stage Assessments by ethnic group and gender 2004*

Ethnic group	Personal, social and emotional development			Communication, language and literacy			Mathematical development			Knowledge and understanding of the world			Physical development			Creative development		
	B	G	All	B	G	All	B	G	All	B	G	All	B	G	All	B	G	All
White	n/a	n/a	n/a	n/a	n/a	n/a	n/a	n/a	n/a	n/a	n/a	n/a	n/a	n/a	n/a	n/a	n/a	n/a
Mixed Race White/African Caribbean	−7	−1	−4	−4	−4	−3	−5	−3	−3	−5	+1	−2	+3	+1	+2	+3	+4	+4
Mixed Race White/Asian																		
Asian	−9	−5	−8	−1	−8	−5	−5	−11	−8	−11	−2	−8	−6	−7	−6	−9	−1	−7
Mixed Race Other	−10	−7	−8	−7	−10	−8	−10	−9	−9	−11	−9	−10	−4	−3	−3	−11	−7	−10
Indian	−7	−7	−7	−5	−9	−7	−8	−12	−10	−15	−13	−14	−5	−8	−6	−12	−9	−11
Pakistani	−16	−14	−15	−20	−24	−12	−23	−22	−22	−24	−24	−24	−9	−8	−8	−20	−15	−18
Bangladeshi	−15	−19	−17	−26	−29	−27	−26	−29	−27	−28	−28	−28	−10	−7	−8	−22	−17	−20
Asian Other	−7	−8	−7	−6	−11	−8	−12	−10	−10	−12	−12	−12	+1	=	+1	−6	−14	−10
Black Caribbean	−13	−7	−10	−14	−11	−12	−9	−7	−7	−8	−10	−9	−2	−4	−2	−5	−5	−5
Black African	−16	+2	−6	−23	−11	−15	−17	−7	−11	−28	−12	−20	−1	=	=	−18	+3	−6
Chinese	−9	−5	−6	−2	+2	+1	−5	−4	−4	−16	=	−8	−1	=	=	+10	−4	+3
All Groups	−7	−6	−6	−8	−10	−9	−9	−9	−9	−10	−9	−10	−4	−3	−3	−8	−6	−7

Note:
* shows proportion of pupils achieving the majority of Early Learning Goals in each area of learning (percentage points comparison with White pupils).

lower than their White counterparts. There are just 15 cells where minoritized students are ranked higher than Whites and most of these are within the areas of 'Physical development' and 'Creative development': domains where traditional stereotypes would more easily accept (generate?) such performance.

It gets worse…

In September 2005 I made these findings public as part of a keynote address at the annual conference of the British Educational Research Association (BERA). I had hoped that by generating some publicity about the effects of the new assessment, serious questions would be raised about the FSP, possibly leading to a review of procedures or even calls for its suspension. I have been in the field long enough to know that most education news stories have little or no impact on policy but, in view of the high profile of the earlier Ofsted report and the sheer scale of the turn-around in results, I hoped that this case would be different. I was wrong.

Although the story received some coverage in print media[36] it had little or no tangible effect. I have been told that questions were raised within the Education Department but no serious investigation was carried out. Indeed, the Department publicly dismissed my concerns:

> A DfES spokesman says, 'The original baseline assessments that Professor Gilborn [*sic*] refers to are from six local authorities and from a time when there was no national system or system for moderation. Those figures cannot be compared with the figures published earlier this year, which were national and moderated. A key principle of the Foundation Stage is that no child should be disadvantaged because of ethnicity, culture or religion, home language, family background, special educational needs, disability, gender or ability.'[37]

This is a disturbing quotation. First, the spokesperson uses the national remit and 'moderation' of the FSP as the basis for asserting its superiority. There is no acknowledgement here of the 'limited and variable training' and 'patchy' moderation (the Department's own words) that led the DfES to originally label the same data as 'experimental'.[38] In addition, the spokesperson asserts that a 'key principle' is that no child should be 'disadvantaged' by factors such as ethnicity, language, etc. No evidence is marshalled to defend against the accusation of institutional racism: in an echo of the failure to act on the new laws that arose from the Lawrence Inquiry (see Chapter 6) it appears that for the Education Department good intent alone is sufficient. On average the new assessment has placed *every* minoritized group below their White peers, but the Education Department is content.

And worse still…

Since I first raised questions about the FSP additional data has become available on subsequent cohorts. In view of the 'improvements' that the Department claims have been made in moderation and training[39] we might have hoped that the scale of some of the race inequalities would have fallen. In fact, the opposite is true.

Data for 2004 and 2005 showed numerous minoritized groups still achieving below the national average. In fact, this was true in *all* 13 FPS scales for *both* years for students in 9 of the 17 different census categories that the Department recognizes, including Black Caribbean, Black African, Black Other, Pakistani and Bangladeshi students.[40] Worse still, in most cases the size of the inequalities actually *grew* between 2004 and 2005 (see Exhibit 5.9).

It would appear, therefore, that improved training and moderation has only deepened the race inequality that appeared with the introduction of the FSP. This change in patterns of attainment is hugely important. It is these scores that schools will use to judge the progress of the students in later assessments. Potentially, the lower attainments of Black students in subsequent stages of the education system will no longer be viewed as a relative *drop* in performance; they may simply be viewed as performing in line with their now lower starting points. And, in case you are in any doubt about how quickly the political and educational systems are

Number of FSP scales where the inequality of attainment rose between 2004 and 2005*

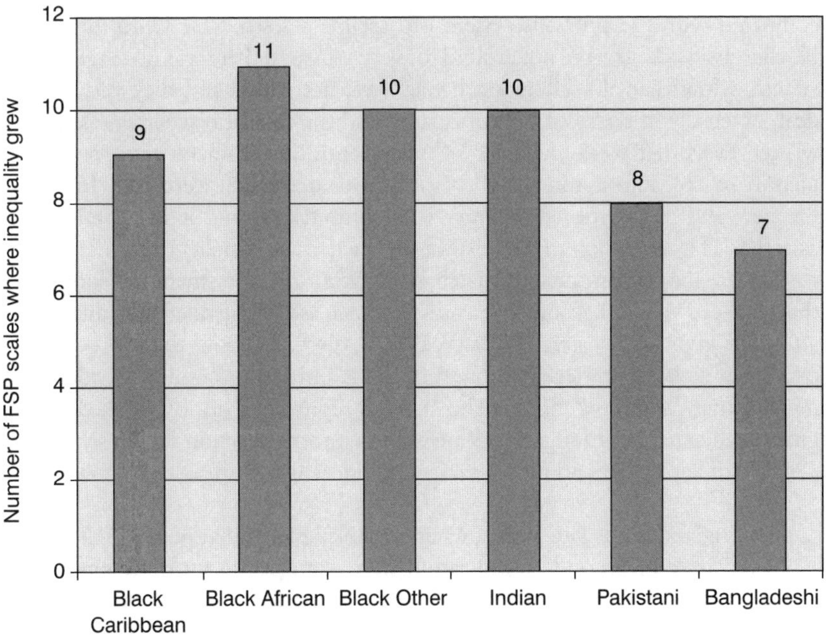

Source: adapted from DfES (2006a): Figure 21.

Note:

* defined officially as where the gap widened between the percentage of students in the group and the average for all students who have met or are working beyond the Early Learning Goals.

Exhibit 5.9: Widening gaps in the FSP, 2004 to 2005

adapting to the new story written by the FSP, consider the following. In 2006, around two years after the first ethnic analysis of FSP, a new cross-departmental report set out the Government's intention to improve race equality across society. The chapter on education includes the following section:

> **Identifying reasons for the poor start**
> Data from the Foundation Stage Profile (FSP) results show that some minority ethnic groups of children tend to perform less well than their peers. Local authorities will have to identify the reasons for this and address common factors that may be obstacles to the development of young children in their area.[41]

And so the old story of Black educational success at age five has been entirely rewritten. The new assessment has established Black failure as, once again, the norm. The change has been accepted as an unfortunate fact and the Government is asking LEAs to 'address' it.

How did we get here?

Clearly, these developments raise a series of important questions, most obviously why does the FSP produce such markedly different results for Black students when compared with the previous system of baseline assessments? Unfortunately, the baseline assessments were not around for very long and there was no single national system. More than 90 different schemes were accredited and they varied a great deal, especially in terms of their formality and the mix of teacher assessment and written tasks that were involved.[42] Consequently, it is difficult retrospectively to identify reliable information on the various approaches that were used. In contrast, the new FSP is a national scheme; it is compulsory; and it is entirely teacher assessed. This latter point (the reliance on teacher assessment) may offer a clue to part of the mechanism behind the changes. Work on assessment has long argued that teachers' views of group characteristics (such as class, gender and ethnicity) can affect the scores they give.[43] I have already discussed how these processes can operate at a classroom level (through tracking and setting) and it is widely documented that Black students tend to be over-represented in low ranked teaching groups when teachers' judgements are used to inform selection within schools.[44] In a review of key debates about assessment, Sanders and Horn note the following:

> In England in the late 1980s, when the assessments that make up the General Certificate of Secondary Education were changed to put more emphasis on performance tasks (which are assessed by classroom teachers) and less on written answers, the gaps between the average scores of various ethnic groups increased rather than narrowed.[45]

In addition, the change in the *timing* of the FSP may be implicated in the new pattern of results. The new assessment is completed by teachers at the *end* of the children's reception year whereas most baseline assessments were completed within the first few weeks of children entering school. Some antiracist practitioners have suggested to me that the relative deterioration in Black students' scores (noted previously in assessments that were spaced years apart; see Exhibits 5.4 and 5.5) may actually take effect during this first year. They report that Black students are often viewed as relatively advanced when they first enter school: unlike many White students, they can frequently write their names and read simple sentences (a sign of the high value placed on education in minoritized households). However, it is possible that even during the very first year of schooling such positive evaluations are overridden by teachers who come to see them stereotypically as a source of trouble while, on the other hand, their White peers have time to catch up and show what they are capable of.[46]

How these changes in outcome have come about, therefore, is an important question but even more important is the fact that the changes occurred without apparent disquiet and possibly even without being recognized: there is nothing to suggest that the FSP results raised any eyebrows at the DfES. Indeed, the Department's public response was to question the validity of the earlier baseline assessments (in which Black students performed well) and to assert the validity and good intent of the new system.

Boldly stated, the facts are simple: in recent years Black students' attainments at the start of school appear to have radically decreased relative to their White peers; this has coincided with the reform of assessment procedures at that stage and yet the pattern is reported officially without query and without further comment. This looks suspiciously like the imaginary racist society in my earlier story.

However, there is a key difference. Unlike the society in that story, I have no evidence that the changes in England were manufactured deliberately. This is not to deny their impact and severity: the changes that have happened are clearly racist in their outcome; Black students, in particular, have been markedly disadvantaged. And, although the racist impact of the original changes may not have been planned, it is certain that a decision has subsequently been made to defend the changes and resist calls for change; the Department's own statements and actions provide ample evidence of this. Consequently, the most *generous* interpretation of these events is that they arose from the normal workings of the education system: a system that places race equality at the very margins of debate and robustly defends a new assessment that produces results that leave all minority groups in the wake of the White majority. Mainstream education policies are enacted with little or no regard to how they will impact on minoritized students. This is demonstrably the case in relation to GCSE tiering and setting within schools, and it is true of the assessment system more generally. One question suggests itself: Is it possible to imagine a contrary situation where no action would be taken if a new assessment system resulted in White children being out-performed by their peers in every minority group?

Before moving on it is necessary to examine one more area where assessment operates to re-inscribe and legitimate racist inequalities of educational opportunity and achievement. Tests of 'cognitive ability' (otherwise known as 'intelligence tests') arise from an area of supposedly scientific exploration that is continually discredited but always resurfaces. Most worrying of all, the fundamental assumptions are widely accepted as common sense and are used to justify a growth in 'gifted' education that represents one of the most extreme forms of racist assessment.

Ability, intelligence and the 'new eugenics'

> When two dozen prominent theorists were recently asked to define intelligence, they gave two dozen somewhat different definitions.
>
>

Task force established by the Board of Scientific Affairs
of the American Psychological Association[47]

> We must make sure that every pupil – gifted and talented, struggling or just average – reaches the limits of their capability.
>
> Department for Education and Skills[48]

The scientific study of human abilities is an area fraught with complex and bitterly contested divisions. When national bodies have attempted to clarify what is reliably established they have usually drawn attention to how little is agreed even concerning the most basic issues (such as the meaning of 'intelligence'). Despite this policymakers, advisers and many teachers continue to behave as if the meaning of intelligence/ability is plainly obvious.

The first quotation (above) demonstrates the lack of any firmly agreed position on intelligence, even among psychologists. The second quotation shows that the British Government not only believes in a clear and hierarchical notion of intelligence; it also knows how many groups exist. The quotation is taken from one of the Government's most high-profile education reform documents. Published with a flurry of publicity in 2005, 'Higher Standards, Better Schools for All' was meant to mark a new stage in Labour education reforms: summing up past achievements and setting out fresh approaches for the future. But much of the document embodies the kinds of assumption about ability (what it is and how it is distributed) that were dominant more than 60 years ago and have since been repeatedly debunked.

Racist pseudo-science and contemporary education policy

From the late 1940s to the 1960s secondary education in Britain operated a selective entry system – still maintained in a few LEAs – where access to the favoured 'grammar schools' was granted to children who passed the 11-plus exam. On average, girls scored higher than boys, which logically would have meant that girls outnumbered boys in grammar schools. However, most LEAs operated separate pass lists to ensure equal numbers of each sex: at least one LEA made sure that boys outnumbered girls! Consequently, in most parts of the country girls had to score more highly than boys to 'pass' the same test.[49] LEAs tried to justify their actions in numerous ways and legal challenges dragged on for years.[50] It is known that such tests systematically place a disproportionate number of Black students as failures but no LEA chose to make good this anomaly by setting a lower pass rate for Black students and no legal challenge was brought against a biased exam. *In short, a gender inequality was viewed as problematic but a race inequality was taken for granted.*

And now, in the twenty-first century, the government's aim 'that every pupil – gifted and talented, struggling or just average – reaches the limits of their capability'[51] takes for granted that people have different degrees of potential and, indeed, that these 'limits' can be identified. Second, and most disturbingly, the statement assumes a three-way split between the 'gifted and talented' at the top end of the distribution, the 'struggling' at the bottom, and the 'just average' in the middle. This three-way division is heavy with historical significance: the selective post-war education system in England was modelled on a tripartite division that was justified in relation to the psychometric theories of the day. Based on the now discredited work of Cyril Burt,[52] the Norwood Report of 1943 famously described three types of child, using language full of class and gendered bias:

> *[T]he pupil who is interested in learning for its own sake*, who can grasp an argument or follow a piece of connected reasoning … who is sensitive to language as expression of thought … He can take a long view and hold his mind in suspense … He will have some capacity to enjoy, from an aesthetic point of view, the aptness of a phrase or the neatness of a proof …

> *[T]he pupil whose interests and abilities lie markedly in the field of applied science or applied art* … He often has an uncanny insight into the intricacies of mechanism whereas the subtleties of language construction are too delicate for him …

> *The pupil [who] deals more easily with concrete things than with ideas* … Because he is interested only in the moment he may be incapable of a long series of connected steps; relevance to present concerns is the only way of awakening interest, abstractions mean little to him.[53]

Significantly, a three-way division has also proven alluring to contemporary theorists who propose a *genetic racial* basis for intelligence. J. Philippe Rushton's 'gene-based evolutionary theory', for example, asserts three basic groups, each naturally selected and ordered hierarchically; he places 'people of east Asian ancestry' (whom he calls 'Mongoloids' or 'Orientals') at the top; those of 'European ancestry' in the middle; and 'people of African ancestry (Negroids, blacks)' at the bottom.[54] Rushton is the current president of the Pioneer Fund, a 'not-for-profit' organization established in 1937 with the purpose of 'race betterment, with special reference to the people of the United States'.[55] The Fund describes its aim as:

> … furthering the scientific study of human ability and diversity. We are resolved to promoting better understanding of our similarities, our differences, our past, and our future through scientific research and dissemination of that information to the public – no matter how upsetting those findings may be to any entrenched religious or political dogmas.[56]

The Pioneer Fund has made substantial grants to many of the most influential writers in the hereditarian tradition (including Rushton, Richard Lynn, Hans

Eysenck and Arthur Jensen) all of whom have asserted a genetic component to human intelligence which they argue, on average, places Black people substantially behind Whites in measured intelligence.[57] Charles Lane estimates that the Pioneer Fund made grants totalling more than $4 million to many of the key authors (13 in total) whose work is cited in Herrnstein's and Murray's infamous tract about the supposedly genetic basis of race and class inequality in the US, *The Bell Curve*.[58] Indeed, Jean Stefanic and Richard Delgado argue that 'racial pseudo-science, like that popularized in *The Bell Curve*, can only be carried out with funding from elite conservative organizations'.[59] In *The Bell Curve*, Herrnstein and Murray argue:

> *Putting it all together, success and failure in the American economy, and all that goes with it, are increasingly a matter of the genes that people inherit.*

> *[T]he average white person tests higher than about 84 percent of the population of blacks … the average black person tests higher than about 16 percent of the population of whites.*[60]

The Bell Curve sparked huge controversy in the 1990s with its claims that African Americans (and 'underclass' Whites) were genetically predisposed to lower intelligence and higher criminality.[61] In 1994, as the public controversy raged on, a group of 52 professors (including Rushton, Lynn, Eysenck and Jensen) presented themselves as 'experts in intelligence and allied fields' and signed a statement that was published in the *Wall Street Journal* under the title 'Mainstream science on intelligence'.[62] Among the statements of supposedly 'mainstream' scientific opinion were the following:

> Genetics plays a bigger role than does environment in creating IQ differences among individuals … The bell curve for whites is centred roughly around IQ 100; the bell curve for American blacks roughly around 85 … black 17-year-olds perform, on the average, more like white 13-year-olds in reading, math, and science, with Hispanics in between.[63]

These views are presented as if distilled from numerous 'scientific' studies and the tone of delivery is somewhat dry.[64] But the meaning is clear. First, the authors are stating that intelligence is largely a matter of genetic inheritance. Second, they are saying that most Whites are naturally more intelligent than most Black people: in fact, that the 'average white' is more intelligent than eight out of ten African Americans!

Despite these authors' claim to 'mainstream' status, and the commercial success of *The Bell Curve*,[65] most policymakers would publicly reject any suggestion of innate racial inferiority. However, the fact is that policymakers in Britain *act* as if they fundamentally accept the same simple view of intelligence (although they substitute the term 'ability') as a relatively fixed and measurable quality that differs between individuals. This is what Deborah Youdell and I have termed 'the new IQism', that is, a view of 'ability' that encodes deeply regressive (and erroneous) assumptions about intelligence, once familiar in the discredited IQism of the 1960s.[66] In fact, this view of ability/intelligence is demonstrably false.

Ability/intelligence is not relatively fixed: there is no measure of potential

> [H]uman abilities are forms of developing expertise ... tests of abilities are no different from conventional tests of achievement, teacher-made tests administered in school, or assessments of job performance. Although tests of abilities are used as predictors of these other kinds of performance, the temporal priority of their administration should not be confused with some kind of psychological priority ... There is no qualitative distinction among the various kinds of measures ...The fact that Billy and Jimmy [*sic*] have different IQs tells us something about differences in what they now do. It does not tell us anything fixed about what ultimately they will be able to do.[67]

This quote is from someone working *within* the psychometric field: Robert J. Sternberg, the IBM professor of psychology and education at Yale, who is a major figure in contemporary 'intelligence' testing and a leading theoretician in the field of human abilities and giftedness. Sternberg has devoted considerable energy to his thesis that 'abilities' are 'forms of developing expertise'. However, Sternberg's central argument is not as revolutionary as some might think. The Cleary Committee, appointed in the 1970s by the American Psychological Association, stated that:

> A distinction is drawn traditionally between intelligence and achievement tests. A naive statement of the difference is that the intelligence test measures *capacity to learn* and the achievement test measures *what has been learned*. But items in *all* psychological and educational tests measure *acquired* behaviour ...[68]

Contrary to popular belief, therefore, there is no test of capacity to learn nor academic potential: *every* test so far conceived measures only what a person has learnt to that point. Despite the 'scientific' façade that surrounds the industry of standardized testing, therefore, we must remember that tests – *all tests* – measure only whether a person can perform well on that particular test at that particular time. If a student is given focused support and preparation for a test, including so-called 'cognitive ability tests' (the preferred term for contemporary IQ tests among those constructing and selling them), then on average their performance improves significantly.[69] This is a hugely important fact that is rarely given the significance it deserves, so let me put it another way.

Ability, intelligence and the driving test

One way to think about assessment in education is to compare our use of school tests with our use of other assessments, such as the driving test. Schools routinely assume fixed differences in potential on the basis of their assessment of students' performance. They separate children into different groups (tracks, sets and tiers) that are treated very differently and, not surprisingly, eventually emerge with markedly different results. But this is the equivalent of saying that people who do not pass their driving test on the first attempt have demonstrated that they cannot attain complete proficiency behind the wheel. Does society deny such people the opportunity to drive or at least limit the engine capacity of their vehicles? Of course not; the suggestion is ludicrous. In reality, people take additional lessons and, on the basis of their improved performance, the vast majority eventually make the grade. Society does not assume that a poor driving test denotes an inner deficiency that can never be made good, but that is precisely how children are treated in terms of their academic potential.

Gifted and Talented: elite and privileged

> [T]he needs of gifted and talented children in inner city schools are not given the priority they deserve … Secondary schools will be expected to develop a distinct teaching and learning programme for their most able five to ten per cent of pupils.[70]

In the late 1990s, the Labour government announced a scheme to reward schools for identifying their 'gifted and talented' children and to provide enhanced teaching and resources to cater to their particular needs. In view of previous work on the racialized nature of selection in schools antiracists warned that Gifted and Talented registers would further institutionalize racism in schools. These warnings were rejected. Responding to public criticism that I had made, for example, the Education Department stated: 'The gifted and talented scheme will identify children by looking at ability, rather than attainment, to capitalise on the talents of the individual child, regardless of ethnic background.'[71] Incredibly, its own rebuttal demonstrates clearly that the Education Department is working under the familiar but mythic belief that 'ability' and 'attainment' are somehow different; as if 'ability' were some inner quality or potential.

   As previous research has demonstrated, regardless of the form of assessment used (whether relying on teachers' judgements or on formal IQ/cognitive ability tests) the odds are stacked against Black children. Exhibit 5.10 shows the scale of the problem. Three years after my initial warning, and the official rebuttal, the DfES published the first breakdown of Gifted and Talented cohorts by ethnicity. The data show that White students are identified as 'gifted and talented' at more than twice the rate of Black Caribbean children and five times the rate for their Black African peers.[72]

The new eugenics

Eugenics – the attempt to engineer a supposedly stronger, more intelligent population by selective breeding and other approaches (including the sterilization of 'inferior' groups) – was dealt a severe public relations blow by the atrocities committed by Nazi Germany in the twentieth century. But eugenics is far from dead. In the words of Bernadette Baker, there is a 'new eugenics' visible in 'the everyday dividing, sorting and classifying practices of schooling' that relate ulti-mately to the '"quality control" of national populations'.[73] Indeed, numerous

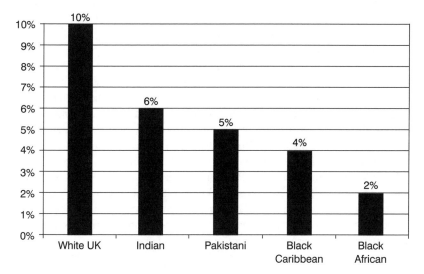

Source: adapted from DfES (2005d): 36.

Exhibit 5.10: Gifted and Talented by ethnic origin

authors, working in different subject specialisms in different countries, have each used the same phrase to describe the renewed popularity of beliefs in genetically patterned and heritable causes of socially constructed inequalities.[74]

In fact, eugenic thinking is remarkably close to the surface in contemporary education. For example, as part of the Gifted and Talented reforms the British government established a National Academy for Gifted and Talented Youth (NAGTY) at a cost of £20 million over the first four years.[75] The NAGTY was consciously modelled on the Center for Talented Youth at Johns Hopkins University in the US.[76] Significantly, the US centre was established by Julian C. Stanley, one of the 52 'experts' who signed the *Wall Street Journal* statement on IQ and race. But establishing a eugenic motive to the NAGTY does not require such detective work, important though the link is. To judge the dangers inherent in the Gifted and Talented programme in general, and NAGTY in particular, we need only consult the organization's website:

> [T]here are reasons that transcend education policy that suggest that a country would be well-advised to give gifted education a more central location. Today's gifted pupils are tomorrow's social, intellectual, economic and cultural leaders and their development cannot be left to chance. Where it is left to chance, evidence from England and elsewhere indicates that educational progress is not so much a question of intellectual merit but rather a question of affluence, with the most affluent receiving the best education and therefore achieving most highly. This suggests significant intellectual ability being untapped and unnoticed.[77]

There are several things of note here. First, the eugenic assertion that 'Today's gifted pupils are tomorrow's social, intellectual, economic and cultural leaders' is clear: NAGTY assumes that it is dealing with the cream of the crop with no doubt about the efficacy or scope of its selection methods. But even more worrying is the attempt to pass off the privileging of those students fortunate enough to have been identified as 'gifted and talented' – and we have seen that the process is deeply racialized – as a victory for equality of opportunity. The statement that 'significant intellectual ability [is] being untapped and unnoticed' sounds laudable but NAGTY's performance, like the Gifted and Talented scheme more widely, offers little hope that anything is changing: the most recent inspection reports have stated that 'only small numbers from Pakistani, Black African and Black Caribbean heritages' appeared on NAGTY courses.[78] Despite the rhetoric of new opportunities and benefits for all, therefore, Gifted and Talented education is operating as an additional even more extreme example of how contemporary assessment produces racist inequalities under the guise of a meritocracy.

Conclusion

> Our society must rationalize a larger and larger disparity – measured by the difference between equality of results and equality of opportunity. Because we want to believe that our country gives every person an equal chance to succeed, we must justify social stratification on other grounds. We turn to genetics since it allows us to explain why whites hold most of the wealth … after all – whites are biologically superior.
>
> Richard Delgado[79]

Richard Delgado has commented that advanced capitalist systems, such as the US, UK and Australia, face a contradiction between their twin attachments to neo-liberalism and free-market economics on the one hand, and equality of opportunity on the other hand. This contradiction threatens the stories that our nations tell about themselves, as lands of freedom and opportunity. The solution lies in assessments that label minoritized groups as inferior and explanations that identify the cause as their own deficiencies.

In this chapter I have described how the systems of setting and tiering operate to deny a disproportionate number of Black students the possibility of gaining the best pass grades in the high stakes tests that mark the end of compulsory schooling in England. Despite the rhetoric of 'higher standards for all', the simple fact is that many Black students are locked into an examination that, by enforcing fixed grade limits for different papers, makes the highest grades literally impossible to attain. I have also described how a new system of assessment for five-year-olds appears to have erased, virtually over-night, the only part of the system where Black children were relatively successful. Perhaps most frightening of all, I have shown how official data suggest that the reinstated Black/White inequality for five-year-olds is growing at the same time that teachers' training in the new system is supposedly reaching new heights. Finally, I reviewed assumptions about the nature of 'ability' and showed how long-discredited beliefs about intelligence are being re-coded and reinforced through contemporary policy that claims to be meritocratic while it enacts a deeply racist approach that amounts to a New Eugenics of Gifted and Talented education for the few – most of whom happen to be White.

In this chapter, therefore, I have used the case of assessment and testing to raise fundamental questions about the possibility of socially just outcomes in an education system dominated by the perspectives of White policymakers and practitioners. The evidence suggests that assessment does more than merely *record* inequality: it is implicated in the processes that *produce* and *sustain* inequality. This offers yet another challenge to the assumption, common to liberal democratic societies, that race inequality is a temporary aberration and that race is a marginal issue in society at large, and the education system in particular. A critical perspective on race and education highlights that – whatever the rhetoric – race inequality is a constant and central feature of the education system. In this chapter I have tried to show how even the most dramatic of set-backs can happen without apparent malice, and even without comment. Until we address the presence of racism, as a fundamental defining characteristic of the education system, the present situation is unlikely to change in any meaningful sense, irrespective of superficial rhetorical commitments to inclusion, civil rights and social justice.

Liberal opponents of Critical Race Theory might argue that such dramatic moves against racism have already occurred. In the US, for example, the civil rights gains of the 1960s are celebrated as historic landmarks; in the UK the Stephen Lawrence case is often held up as showing that the system is capable of addressing racism and launching far-reaching reforms as a result. I address these arguments in the following chapter and show how the consequences of these cases are far less certain than might first be assumed.

6   The Stephen Lawrence case:
An exception that proves the rule?

The Lawrence tragedy is our tragedy.

Nelson Mandela[1]

Introduction

The key driving force behind advances in the rights of minoritized groups is minoritized groups themselves. In England *every* notable development taking forward antiracist education has arisen in some way as a direct result of action by minoritized people. Often the catalyst for change nationally is a major protest or public injustice, frequently involving bloodshed, even death. These are typically presented, by policymakers and media commentators, as if they arise randomly, when some fluke occurrence exposes a problem and action is taken to rectify the anomaly; one more step on the steady road of incremental advance towards ever greater inclusion and social justice. The most notable example in recent British history was sparked by the racist murder of a Black teenager, Stephen Lawrence. Over a period of several years the case grew to occupy a place in British cultural politics at least equivalent to the O.J. Simpson trial and the Rodney King case in the US.

Murdered in cold blood on a London street for no other reason than his race, Stephen Lawrence's killers have never been brought to justice. After a prolonged and painful campaign the Lawrence family eventually won a public inquiry into the police's failure to successfully prosecute his attackers. The catalogue of police racism and incompetence was such that when the inquiry report was published the Government announced its intention to take forward new race equality legislation which ultimately included specific duties that affect every state-funded school in the country. The move was hailed as a turning point in British race relations: now, less than a decade after the Stephen Lawrence inquiry, the education system appears mostly to have ignored its legal duties and Government seems to have abandoned its short-lived commitment to challenge institutional racism across the public services. For ease of reference a detailed timeline, setting the events in their historical context, is provided at the end of the chapter (Exhibit 6.1).

This chapter documents what happened and, using the concepts of 'interest convergence' and 'contradiction-closing cases' – ideas drawn from Critical Race Theory – I hope to shed new light on how apparently revolutionary moments (like the Lawrence case) are quickly recaptured by the racist status quo. This is vital, not only because of the high profile of the Lawrence case (and its symbolic importance as a potential turning point in British race politics) but also because of the wider lessons that it teaches us about the operation of power in a racist society where exceptional breakthroughs can quickly be recolonized in ways that not only betray those involved in the initial struggle but may actually reinforce the very inequities that we are told have been addressed.

What if they changed the law and no-one noticed?

> Looking back now, I am sure that if the government had realised all that would come out of the inquiry, they would not have let it take place.
>
> Doreen Lawrence[2]

Stephen Lawrence was 18 years old when he was murdered by a gang of White youths. His parents' fight for justice, in the face of a racist, incompetent and uncaring police force, made legal and social history. The Stephen Lawrence case led to far-reaching changes in race equality law (that touched every public body in the UK) and elevated the notion of 'institutional racism' to a point in the public consciousness where the term is now frequently used and debated in politics and in the mainstream media. But for all this, serious questions remain about the long-term impact of the case. Before reviewing the key events, therefore, it is worth outlining two concepts which, I fear, shed a great deal of light on the role of such cases within the wider politics of education policy and White racial domination.

Interest convergence and contradiction-closing cases

In Chapter 2 I outlined the concept of 'interest convergence' and noted that it has become a key part of CRT's conceptual toolkit. As Derrick Bell argues:

> On a positivistic level – how the world *is* – large segments of the American people do not deem racial equality legitimate, at least to the extent it threatens to impair the societal status of whites … The interest of blacks in achieving racial equality will be accommodated only when it converges with the interests of whites.[3]

Interest convergence offers a powerful way of understanding the dynamics of race and social policy at certain points, especially where a landmark event appears to have advanced the cause of race equality. The less well-known, but no less insightful, idea of contradiction-closing cases helps to explain what happens after the news headlines have died down and racism returns to its business-as-usual.

When reviewing the key civil rights decisions of the US Supreme Court, Bell shows how, in retrospect, these famous victories can be seen to have operated in much more complex ways than was initially imagined. Hailed as landmark victories that would change the social landscape forever, Bell argues that their progressive impact was not only uncertain and short lived but that, in the long run, their consequence may be to further protect the status quo:

> We can expect that the Court will favor civil rights litigants if the policies they attack are so blatantly discriminatory as to shock (or at least embarrass) the public conscience. This is particularly true when a ruling in favor of black litigants will not impose any costs on identifiable classes of whites … Such cases might be seen as 'contradiction closing' cases … These cases serve as a shield against excesses in the exercise of white power, yet they bring about no real change in the status of blacks.[4]

The idea of contradiction-closing cases has been taken up and used by several writers, most notably Richard Delgado, who argues that they protect the status quo by offering an occasional symbolic victory to minorities that 'allow business as usual to go on even more smoothly than before'.[5] Using the 1954 *Brown v. Board of Education* desegregation case as an exemplar, Delgado argues that a clear pattern can be seen. Initially the case seems to offer a huge breakthrough – things will never be the same again. Those arguing the case rejoice in their victory and many liberals move on to other issues, assuming this one to be solved. However, lower courts may interpret the decision very narrowly; administrators and others in the system 'drag their feet' over any substantive changes; meanwhile, conservatives redouble their resistance and mobilize to have the decision overturned in practice if not principle. Years later the case stands as a 'landmark decision', used to celebrate the country's liberal values and commitment to equality, but on the ground little or nothing has really changed. Fifty years after the *Brown* decision it has been argued that US schools are even more segregated than they were at the time of the original case.[6]

In this chapter I outline the Stephen Lawrence case: from the murder, to his family's fight for justice; the public inquiry; the reform of race equality law; and the piecemeal changes that have followed. Unfortunately, the case stands as the supreme example of a contradiction-closing case in the UK: a case that, after years of the most painful campaigning and mistreatment, was supposed to have changed Britain for ever but which now seems to have left little imprint on the system in general, and education in particular.

The murder, the investigation, the campaign, the inquiry

At around 10.30pm on 22 April 1993, Stephen Lawrence was waiting for a bus home with his friend, Duwayne Brooks. Stephen walked a short distance from Duwayne to see if he could see a bus coming. The public inquiry into the case describes what happened next:

> Mr Brooks called out to ask if Stephen saw the bus coming. One of the [five or six White youths on the opposite side of the road] must have heard something

said, since he called out '*what, what nigger?*' With that the group came quickly across the road and literally engulfed Stephen.[7]

Stephen was stabbed twice. His attackers ran off, leaving him to struggle about 100 yards towards Duwayne before collapsing. A granite memorial stone now marks the spot where Stephen died: it is regularly defaced with racist graffiti.

Stephen was by no means the first Black young man to be murdered in an unprovoked racist attack on British streets, and he was not the last.[8] But his case was set apart by the courage and endurance of his parents, Doreen and Neville Lawrence, who waged a campaign for justice that made national headlines and continues to this day.[9] From the beginning the investigation was dogged by police incompetence, disdain, racism and, possibly, corruption.[10] Shortly after witnessing his friend's murder Duwayne Brooks was questioned by police who thought him 'very agitated' and 'aggressive'.[11] The public inquiry concluded that 'Mr Brooks was stereotyped as a young black man exhibiting unpleasant hostility and agitation, who could not be expected to help, and whose condition and status simply did not need further examination or understanding'.[12]

Stephen's parents were equally badly treated: seen by officers as troublesome and interfering, they too were labelled as aggressive. At the inquiry Doreen Lawrence recalled what happened:

> Basically, we were seen as gullible simpletons. This is best shown by Detective Chief Superintendent Ilsley's comment that I had obviously been primed to ask questions. Presumably, there is no possibility of me being an intelligent, black woman with thoughts of her own who is able to ask questions for herself. We were patronised and were fobbed off …
>
> I thought that the purpose of the meetings was to give us progress reports, but what actually happened was that they would effectively say: 'Stop questioning us. We are doing everything.'[13]

An internal review of the case concluded that 'the investigation has been progressed satisfactorily' but that 'relations were hampered by the involvement of active, politically motivated groups' and the investigation had been 'undertaken with professionalism and dedication'.[14] The review's author, an extremely experienced officer, later admitted to suppressing evidence (that would have been critical of the original investigation) for fear of damaging police morale. The review was ultimately described by the public inquiry report as 'misleading', 'flawed' and 'indefensible': the evidence of its author was considered 'unconvincing and incredible in a number of important respects'.[15]

Undeterred, the Lawrences pursued their case through every legal channel open, including launching a private prosecution. At one point they felt confident that they had sufficient evidence to convince a jury, including surveillance video of the main suspects wielding knives and using violent racist language. One suspect is seen saying: 'I reckon that every nigger should be chopped up, mate, and they should be left with nothing but fucking stumps.'[16] This damning evidence was never shown to the jury: the judge ruled out Duwayne Brook's identification evidence and directed the jury to return 'not guilty' verdicts. Doreen Lawrence recalls:

> Only later did I start to analyse the implications: bringing a private prose-cution was a very rare event, yet here was a black family doing just that, in a case that threatened to show up the Conservative government, show up the Crown Prosecution Service, show up the Metropolitan Police force, show up the entire justice system – the enormous odds against us winning had not dawned on me before. In my mind's eye, I had believed that in the end right was on our side, but the forces lined up against us were too great. I may be wrong; but I know I was naïve to think we could succeed.[17]

Despite these huge set backs, the Lawrences continued their campaign and, following a change of government in 1997, were finally granted the public inquiry they sought.

Much of the inquiry, chaired by Sir William Macpherson of Cluny, was held in public and the nightly coverage in the news media meant that the catalogue of police errors and racism was broadcast nationally, initially to a sceptical public but eventually to a growing sense of outrage.[18] Conscious of the wider issues that were emerging, the inquiry report does not limit itself to the failings of the police in the Lawrence case. Indeed, the inquiry identified changes in the *education system* as fundamental to the issues it had uncovered:

> [T]he issue of education may not at first sight sit clearly within our terms of reference. Yet we cannot but conclude that to seek to address the well founded concerns of minority communities simply by addressing the racism current and visible in the Police Services without addressing the educational system would be futile. The evidence we heard and read forces us to the conclusion that our education system must face up to the problems, real and potential, which exist.[19]

Consequently, among its list of 70 recommendations, the inquiry report includes direct calls for changes in the education system.[20] Of greater significance than any of the individual recommendations, however, is the report's championing of a particular interpretation of 'racism' that moves beyond the crude, limited and obvious notions that usually characterize official approaches.

Institutional racism

> 'Racism' in general terms consists of conduct or words or practices which advantage or disadvantage people because of their colour, culture or ethnic origin. In its more subtle form it is as damaging as in its overt form.
>
> 'Institutional racism' consists of the collective failure of an organisation to provide an appropriate and professional service to people because of their colour, culture, or ethnic origin. It can be seen or detected in processes, atti-

tudes and behaviour which amount to discrimination through unwitting prejudice, ignorance, thoughtlessness and racist stereotyping which disadvantage minority ethnic people.[21]

This is how the Stephen Lawrence Inquiry defines racism and institutional racism. In reaching this position the inquiry took evidence from a range of individuals and organizations, including academics and Black advocacy groups. The definition builds on existing notions of institutional racism in two important respects. First, it condemns the actions both of *individuals* (in their 'conduct', 'attitudes and behaviour') and *organizations* and *agencies* whose 'processes' work against certain groups. In this way the inquiry rejects the familiar official assertion that racism is limited to the actions of a few 'rotten apples'. Second, and most importantly, this approach moves away from endless debates about *intent* by explicitly focusing on the *outcomes* of actions and stating that 'unwitting' and 'thoughtless' acts are equally as problematic as overt racism. The definition removes intent from the equation and focuses simply on the outcomes of actions and policies.

This is not to say, however, that the inquiry ignored the importance of people's perceptions. In fact, the report goes on to define a racist incident explicitly in terms of individual perceptions but, once again, it shifts the balance away from the usual locus of intent: "*A racist incident is any incident which is perceived to be racist by the victim or any other person*" ... this definition should be universally adopted by the Police, local Government and other relevant agencies.'[22] This approach was in direct conflict with the views expressed by the country's most senior police officer, Sir Paul Condon (at that time head of London's Metropolitan Police), who wanted to retain the most basic, crude understanding of racism (in his words the 'normal' view) which, he argued, reflected what an 'average member of the public'[23] would understand:

> I have serious reservations for the future of these important issues if the expression 'institutional racism' is used in a particular way. I am not in denial. I am not seeking weasel words. I have been the first to be critical of police officers and the police service to say things which are unpopular. I am not denying the challenge or the need for reform, but if you label, if this Inquiry labels my service as 'institutionally racist' (pause) then the average police officer, the average member of the public will assume the normal meaning of those words. They will assume a finding of conscious, wilful, or deliberate action or an action to the detriment of ethnic minority Londoners.[24]

The inquiry pushed ahead with the more radical approach and, initially at least, met with success in its attempt to shift public debate on the issue.

The inquiry's reception

On 24 February 1999, almost six years after the murder, the Stephen Lawrence Inquiry report was presented to Parliament by Jack Straw, the home secretary who had established the inquiry. Before that, however, Prime Minister Tony Blair used his weekly Parliamentary question and answer session to praise the Lawrence family, condemn the failures that had been exposed and to promise far-reaching action in the future:

> I am proud that it was this Government who set up the Lawrence inquiry. I am happy to accept its judgment … The publication of today's report on the killing of Stephen Lawrence is a very important moment in the life of our country. It is a moment to reflect, to learn and to change. It will certainly lead to new laws but, more than that, it must lead to new attitudes, to a new era in race relations, and to a new more tolerant and more inclusive Britain. … The test of our sincerity as law makers in this House is not how well we can express sympathy with the Lawrence family, but how well we implement the recommendations to make sure that such an incident never again happens in our country.[25]

Placing the report before Parliament, Jack Straw was even more forthright, making clear that the inquiry's recommendations had the Government's support and, significantly, noting that Condon accepted the inquiry's findings *and* its definition of racism: in the weeks before publication it had been clear that the inquiry would make acceptance of its definition a key factor in taking forward its recommendations, prompting speculation that Condon would be forced to resign. In the event Straw stated:

> The House will share my sense of shame that the criminal justice system, and the Metropolitan police in particular, failed the Lawrence family so badly. The Commissioner of Police of the Metropolis, Sir Paul Condon, has asked me to tell the House that he shares that sense of shame. He has also asked me to tell the House that, as head of the Metropolitan police service, he fully accepts the findings of the inquiry, including those relating to him. … I have asked Sir Paul to continue to lead the Metropolitan police to deliver the programme of work that is now required. He has agreed.[26]

On its publication the report dominated the media. Most coverage focused on the Metropolitan police, the principal subject of the inquiry, but education also featured prominently. This was prompted by the last four of the inquiry's 70 recommendations, which were entitled 'prevention and the role of education'. Among the actions called for by Macpherson were changes to the National Curriculum 'aimed at valuing cultural diversity and preventing racism'; a higher profile for these issues in Ofsted school inspections; and new duties on schools and local education authorities to address racism. The latter included a call for all 'racist incidents' to be monitored and for the publication of these data annually and on a school-by-school basis.[27] Many daily newspapers included some mention of the education recommendations, including the *Daily Mail*'s headline on an inner page: 'Lessons against prejudice "should be compulsory"'.[28]

The vast majority of the press coverage was favourable, to begin with. Only one of the national daily newspapers, the *Daily Telegraph*, positioned itself firmly against the inquiry report: '[I]t should be stated as clearly as possible that the Macpherson report ... is a misguided and unfair document whose recommendations, if enacted, would do serious harm to race relations and the rule of law.'[29]

This contrasted strongly with opinion elsewhere, as the following headlines indicate:

> The legacy of Stephen: judge's damning report on race murder will change Britain
>
> *Daily Mail*[30]

> Stephen Lawrence's legacy: confronting racist Britain
>
> *The Guardian*[31]

> A family tragedy, a police force disgraced and a nation shamed
>
> *The Independent*[32]

> Nail them: Mirror offers £50,000 to catch Lawrence killers
> Damning verdict that shames the nation
>
> *Daily Mirror*[33]

As the *Daily Mail* headline suggests, even right-wing papers, including *The Sun*, were generally supportive.[34] Elsewhere, for example, a column concerned with the media's response caught the mood in its title: 'Case united every shade of opinion'.[35] This near unanimity reflected the widespread disgust that the inquiry's evidence had engendered. The mood of agreement and a desire for change, however, did not last long.

The following day news broke that an appendix in the first copies of the report had included the names and addresses of people who had testified against the White murder-suspects. Although this information had always been available to the suspects' lawyers, the report that had been so critical of police incompetence was now an easy target for similar charges. By the weekend the tide was turning, with several Sunday papers carrying strongly worded opinion pieces attacking the report and its author. Stewart Steven, in the *Mail on Sunday*, provides an instructive example. First, he was keen to make clear his revulsion at racism (by which he meant deliberate, callous acts of race hatred), but he saw the inquiry report as equally if not more dangerous:

> There are no grounds ... for complacency, but that doesn't mean that we should allow the warped imagination of bigoted white low-lifes, whom we have inadequately educated to destroy that edifice of tolerance which the rest of us have built up over the years. I fear that may happen if Sir William Macpherson's definition of institutional racism is allowed to stand ... One

can't be an unwitting racist any more than one can be an unwitting burglar and to pretend otherwise is to put back the cause of multiculturalism for years.[36]

In this way racism is equated with 'bigoted white low-lifes' while the majority of the population and all its major institutions are safe in their well meaning 'tolerance'. This kind of argument is important because it challenges some of the most significant aspects of the Lawrence Inquiry and the most incisive of its criticisms. The whole point about the inquiry's definition of racism is that it moves beyond questions of individual intent to address deep-seated inequalities that are born of 'common-sense' assumptions and actions that *actually* disadvantage minoritized people. It is more widespread and much harder to identify (in others and in oneself) than the simple obscene brutality of a few 'bigoted white low-lifes'.

This assertion of a minimalist understanding of racism was repeated in the educational press which, just 48 hours after the inquiry's publication, carried critical statements by representatives of several teacher unions:

> It is too easy to be politically correct without facing teachers' pressures. As important as racism is, if teachers had to put every social concern first eight days a week, 25 hours a day wouldn't be enough.
>
> Peter Smith, Association of Teachers and Lecturers[37]

> I do not believe there is a school in the country which would not take urgent steps to stamp out racism.
>
> David Hart, National Association of Head Teachers[38]

Within a few weeks more union leaders joined the public scepticism about the idea that schools might be institutionally racist. Doug McAvoy, leader of the National Union of Teachers (NUT), the largest and generally most supportive of the unions, echoed Condon's earlier worries about how the charge would be interpreted, again shifting the debate away from those experiencing the injustice (minoritized students) and focusing concern on those responsible for it: 'Teachers will interpret the term "institutional racism" as an attack on them. Teachers are not racist. We need to be very careful how language is used. It can alienate rather than include.'[39]

The next largest union, the National Association of Schoolmasters/Union of Women Teachers (NASUWT) argued that race was being given too much emphasis[40] and its general secretary, Nigel de Gruchy, reportedly described institutional racism as 'gobbledegook'.[41] Over time the resistance of teaching unions was bolstered by concerted attacks on the Lawrence Inquiry in general, and its definition of racism in particular. Civitas, a right-wing 'think tank', was especially vitriolic, describing the inquiry as a 'kangaroo court'[42] and claiming that the process had been hijacked by antiracist organisations.[43]

Privately, there were soon signs that the Education Department was not keen on pushing forward the Lawrence agenda. A couple of weeks after the Inquiry report was published an official report by Ofsted, the schools inspectorate, focused on race inequality and at the press launch a senior inspector described the education system as 'institutionally racist'. *The Guardian* newspaper reported that: 'Ministers found the language of Ofsted's comments extremely unhelpful. Instead of a "futile argument" about how to describe the problems faced by some ethnic minorities in schools, there should be more effort to improve standards.'[44]

And so, two weeks after the Lawrence Inquiry had (in the words of politicians and media) 'shamed' a nation, the Education Department was privately equating discussion of racism with a question of semantics – as if racism were merely a *word* rather than a structured, recurrent and deeply embedded *reality*. To consider the issue nothing more than a 'futile argument' about terminology betrays a total failure to engage with the substance of the inquiry's analysis. This suspicion was confirmed when the Government published its 'action plan' for taking forward the Lawrence recommendations. The Education Department's view was that most of the recommendations were already in motion and nothing new was needed. Macpherson's first education recommendation, for example, was that the National Curriculum change so as to ensure 'valuing cultural diversity and preventing racism, in order better to reflect the needs of a diverse society'.[45] In reply the Department stated:

> The Department has taken a number of actions to date. The National Curriculum addresses and values the diverse nature of British society … all subject documents are designed to provide teachers with flexibility to tailor their teaching to stimulate and challenge all pupils, whatever their ethnic origin or social background.[46]

Hence the Department formally claimed to 'accept' the recommendation while actually asserting that things were fine already. Perhaps the most cynical example of this approach was the repackaging of citizenship education by the then education secretary, David Blunkett. On the same day that the Lawrence Inquiry was published, Blunkett issued a press release entitled 'Ethnic minority pupils must have the opportunity to fulfil their potential':

> Mr Blunkett said the Department for Education and Employment would be carefully considering the Inquiry Report's recommendations.

> Mr Blunkett said: 'The tragedy of Stephen Lawrence's death shows how much more needs to be done to promote social justice in our communities. This is about how we treat each other and, importantly, how we learn to respect ourselves and one another as citizens … That is why we are promoting the teaching of citizenship at school, to help children learn how to grow up in a society that cares and to have real equality of opportunity for all.'[47]

With the ink barely dry on the Lawrence Inquiry report, the Education Department took the opportunity to repackage its already existing plans for citizenship education as if they were an answer to institutional racism in the system.

Worse still, the development did nothing to advance antiracist education: it simply provided for basic civics lessons and institutionalized a weak understanding of discrimination that is entirely at odds with the thrust of the Lawrence Inquiry.[48]

The Race Relations (Amendment) Act 2000

Tony Blair's commitment to Parliament to bring forward new legislation as a result of the Lawrence Inquiry was made good when the Race Relations (Amendment) Act (RRAA) was passed in November 2000. The Act extended the existing race equality legislation to apply to more than 45,000 public bodies, including all state maintained schools and universities. The Act placed a duty on public bodies to pro-actively work towards the eradication of race discrimination and, specifically, required that every school should:

- have a written policy on race equality;
- monitor their activities for signs of bias (especially focusing on student achievement);
- actively plan to eradicate race inequality.

These duties are *mandatory* and, on paper, the new law looked like a major step forward. Unfortunately, signs soon emerged that the education sector in general, and schools in particular, were lagging behind other public authorities. Around a year after the new education requirements became active, for example, the Commission for Racial Equality (CRE) published survey findings that highlighted the slow pace of change in education.[49] In a survey of more than 3,000 public authorities, schools were the least likely to reply: only 20 per cent of schools replied, compared with an overall rate of almost 50 per cent. Of course, nothing substantial can be read into a return rate alone. For example, among countless possible explanations, it might be thought that schools were not interested in race equality or that they were more fearful of responding to a survey sponsored by the CRE: the body which – at that time – policed the legislation. The most obvious explanation, in the eyes of some teachers with whom I've discussed this, is simply that schools are too busy to fill in questionnaires. Any or all of these might have a grain of truth. Looking ahead, however, we might assume that since so few schools responded, then at least the ones that *did* participate would be among the most committed. If that is true their responses make even gloomier reading. More than half of respondents in the education sector had not identified clear 'goals' or 'targets' for improvement. In relation to differences in attainment, which is especially prominent in the legislation, only one in three schools had set any clear goals for change.[50]

The survey found schools to be among the least positive respondents when considering any changes they had made: 65 per cent of respondents in schools believed their race equality work had produced positive benefits, compared with 74 per cent of those in criminal justice and policing, 80 per cent in further and higher education, and 89 per cent in central government.[51] Perhaps most worrying of all, despite the relatively poor response so far, is that people working in education were the *least* likely to express a need for further guidance.[52] Put simply, the survey suggested that many schools were inactive on race equality: at best, they might be thought to be 'too busy'; at worst, they appear to be complacent about their legal duties and uninterested in further progress.

The national system of regular and punitive school inspections is widely recognized as one of the key mechanisms by which government has pressured schools into taking certain actions. Ofsted inspection reports are made public and, if the school raises serious cause for concern, inspectors have the power to trigger a series of 'special measures' that include increased scrutiny and, eventually, can lead to closure if sufficient improvements are not delivered. Wisely, the Lawrence Inquiry reflected the inspectorate's key role by explicitly recommending that Ofsted inspections should check on the implementation of race equality work.[53] Predictably, Ofsted officially accepted this recommendation and stated that 'Ofsted … will ensure that the important issues raised in the Report are addressed during inspections, and that appropriate training is put in place for inspectors.'[54]

Although Ofsted has issued occasional special reports that focus explicitly on race equality issues, its programme of school inspection reports has been heavily criticized for failing to give race equality a central position.[55] In 2004, for example, a research report found that 'Ofsted school inspections rarely comment on disproportionality in exclusions', despite this being one of the most pressing issues for Black communities.[56] The report notes that even where evidence of over-representation is contained *within* reports themselves, say in quoted statistics, the issue is usually absent from the conclusions and recommendations for action: 'None of the seven Ofsted inspection reports published on secondary schools [in the sample] commented on disproportionality of minority ethnic exclusions, which was evident in the tables published in six of them.'[57]

The low priority given to race equality in the inspection regime is confirmed by an Education Department review of the Black/White gap in exclusions, which states: 'Special Measures, LA [local authority] Warning Notices and other measures that lead to the closing of a school are not appropriate here: realistically, we would never invoke them over an exclusions gap alone.'[58] As this quotation suggests, the inaction of schools and the inspectorate is compounded, and legitimized, by the stance of the central Government which, just a few years after the lofty promises to the House of Commons, seems to have abandoned any meaningful concern with race equality. In the summer of 2004, for example, the Education Department published its 'Five year strategy'. Running to 110 pages, the strategy set out the future priorities and policies for education, yet the word 'racism' did not appear at all.[59] Even the more anodyne terms 'prejudice' and 'discrimination' were conspicuously absent. In contrast, 'business/es' appeared 36 times and 'standards' warranted 65 appearances – prompting an obvious question: *standards for whom?*

This remarkable absence is all the more worrying because one of the key lessons of the Stephen Lawrence Inquiry was the importance of facing up to racism (in all its forms) and challenging it openly and honestly. As the inquiry report argued: 'There must be an unequivocal acceptance of the problem of institutional racism and its nature before it can be addressed, as it needs to be, in full partnership with members of minority ethnic communities.'[60]

A change of mind? The retreat from the Lawrence Inquiry

Exhibit 6.1 documents how quickly the Government retreated from the substance of the Lawrence Inquiry. Less than a year after the RRAA duties were activated David Blunkett, by now promoted from education secretary to home secretary (and therefore the politician with personal oversight of the relevant legislation), questioned the usefulness of 'institutional racism'; reportedly describing it as a 'slogan' that 'missed the point'.[61]

A few weeks later another inquiry began, this time into the death of David 'Rocky' Bennett, a black patient who died in psychiatric detention. The Bennett report, published in 2004, found that David had been treated as 'a lesser being' when he was killed by the use of 'unacceptable and unapproved methods of restraint'.[62] The Bennett Inquiry, like the Lawrence Inquiry, had only come about as a result of a prolonged family campaign, in this case led by David's sister, Dr Joanna Bennett. The Bennett Inquiry adopted the Lawrence definition of institutional racism and called for 'Ministerial acknowledgment of the presence of institutional racism in the mental health services and a commitment to eliminate it'.[63] In 2005, almost a year after the Bennett report was released to the public, the Health Department issued a response that did not acknowledge institutional racism but restated a bland commitment to 'reshape front line services'. Later the same year the Home Office disbanded the advisory committee that had helped push for firmer implementation of the Lawrence Inquiry recommendations.

Five years after the publication of the Lawrence Inquiry, therefore, institutional racism was increasingly a term used by critics but notably absent from official statements, let alone formal policies. The abandonment of the Lawrence commitments, in practice if not in principle, became obvious through decisions that were highlighted by the press – and never officially acknowledged (nor denied) – in late 2006 and early 2007.

First, in December 2006, the *Independent on Sunday* newspaper carried extensive quotations from an internal Education Department review of the reasons for Black over-representation in exclusions from school.[64] The story quoted the review as stating that the problem was mostly the result of 'largely unwitting, but systematic racial discrimination', concluding that 'a compelling case can be made for the existence of "institutional racism" in schools'.[65] However, the same document warned that the term was potentially explosive: 'If we choose to use the term "institutional racism", we need to be sensitive to the likely reception by schools [but] if we choose not to use the term, we need to make sure that the tone of our message remains sufficiently challenging.'[66]

When the story broke, the Education Department briefed journalists that 'ministers had concluded that it would be inaccurate and counterproductive to brand the school system racist'.[67] The report remained unpublished until months later. Following the embarrassment of the leak, it was quietly released (without any press notice) on the 'Ethnic minority achievement' part of the departmental website. Significantly, it was accompanied by a short ministerial statement, authored by Schools Minister Jim Knight, which is a classic case of 'Gap Talk' (see Chapter 3): it quoted two-year-old data and erroneously inflated the size of the claimed improvement.[68]

Early in 2007 the BBC reported that 'the Department of Health now regards the term [institutional racism] as "unhelpful" and believes that "the solutions lie in the hands of individuals not institutions"'; there was no official comment.[69] And so in health, as in education, following a long and traumatic family campaign, an inquiry into the horrific death of a Black man had finally established racism as a key systemic factor in a public service and yet, regardless of the Lawrence and Bennett Inquiries, by 2007 'institutional racism' had been erased from the policy lexicon.

'Modernizing' equality: the final blow

The last act in the official retreat from the Lawrence Inquiry came in mid-2007 when the Government published proposals for a Single Equality Act that would 'modernise and simplify equality legislation'.[70] This was to be achieved by combining existing equalities legislation into a single duty, mirroring the move to establish a single equalities body (the Commission on Equality and Human Rights – CEHR).[71] In one of its final acts before being replaced, the Commission for Racial Equality issued a strongly worded attack on the proposals:

> [T]he Government's proposals for a new single equality duty ... regress entirely unnecessarily from the Macpherson Report [Lawrence Inquiry] and constitute a piecemeal approach to addressing discrimination and promoting equality ... The CRE is concerned that the Government's proposals on equality duties will render them pretty well unenforceable.[72]

In the classic Orwellian style of 'Doublethink' (see Chapter 4) the Government stated that a guiding principle for the reforms was that 'we do not erode existing levels of protection against discrimination': [73] the document then went on to not only erode existing protection but to wash much of it away entirely by downgrading the post-Lawrence duties (allowing public bodies themselves to decide what is relevant) and removing the legal right for members of the public to challenge public bodies under the Act.[74] As the CRE argued, the proposals abandoned the notion of 'mainstreaming' and returned to a position where race equality was officially placed on the margins of policy and practice. This was achieved by enshrining the principle of 'proportionality'. The Government's proposals stated that:

The duty is designed to help all public authorities to do what they do better, not stop them operating effectively or weigh them down with bureaucracy. The duty should not lead any public authority to feel it needs to take any action which might be disproportionate to the benefits the action would deliver.[75]

In this way an institution would be free to decide whether it thinks race equality is worth pursuing. A school could, therefore, acknowledge that there were persistent race inequalities in achievement and opportunity (say in exam results and its use of exclusions and setting) but determine that the effort required to address them was too bureaucratic or out of proportion to any likely benefits. The shift in duties is made clear in one of the Government's stated examples:

> For example, a school might identify three actions to:
> • narrow achievement gaps by addressing under-achievement by pupils from particular groups;
> • make sure that anti-bullying strategies protect pupils who may be bullied because of a particular characteristic; and
> • encourage parents to be involved in their children's education, in particular parents from groups who do not normally attend parents' evenings (e.g. often fathers).[76]

Notice that these are things a school 'might' wish to do. There is no compulsion to narrow existing achievement gaps. The reference to 'particular groups' leaves it to schools to decide which kinds of inequality are important. Under the proposed changes a school could argue, for example, that it would focus on gender gaps (raising boys' achievement) but take no action on race because it had too few minoritized students, or because a race focus would spoil its harmonious (colour-blind) philosophy, or even that it could only deal with one inequality at a time. The proposals signal a clear end to the period where equalities policy was drawn up with any meaningful reference to the Lawrence Inquiry.

Conclusion: 'just the right amount of racism'?

> Civil rights laws efficiently and smoothly replicate social reality, particularly black–white power relations. They are a little like the thermostat in your home or office. They assure that there is just the right amount of racism. Too much would be destabilizing – the victims would rebel. Too little would forfeit important pecuniary and psychic advantages for those in power. So, the existing system of race-remedies law does, in fact, grant minorities an occasional victory … Particularly in areas where concessions are not too costly …
>
> Richard Delgado[77]

The Stephen Lawrence case is one of the single most important episodes in the history of British race relations and yet, less than a decade after the inquiry report was published to such glowing tributes and heartfelt promises from politicians, the Lawrence legacy is more uncertain than ever. The concept of institutional racism has enjoyed an increased public profile but the evidence suggests that the majority of schools have been inactive on their new legal duties and the Departments of Education and Health both appear to have dropped the term altogether (imagining it to be 'unhelpful' or a question of semantics). When I speak to teachers and/or local education officials (who are usually White) it is not unusual for them to roll their eyes at the mention of 'institutional racism', as if the concept (and the problem) is somehow out-dated or has 'been done' already. The mere fact of the Stephen Lawrence and David Bennett Inquiries – and the attendant press coverage – is assumed by some observers to denote change.

This is exactly what Derrick Bell and Richard Delgado have warned about in relation to 'contradiction-closing cases'. The fact that institutional racism has been named explicitly as a factor in Britain's police, education and health services is not a solution, it is merely a diagnosis. But in education the diagnosis has been ignored or rejected in most schools while the system rolls along in its familiar racist fashion, treating race inequality as if it were a temporary phenomenon of marginal importance, arising mainly from the minoritized groups themselves, and entirely oblivious and/or uncaring about the active role that policy and assessment play in creating and legitimating such injustices (see Chapters 3, 4 and 5). It is in this sense that the Lawrence Inquiry is an exception that proves the rule of White racial domination in the UK. However, it would be wrong to imagine – as some do – that recognizing this state of affairs is somehow contrary to future political struggle and progress towards greater race equality.

Victory upon victory: The Stephen Lawrence case in context

Critical Race Theory is often accused of prompting despair and being devoid of hope. In the US, Derrick Bell was met with hostility when he first argued that the famous *Brown v. Board of Education* desegregation case could be understood as a point at which White interests were best served in the long run by a short-term appeasement of civil rights claims. As Richard Delgado notes: '[T]hat outraged many of Bell's readers … They found his thesis cynical and disillusioning, preferring to think of *Brown* as a great moral breakthrough, not a case of white people doing themselves a favour.'[78]

Similarly, critical race theorists have been accused of bad-mouthing their forebears, as if any reassessment of the impact of the civil rights movement amounts to political heresy.[79] I am aware that my analysis of the Stephen Lawrence case could be seen in the same way, as disrespectful of the Lawrence family's continuing battle for justice and belittling of the victories that have been won along the way. This is not my intent nor, I hope, the outcome of my analysis. I have shown how the Stephen Lawrence Inquiry has been used as a contradiction-closing case to serve the interests of the already powerful: this is not news to those involved in the campaign. Doreen Lawrence continues her fight to bring Stephen's killers to justice and, through a charitable trust in her son's memory, works to advance Black achievement despite the odds.[80] It is entirely predictable that a system of race exclusion and exploitation as firmly rooted as the British case would attempt to recapture any gains given up when the force of antiracist calls for justice become, momentarily at least, irresistible.

The Stephen Lawrence case has not removed institutional racism from the British state; no-one involved in antiracist politics ever imagined that it would. But it has involved *several* significant victories:

- Winning an official inquiry, after years of struggle and obstruction by the Government, the police and the judiciary, was a huge victory in itself;
- Ensuring that the wider public heard evidence of the scale of racism in the police force was a major victory: accusations of racism and incompetence that were previously dismissed out of hand were suddenly less ridiculous to a public shocked by the sheer scale and number of incidents that the inquiry catalogued;
- Putting the notion of 'institutional racism' into the public domain – despite all the subsequent setbacks and falsehoods – was a victory. Antiracism suddenly gained a degree of respectability that it had never before enjoyed (albeit a status that is unstable and constantly questioned). This has been used positively by numerous advocacy groups and antiracist practitioners who have sought to build upon the opportunities that the Lawrence case has opened up;
- Having the law changed was an unprecedented victory. Although the advances are constantly under threat, the changes have created the potential for significant strides forward that would have been unimaginable before.

The lesson of contradiction-closing cases, therefore, is not that change is impossible but that change is always contested and every step forward must be valued and protected. A victory won is not a victory secured. The reaction of teachers' unions and conservative commentators, plus the state's use (and abuse) of the Stephen Lawrence Inquiry, emphasize the importance of constant vigilance to maintain and build upon each victory.

Optimism, hope and 'pure politics'

> 'I'll let you decide,' said Rodrigo. 'Here's my thought. For minorities – ordinary people, not the elites – hope is not the way to emotional wholeness. For whites, it is. They need, above all, guilt-assuagement, the sense that they are not responsible, or if they are, at least things are getting better … If they are [getting better] it should follow that in time, people of color will be on a par with whites. Nothing special need be done. Whites can go about their business … So, for whites, the tonic is optimism and faith in progress … For minorities … it's realism.'
>
> Richard Delgado[81]

At a conference recently I was discussing my work with an academic colleague who said that they yearned for a more optimistic view of things: they complained that there was 'no hope' in my analysis. It is interesting that I rarely, if ever, hear such complaints from Black advocacy groups: it is as if they immediately see the relevance and usefulness of a critical understanding of what is happening. This seems common to those with first-hand experience of antiracist politics. Terezia Zoric, for example, has spent several years working against the status quo in Toronto, Canada, initially as a teacher and then as 'coordinator of equity' at the Toronto District School Board – one of the most ethnically diverse school districts on record. She has written about the struggle to create and implement a radical equity policy that could have lasting impacts despite the ever-present threat of reversal at the hands of neo-liberal politicians and popular authoritarianism:

> Our equity policy allowed me to disseminate materials into schools on antiho-
> mophobia education, books that had been banned in other provinces. We
> could remove hate materials because they were contrary to the policy. We
> created a cadre of defenders of equity … school principals who had never
> talked about equity before began to understand the difference between
> treating everyone the same and treating people according to their needs in
> order to achieve similar outcomes … [T]he key is not so much the high
> quality of the policies you produce, as the leverage of the policies when they
> hit the ground.[82]

Zoric highlights the importance of translating equity policies into action and reminds us that, as critical educators, we must *use* the changes constructively to maximize their impact in the short time that they hold sway. Which brings me back to a more realistic measure of success and our chances for further change in the future. The Lawrence Inquiry proves the worth of what Girardeau Spann calls 'pure politics': a recognition that political mobilization takes numerous forms and is often most effective when it occurs outside the traditional electoral channels, such as in 'the form of demonstrations, boycotts and riots'.[83] The Lawrence Inquiry was not granted by a benign state that perceived a previously unknown injustice and wished to do the right thing; it was granted by an incoming Labour Government after years of Conservative refusals and high-profile protests and public demonstrations, including support from Nelson Mandela (the world's most respected Black politician: a man, of course, who might have been executed decades earlier for his direct action against White oppression in his homeland). The Lawrence Inquiry has delivered considerable advances and holds out the possibility of further progress, but it is a start not an end. Recognizing this reality is neither defeatist nor hopeless, it is a necessary step in understanding what we – as critical educators, parents and/or activists – are up against. As Derrick Bell argues:

> [W]e can only *de*legitimate it [racism] if we can accurately pinpoint it. And
> racism lies at the center, not the periphery; in the permanent, not in the
> fleeting; in the real lives of black and white people, not in the sentimental
> caverns of the mind.[84]

But, of course, there are many commentators and observers who refuse to acknowledge racism as anything but a minor aberration. Claims of systematic institutional racism are frequently dismissed with reference to the supposedly exemplary actions and achievements of particular minoritized groups, who are seen as an ideal for others to copy. The construction and political deployment of such 'model minorities' is the subject of the following chapter.

Exhibit 6.1: Stephen Lawrence timeline

Date	Event	Notes
1993		
22 April	**Stephen Lawrence is murdered**	
April–May	Relations between the Lawrence family and the police become strained	Vital leads go unchecked; Stephen's friends are quizzed about which 'gang' he belonged to (the answer 'none' is greeted with surprise); and police surveillance officers see the prime suspects disposing of large rubbish bags but they do not check on their contents.
		The police accuse the family of being unhelpful and resent their solicitor asking questions about the progress of the investigation.
6 May	Doreen and Neville Lawrence meet Nelson Mandela in London	In a statement to the press Mandela says: 'The Lawrence tragedy is our tragedy. I am deeply touched by the brutality of the murder – brutality that we are all used to in South Africa, where black lives are cheap.'[85]
		Doreen Lawrence says: 'Why is it that a leader from a foreign country shows us sympathy when our government has expressed no interest at all? … They [Stephen's killers] are walking, eating and drinking and my son is lying on some slab.'[86]
7 May	Three arrests	Neil Acourt, Jamie Acourt and Gary Dobson are arrested.
10 May	Fourth arrest	David Norris is arrested.
3 June	Fifth arrest	Luke Knight is arrested.
June	Two men appear in court charged with Stephen's murder	Seven hundred people gather at a memorial service for Stephen.

Date	Event	Notes
29 July	Charges dropped	Charges against two youths are dropped as the Crown Prosecution Service (CPS) declares there is insufficient evidence to continue.
15 August	Metropolitan Police announce review of the investigation (Barker review)	Det. Ch. Sup. Barker meets with the Lawrence family and assures them he will 'get to the bottom of the case'[87] and personally feedback his results. The family hears nothing until November, when the press report the review as concluding that 'the investigation has been progressed satisfactorily', that 'relations were hampered by the involvement of active, politically motivated groups' and the investigation had been 'undertaken with professionalism and dedication'.[88]
		The review is later discredited by a Kent police investigation. The final inquiry report describes the review as 'misleading', 'flawed' and 'indefensible' and the evidence of its author 'unconvincing and incredible in a number of important respects' (para 28.15).[89]

1994

15 April	New evidence rejected	CPS rules new evidence, uncovered by the family, 'insufficient to support murder charges'.[90]

1995

April	Lawrence family launches private prosecution	David Norris, Jamie Acourt, Neil Acourt and Luke Knight appear at Greenwich Magistrates Court.
September	Two sent for trial	Neil Acourt and Luke Knight are sent for trial at the Old Bailey.
December	Third man sent for trial	Gary Dobson is sent for trial.

1996

April	Private prosecution collapses	Mr Justice Curtis rules key identification evidence as unreliable and directs the jury to return 'not guilty' verdicts.
		The case ends before the jury can view surveillance videotape of the accused brandishing knives, saying that 'every nigger should be chopped up'[91] and routinely leaving home with concealed knives.

1997

10 February	Inquest rules 'unlawful killing'	In an unprecedented verdict the jurors state 'Stephen Lawrence was unlawfully killed in a completely unprovoked racist attack by five white youths'.[92]
13 February	Lawrence family registers a formal complaint against the Metropolitan Police with the Police Complaints Authority (PCA)	
14 February	*Daily Mail* accuses five men of Stephen's murder	Above pictures of Dobson, Knight, Norris and the Acourts, the newspaper's front page headline reads: *MURDERERS: the Mail accuses these men of killing. If we are wrong, let them sue us.*[93]
March	Police Complaints Authority announces inquiry	A team led by officers from Kent police investigates the Lawrences' complaint.
April	The Lawrences meet with Jack Straw MP	Straw (shadow home secretary) meets with the Lawrences to discuss their case: Michael Howard MP, the Conservative home secretary, has repeatedly refused to meet with them.
1 May	General election: Labour form a new government	The Conservative Government, that had refused all calls for a public inquiry into the case, is replaced by 'New' Labour led by Tony Blair.
31 July	**Public inquiry announced**	Jack Straw (now home secretary) announces a public inquiry to be led by Sir William Macpherson.
15 December	PCA Report	PCA's report does not find evidence of overt racism but identifies five officers who would have faced disciplinary charges had they not by now retired. The Macpherson Inquiry report later draws attention to the limited definition of racism used in the PCA report.

1998

24 March	**Public hearings begin**	
20 July	Suspects questioned by the inquiry	Macpherson later describes them as 'arrogant and dismissive, evasive and vague'.[94]
1 October	Head of the Metropolitan Police apologizes for failure to prosecute the killers but denies institutional racism in the force	

Date	Event	Notes
30 October	David 'Rocky' Bennett dies in an NHS medium secure unit	Mr Bennett, a 38-year-old Black man, dies following control and restraint procedures applied by five nurses at the Norvic Clinic, Norwich.
1999		
24 February	**The Stephen Lawrence Inquiry report is presented to Parliament and published**	Tony Blair (prime minister) tells Parliament: 'I am proud that it was this Government who set up the Lawrence inquiry. I am happy to accept its judgment.' He states: 'The test of our sincerity as law makers in this House is not how well we can express sympathy with the Lawrence family, but how well we implement the recommendations ...'[95]

Jack Straw (home secretary) announces that the Race Relations Act 1976 will be extended and states: 'The report makes 70 wide-ranging recommendations, and I welcome them all.'[96] |
23 March	'Home Secretary's Action Plan' published	Thirty-eight pages long, the document sets out action to be taken on every one of the inquiry report's recommendations and commits the home secretary to 'take personal responsibility for oversight of this programme'.[97]
2000		
February	First annual report on progress (Home Secretary's Action Plan) published	Forty-one pages long, the report includes details on forthcoming changes to race relations laws and addresses every recommendation separately and in detail.
30 November	**Race Relations (Amendment) Bill enacted**	The Act places increased general and specific duties, including the need to proactively seek the elimination of race discrimination, on more than 45,000 public bodies (including all maintained schools and universities).
5 December	Black academic attacks prominence given to institutional racism	In the latest of several well publicised attacks, Dr Tony Sewell is quoted in the *Daily Mail* attacking 'the "pathetic cry" of institutional racism by black community leaders and "spineless" white academics'.[98]

2001

21 February	Second annual report on progress is published	Forty-four pages long. The introduction focuses on reforms in the prison service and police service. The education sections emphasize citizenship education and recent improvements in GCSE scores.
17 May	Rocky Bennett Inquest verdict	The inquest hears that Mr Bennett was held down for at least 20 minutes and subject to 'unacceptable and unapproved methods of restraint'.[99] After eight days of evidence, the verdict is 'Accidental death aggravated by neglect'.
7 June	David Blunkett replaces Jack Straw as home secretary	Straw moves to the Foreign Office following Labour's re-election.
11 September	Terrorist attacks on the US	Around 3,000 people die in coordinated attacks on four targets in the US.

2002

May	**Specific duties under the Race Relations (Amendment) Act 2000 become active**	All schools and universities in England and Wales must now have a race equality policy and take measures to eliminate race discrimination (including the areas of staff appointment and retention, and student access and achievement).
25 June	Third annual report on progress	Seventeen pages long, the third progress report breaks with the previous format: it no longer itemizes action separately under each of the Macpherson recommendations. The education recommendations are dealt with in less than a page.
September	Two of the murder suspects are jailed for a racist attack on an off-duty detective	David Norris and Neil Acourt are convicted of a racist attack on the same road where Stephen was murdered.
		The Guardian newspaper reports: 'Norris, a passenger in a car driven by Acourt, threw a drinks carton and shouted "nigger" at an off-duty detective constable, Gareth Reid, as he was crossing the road. They were sentenced to 18 months in prison, later cut to a year on appeal. Passing sentence, the judge said Norris and Acourt were both "infected and invaded by gross and revolting racism".'[100]

Date	Event	Notes
November	Amended race equality duties become legally enforceable in Scotland	Public authorities in Scotland become subject to the new specific and general duties within the Race Relations (Amendment) Act 2000.

2003

Date	Event	Notes
14 January	Home secretary says that institutional racism 'missed the point'	David Blunkett (home secretary) appears to demonstrate a total failure to understand the Stephen Lawrence Inquiry report when he says 'the slogan created a year or two ago about institutional racism missed the point … [I]t isn't institutions, it's patterns of work and processes that have grown up. It's people that make the difference.'[101]
10 February	Independent review finds 39 per cent of English universities do not comply with their race equality duties	Of 130 higher education institutions surveyed, 21 show signs of 'significant areas needing attention'; 10 have 'major work remaining to be done'; and 20 do not meet the law's basic requirements and 'urgent revision is needed'.[102]
March	David 'Rocky' Bennett Inquiry opens	Mr Bennett's sister, Dr Joanna Bennett, campaigns for a full public inquiry but the minister decides on an 'extended form' of the usual inquiry following a death in psychiatric detention.
17 March	Fourth annual report on progress	Twenty-six pages (including 14 pages of appendices). The education recommendations are, again, discussed collectively in less than a page of text.
July	Evaluation reveals little progress in education	An evaluation conducted for the Commission for Racial Equality (CRE) suggests that schools have been relatively inactive compared with other public bodies and that they see little need for further guidance on race equality.

2004

Date	Event	Notes
12 February	David 'Rocky' Bennett Inquiry reports on institutional racism in the NHS	The inquiry reports that Mr Bennett 'was not treated by nurses as if he was capable of being talked to like a rational human being, but was treated as if he was "a lesser being"'.[103] The report adopts the definition of 'institutional racism' set out in the Stephen Lawrence Inquiry report and calls for 'Ministerial acknowledgement of the presence of institutional racism in the mental health services and a commitment to eliminate it'.[104]

8 July	Five-year plan for education makes no reference to race equality	Published in a blaze of publicity, the 'Five Year Strategy for Children and Young Learners' runs to 110 pages. It mentions 'standards' 65 times; 'business/es' 36 times; 'racism', 'prejudice' and 'discrimination' do not appear.[105]
12 August	Fifth progress report	Thirty-three pages long, the document has ceased to be the home secretary's report and is now entitled 'Lawrence steering group 5th annual report'. The education recommendations are, as is now usual, dealt with in a single page.
14 December	Independent report finds serious race discrimination in the Metropolitan Police	Report commissioned by the Metropolitan Police Authority, chaired by Black trade unionist Sir Bill Morris, raises several concerns including disproportionality in disciplinary action against minority officers.
16 December	Charles Clarke appointed as home secretary	Reshuffle made necessary by David Blunkett's resignation as home secretary.
2005		
15 January	Government publishes response to the Bennett Inquiry	'Delivering race equality in mental health care' responds to each of the Bennett recommendations. The report accepts the need for better training 'if [staff] are to give all their patients culturally sensitive and safe care'.[106] However, the report falls short of the ministerial acknowledgement of institutional racism that the inquiry called for.
		The Government response states: 'It is possible to hide behind the label of institutional racism – to confuse the act of recognising it with real action to reform services. … The Government accepts its share of that responsibility and offers its support to those who must reshape front-line services.'[107]
		Health minister Rosie Winterton is quoted saying: 'Racism, discrimination, or inequalities have no place in modern society, and they certainly have no place in the modern NHS.'[108] Critics argue that the proposals are high on rhetoric but low on concrete changes.
7 July	London bombings	Fifty-two people are killed in attacks on London transport targets.

Date	Event	Notes
21 July	Attempted London bombings	Four bombs fail to explode in attempted attacks on London transport targets.
22 July	Jean Charles de Menezes shot dead by armed officers	Brazilian electrician is followed and then shot dead by armed officers on a London tube train. The metropolitan police initially suggest that he was acting suspiciously and had tried to evade officers. This is later revealed to be a lie and the police acknowledge that he is wholly innocent. The Government repeatedly refuses requests from the Menezes family for a public inquiry.
29 July	Anthony Walker murdered	Black teenager Anthony Walker is murdered in Liverpool, the victim of a racist attack by two White youths.
19 September	**Home secretary disbands Stephen Lawrence Advisory Committee**	The group, established by Jack Straw to advise on taking forward the Macpherson recommendations, is told it is being disbanded. The National Black Police Association (one of the most important drivers for race equality reform) is said to be 'shocked and disgusted'.[109] Richard Stone, an adviser to the Lawrence Inquiry and member of the group says: 'All these New Labour apparatchiks are in the same boat. They don't want anything to do with race.'[110] A Home Office spokesperson is quoted saying: 'the decision … will not affect the Home Office commitment to the race equality agenda'.[111]
16 October	Doreen Lawrence says Labour have let Stephen down	In an interview Mrs Lawrence notes: 'David Blunkett … wasn't that committed to the steering group and there were times that we had to question the amount of time he attended meetings … Since Charles Clarke has taken over, it's been even more obvious.'[112]
8 November	Sixth annual progress report	Forty-one pages, discussion of the education recommendations covers two pages.

		In the foreword Charles Clarke notes that this is 'the first report since I became Home Secretary and I am personally committed to the continuing delivery of this Action Plan and outlining how the Government intends to take forward the race agenda'.[113]
		No further progress reports are published.
November	Two jailed for murder of Anthony Walker	Paul Taylor convicted of murder; Michael Barton jailed for supplying the weapon.

2006

26 July	BBC TV documentary accuses a police officer of corruption and sabotaging the Lawrence murder investigation	'The Boys Who Killed Stephen Lawrence' airs at 9pm on BBC 1. It presents new evidence that challenges the accused men's alibis and names former Detective Sergeant John Davidson as receiving money from Clifford Norris, father of one of the accused.
		The TV programme is front-page news in three national newspapers: the *Daily Mail*, *Daily Mirror* and *The Sun*.
10 December	**Education Department refuses to accept 'institutional racism' verdict on Black exclusions**	The *Independent on Sunday* newspaper publishes extensive extracts from an internal review of the reasons for the disproportionate expulsion of Black students.
		The extracts suggest a 'compelling' case for seeing the problems as 'caused by largely unwitting, but systematic racial discrimination'.[114] The relevant minister, Lord Adonis, reportedly argues that 'since the report does not baldly conclude that Britain's entire school system is "institutionally racist", the term – and the issue – could be quietly shelved'.[115]

2007

| 2 March | Education Department releases the exclusions report with no press coverage | The exclusions review, leaked to the press the previous December, is placed on the Department's website. There is no official press release. |
| | | In an accompanying statement, schools minister, Jim Knight, expresses pleasure at improved Black exam achievement: he mistakenly quotes data from two years ago that suggest an improvement almost four times the actual current rate. There are no new commitments to action and 'institutional racism' is not mentioned. |

Date	Event	Notes
31 March	Department of Health describes the term 'institutional racism' as 'unhelpful'	The *Today Programme* (BBC Radio 4) reports that 'the Department of Health now regards the term [institutional racism] as "unhelpful" and believes that "the solutions lie in the hands of individuals not institutions"'.[116]
12 June	**Government launches consultation on a Single Equality Bill to 'modernise and simplify equality legislation'**	The Commission for Racial Equality, in one of its last acts before abolition, describes the proposals as 'pretty well unenforceable'.[117] It states that the plans 'regress entirely unnecessarily from the Macpherson Report and constitute a piecemeal approach to addressing discrimination and promoting equality'.[118]

Note

In this timeline I trace the key events in relation to the Stephen Lawrence case and the status of 'institutional racism' in public policy. I include the David 'Rocky' Bennett case because it adds further vital information on the issue of institutional racism. During this time period, however, there were additional cases that raise further questions and should not go unrecorded:

Zahid Mubarek, a South Asian teenager, was fatally attacked on the day he was due to be released from Feltham Young Offender Institution. A public inquiry was held only after the victim's family appealed successfully to the House of Lords to overturn a rejection by the then home secretary, David Blunkett. The inquiry found a catalogue of failings that meant the murder could have been prevented. Among the problems was deep racism: the report noted 'explicit racism on the part of individual officers was found to be prevalent … BME [Black & Minority Ethnic] prisoners were called "monkeys" and "black bastards"… And BME staff would sometimes turn a blind eye to what was happening in order to fit in.'[119]

Christopher Alder, a 37-year-old Black former paratrooper and father of two, died after being left face down and unconscious on the floor of a police station custody suite for 11 minutes: CCTV footage showed five police officers standing nearby laughing and joking during the relevant time period, ignoring Mr Alder's clear (and audible) signs of distress. The home secretary refused appeals for an official inquiry, preferring instead to request a report by the Independent Police Complaints Commission (IPCC). The IPCC chair has commented that 'the fact he was black stacked the odds more heavily against him … The officers' neglect undoubtedly did deny him the chance of life.'[120] Nevertheless, none of the officers has ever been successfully prosecuted and four of them have since been granted early retirement.[121]

7 Model minorities

The creation and significance of 'ethnic' success stories

> If there was this *racism* in schools – operating to the extent that has been suggested – one would expect that Asian children too would suffer from it … The fact of the matter is that Asian children not only *behave* better than white children and black children … they also *achieve* better than white children and black children. So why are they immune if there's this underlying racist tendency so strongly in our schools?
>
> Local politician[1]

> The performance of Indian, Chinese and other Asian pupils continues to outstrip those of white children.
>
> So why all the fuss? Those who have driven the debate do not want primarily to equip children for the world, but to change the world.
>
> *The Times*[2]

Introduction

The quotations that open this chapter are taken from the 1980s and 1990s respectively but identical sentiments are still repeated frequently in the British media by commentators, politicians, teachers, union leaders and academics. Indeed, whenever activists, parents and/or critical scholars point to the huge inequities experienced by Black students the odds are that many responses will feature some version of the familiar cry, 'Ah, but what about the Indians and Chinese?' The relatively high educational achievement of these groups has become a well known fact of British education that features prominently in educational and political discourse although, as I will show, many of the 'facts' that commentators assert are actually incorrect. In this chapter, therefore, I want to examine this issue more closely and reflect on how the image of certain 'model minorities' is manufactured. I begin by examining what we know about Indian and Chinese students' experiences and achievements in school. I then consider the broader question of who benefits and who loses from the creation of these stereotypes. The chapter ends with a brief account of how a model minority was created, mistreated and abandoned; a case that suggests a disposable character to model minorities who no longer serve the interests of powerholders.

The profile and educational experiences of Indian and Chinese students

It is only recently that detailed data have been available on school students of Indian and Chinese ethnic heritages. From 2002 the Pupil Level Annual Schools Census (PLASC) has gathered information on each child in the state system but before that no reliable national data on Chinese students existed. The Youth Cohort Study (YCS) has produced information on a nationally representative sample of students since the 1980s but Indians were only disaggregated from a general 'Asian' category in 1992 and Chinese students do not figure at all in the YCS: this reflects the fact that people identifying as 'Indian' are the largest minoritized group in Britain but the Chinese group is one of the smallest.[3]

As with all racial/ethnic labels, these groups are also subject to simplification and a false assumption of homogeneity. A major report by the Runnymede Trust, for example, notes that the 'Chinese community has been formed from a range of countries and cultures'.[4] Similarly, a Cabinet Office report into labour market inequalities notes the variety of experiences between the various groups that are a part of the Indian diaspora, disaggregating Indian Hindus, Muslims and Sikhs – where Indian Muslims are considerably more likely to be unemployed.[5]

A range of official statistics indicate that, overall, the social class composition of the Chinese and Indian groups is somewhat higher than other minoritized groups in Britain. For example, official indicators of social disadvantage are lowest for these two groups;[6] similarly, these are the only two ethnic groups to have a smaller proportion of students in receipt of free school meals (FSM) than White students in both primary and secondary schools.[7] Additionally, among the ethnic groups identified in the YCS, Indian students are the most likely to be educated privately: at twice the White rate and five times the rate for Black students.[8] In view of the strong association between social class and educational achievement, therefore, it is not surprising that Indian and Chinese students tend to do well in relation to crude measures of achievement. These facts also explode one of the myths that is often associated with these groups; namely that they achieve well despite high levels of social disadvantage. In 2005 the *Daily Mail* reported:

> Attacking 'the simplistic argument' that underachieving black boys are the victims of the 'racist attitudes', [Trevor Phillips] pointed out that Chinese and Indian children, who are just as likely to come from poor backgrounds and to face racism, typically do nearly three times as well as black boys.[9]

Although Indian and Chinese students undoubtedly face racism, sometimes of the most vicious kind *it is not the case that they 'are just as likely to come from poor backgrounds' as Black students or other lower-achieving minoritized groups*. Significantly fewer Indian and Chinese students come from poor or working-class households. Nevertheless, it is the case that even those who *do* meet current indicators of poverty (such as receipt of free school meals) tend to achieve more highly than peers of the same gender and FSM-status in other ethnic groups.

Chapter 3 includes data on the higher than average overall attainment of Indian and Chinese students. Exhibit 7.1 compares the attainment of Chinese, Indian and Dual Heritage (White/Asian) students in relation to the White majority. In each case the White students are the least likely of the four groups to achieve the GCSE benchmark while Chinese students achieve the best results. The levels of performance are such that FSM Chinese students are more likely to achieve five higher grade passes than their White peers who are *not* in receipt of free school meals.

Exhibit 7.1: Educational achievement of Chinese, Indian, Dual Heritage (White/Asian) and White students by gender and free school meal status: England, 2006

Percentage gaining five or more higher grade GCSE passes (any subject)

	Chinese		Indian		Dual Heritage White/Asian		White	
	Girls	Boys	Girls	Boys	Girls	Boys	Girls	Boys
Free school meals (FSM)	80.0%	65.0%	62.6%	48.3%	42.9%	34.4%	31.3%	24.0%
Non-FSM	84.9%	75.8%	78.3%	69.2%	77.4%	70.2%	65.6%	56.0%

Source: adapted from DfES (2006b): Table 32.

When it comes to explaining the higher than average attainments of Indian and Chinese students many commentators (and some academics) are quick to seek explanations that locate the source solely within the students and their families:

> WHITE children are being left behind by their Asian classmates in exam performance, according to the latest figures. … *Education experts believe traditional family values and hard work are responsible for the outstanding school performance of Young Asians.*
>
> *Daily Mail*[10]

> [T]hey found that Chinese and Indian pupils began with better key stage 1 results, pulling further ahead as they got older. … Dr Wilson's team believes that, because the differences in progress appear nearly uniform across the country, non-school factors are likely to be more significant. She said: 'We think it's more about (pupil) aspiration.' The research revealed that *Asian families in particular placed a strong emphasis on education as the key to getting on in life.*
>
> *Times Educational Supplement*[11]

The latter quotation is especially interesting. First, it should be noted that the article reports on a quantitative research study and such approaches have proven particularly unsuited to identifying inequalities in treatment, expectation and support within schools.[12] Second, it is important to note that such blanket conclusions are not always supported when the detailed findings are interrogated fully. A report whose lead author is quoted in the *TES* story above, for example, states at the outset: 'We address some of the usual factors invoked to explain attainment gaps: poverty, language, school quality, and teacher influence. We conclude that our findings are more consistent with the importance of factors like aspirations and attitudes.'[13]

And yet the detail of the same report notes that these arguments are *not* valid for Black groups – a vital difference that is absent from both the report's abstract and the attendant press coverage:

> [T]he average improvement that we have shown above is close to universal for most ethnic groups. ... The two groups for which this is not true are students with Black Caribbean or other Black heritage. ... These findings suggest that different school processes and practices may have an important influence on outcomes for Black Caribbean or other Black heritage students.[14]

The report's main summary, therefore, seems to suggest that low Black achievement might be a reflection of their lower 'aspirations and attitudes': the fact that the study data do not support this view is only revealed 20 pages later in the body of the text. Significantly, the word 'racism' is absent from the entire 65-page report, which confirms the difficulty that quantitative approaches have when exploring complex and often hidden processes that create and sustain race inequality.

A further problem is the snapshot nature of many accounts. By focusing on statistics or interviews at a single time point there is a tendency for researchers to assume that high achievement has always been present and, therefore, that its causes must be relatively stable, such as community-based factors. Taking a longer timespan into account, however, suggests that this is a more dynamic process than is usually recognized. Exhibit 7.2 illustrates the growing gap between Indian and White students since the early 1990s. This rise has coincided with the increased emphasis on attainment in standardized tests as a crude indicator of 'standards' in published school league tables (see Chapter 3).

In previous research, co-authored with Deborah Youdell, I have shown how annual increases in performance have been bought at great cost.[15] In a pattern that has since been widely recognized, including in the US and Canada, we showed how schools have turned to increased use of internal selection as they try to maximize their position in the 'A-to-C economy' that the league tables have created.[16] In this situation schools are not only competing against each other, they are also competing against themselves because failure to improve on the previous year's performance could lead to accusations of 'coasting'. Schools as institutions, and teachers as individuals, respond by rationing education through a process of 'educational triage': they focus on students who they believe offer the best chance of attaining the benchmark level that counts towards the externally mandated performance indicators. In this context teachers' beliefs about the natural innate

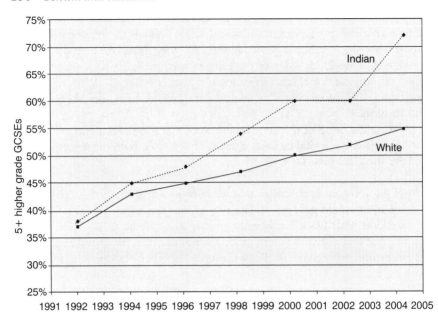

Source: DfES (2005a).

Exhibit 7.2: Educational achievement of Indian and White students: England and Wales, 1992–2004

'ability' and motivation of certain groups pay dividends in terms of students' like-lihood of being selected for the highest ranked teaching groups and receiving all the other benefits that accrue to those who embody (literally) the school's hopes of academic success.

In our joint research Deborah Youdell and I focused mainly on how class and race combined to ensure the success of middle-class White students whilst placing considerable additional hurdles in the way of their Black peers, who were deemed to be lacking sufficient ability and/or motivation to succeed.[17] In her subsequent research Youdell has explored the minutia of these processes in greater detail and, in particular, broadened her analysis to include an additional national site (Australia) and a greater range of minoritized groups.[18]

Focusing on how particular identities are constituted (made, remade and contested) in the everyday interactions of students with peers and teachers in school, Youdell offers a more nuanced and critical understanding of how particular roles and expectations are policed on a day-by-day, minute-by-minute basis. She builds upon, and extends, Howard Becker's notion of the 'ideal client'[19] to show 'that under-standings and identifications of students' by teachers and peers are not merely descriptive of students, they are 'implicated in *creating* students in these terms'.[20]

From the perspective of this chapter Youdell's work with Indian girls is especially important. Through detailed engagement with the daily life of schools and class-rooms, she charts the girls' experiences as particular versions of raced- and (hetero)sexed- identities are constituted. Despite the girls' attempts to move outside the boundaries identified for them by teacher- and student-stereotypes, they are ultimately subject to the wider processes through which their 'Indian-ness' is constituted and constitutes them: as 'good students and acceptable (that is hard working and attaining but not intrinsically gifted) learners'.[21] Crucially, Youdell links these processes to wider cultural and structural operations of racism and builds on Said's work to note the continued operation of 'Orientalist discourses of Asian submission and work ethic'.[22] These assumptions, of course, are in marked contrast to the growing Islamophobic anti-Muslim discourses that have always been present but exploded as a result of the so-called 'War on Terror' (see Chapter 4).[23]

The expansion of qualitative research in recent decades has been reflected in an increasing range of scholarship that reveals the complex social identities of students who too often face simplistic, one-dimensional labels in their school life. Research by Ghazala Bhatti and Farzana Shain, for example, has been especially important in revealing the contrast between teachers' predictable and often oppressive stereotyping of 'Asian' students and the rich, varied reality of their lives in school, at home and on the streets with their peers.[24] As Farzana Shain argues, 'rather than being the passive victims of oppressive cultures, the girls are actively engaged in producing identities that draw on both the residual cultures of the home and the local and regional cultures they now inhabit.'[25]

Louise Archer and Becky Francis map similar territory in their interview-based study of the educational experiences of Chinese students in London. They build on previous work (by Chau and Yu, Parker, and Song) in an exploration of the myriad possible influences behind Chinese academic 'success'.[26] They emphasize a range of factors and note the exceptionally positive views that many teachers hold of Chinese students and their universal attribution of this to 'home' and 'cultural' influences.[27] Frequently teachers contrast their positive evaluation of Chinese students against their negative expectations of other, less highly achieving, minoritized groups: 'I particularly work with Afro-Caribbean groups and I know there's huge problems within that, you know, culture there, to try and get the kids motivated, especially boys.'[28] The level of teachers' positive expectation of Chinese students is so exceptionally high that Archer and Francis note: 'A number of other teachers also expressed concern over whether particular British-Chinese boys were achieving their "whole potential" where their achievement was average or good, rather than outstanding.'[29]

I have already noted the dangers of teachers' assumptions about innate racialized 'potential' in previous chapters: at this point it is sufficient to note the stark contrast that the research evidence suggests between White teachers' views of different minoritized groups and the institutional force that such evaluations carry at a time of increased internal selection and separation (see Chapters 4 and 5).

Model minorities: winners and losers

Pyon Gap Min, of City University of New York, describes the 'model minority' thesis as 'probably the most frequently cited concept in the Asian American school science literature over the past two decades'.[30] It is a concept that generates considerable controversy. Put simply, the model minority thesis suggests that 'Asian' Americans, particularly those of Japanese and Chinese ethnic heritage, provide a model of hard work, family stability and self-sacrifice that illustrates the best way for any migrant community to achieve social mobility by taking advantage of the freedoms and opportunities afforded to all in the USA. *Asian American scholars are among the sternest critics of the model minority thesis.* They argue that it over-simplifies the experiences and achievements of Asian Americans by ignoring areas of inequality and deep-rooted disadvantage; operates to the detriment of other minoritized groups who are demonized and scapegoated as poor reflections of the Asian American stereotype; and that the image is detrimental to Asian Americans themselves, not least because it masks their own experience of racism and marginalization.[31] Each of these criticisms can equally be applied to the popular image of Indian and Chinese success in the UK. I have shown that British Indian and Chinese students are much more diverse and complex groups than is usually assumed. In this section I wish briefly to explore some of the other consequences of the popular presentation of these groups as British model minorities.

Model minorities: the benefit to the status quo

I have already indicated some of the ways in which the achievement of Indian and Chinese students is positioned in public debates on race and education: at this point it is worth considering the process a little further. The public image of successful hard-working Indian and Chinese students has become a discursive resource that is deployed whenever the question of racism in education is raised. There are two key ways in which this happens: first, the mere fact of minority success is positioned as if it automatically disproves the charge of racism against any and all minoritized groups; and second, comparisons are made with 'under-achieving' groups so that the latter are cast as deficient and even dangerous.

The notion of institutional racism, as operationalized in the Lawrence Inquiry report, has been subject to huge controversy and wilful misrepresentation (see Chapter 6). Although the concept clearly attempts to recognize the complex (sometimes hidden) nature of racism, a great deal of White comment seems to ignore this dimension and equate *every* mention of 'racism' with race hatred of the most conscious, violent and one-dimensional kind. Within this simplistic world view *any* minority success is assumed to be incompatible with the charge of racism:

> Whatever failings teachers have, racism – institutional or otherwise – is not one of them … We have known for some time that in secondary schools, pupils of Asian and Chinese origin make better progress than their white peers.
>
> Professor Anthony O'Hear[32]

The infamous definition, produced by the Macpherson inquiry into the murder of Stephen Lawrence, is demonstrably ridiculous here. For the report shows that while Bangladeshi and black Caribbean children do worse than white children, Indians and Chinese do very much better. It's a strange kind of institutional racism that actually favours some ethnic minorities.

Melanie Phillips[33]

I'm no educationist, but if you examine the statistics it is certainly difficult to conclude that our schools discriminate against ethnic minorities, even unwittingly. Chinese and some other Asian pupils excel, easily outperforming the whites.

Rod Liddle[34]

Reading statements like these it is sometimes difficult to believe that the opinions are serious: do commentators (regardless of their own Whiteness and lack of research understanding) genuinely think that success by one or two minority groups necessarily disproves the presence of racism across the board? Are they really so convinced of the system's colour-blind meritocratic principles? Each of the writers noted above has been an outspoken critic of the state education system and yet they cannot conceive that some minoritized groups are systematically discriminated against in the same system they are so swift to decry at other times (on other topics). These quotations are especially revealing because each of the articles references the Lawrence Inquiry, either directly or indirectly, and yet completely fails to understand even the most basic reality of how racism operates. Statements such as these trade on the crudest possible notion of racism and are entirely at odds with the research evidence from schools.

As I have noted, there is a large and growing body of work that clearly documents how teachers' perspectives differ depending on the particular minoritized group they are dealing with. *Racists have always played favourites*, viewing some groups as exotic, mysterious and alluring, while others are seen as bestial, savage and threatening: the same processes are at play in contemporary classrooms and staffrooms.[35] The exceptionally high expectations that many teachers hold about Indian and Chinese students are the flip side of the same coin that involves the demonization of Black students. Indeed, many commentators and 'experts' display these same tendencies in their readiness to use the model minority stereotype of Indian and Chinese students as licence to further denigrate and assault Black students, their parents and communities:

There's certainly not institutional racism … If Indian children are doing better than white children then there is not institutional racism. *We have to look at the particular groups themselves and wonder what's happening there.*

Professor James Tooley[36]

Asian and Chinese pupils still manage to get more out of the school experience than do black boys. Alan Hall, a Bradford head teacher, believes: '*The biggest single advantage [Asian pupils] gain from their family background is that they are seldom cynical about school, teachers and education.*'

Yasmin Alibhai-Brown[37]

What these perspectives fail to understand is the absolutely vital importance of education for very many of the minoritized groups that appear at the wrong end of the league table hierarchy. The Black British community, for example, has an *exemplary* history of mobilization around educational issues, not only pushing for better standards in the state system but also organizing and funding literally thousands of 'supplementary' and 'Saturday' schools run by the community, for the community.[38] But this commitment – whilst at least as deep as any other groups' – does not always surface in ways that match the expectations of White teachers and other observers. The headteacher quoted by Yasmin Alibhai-Brown is especially interesting because of his reference to 'cynicism'. Research with Black students and parents, in the US and the UK, reveals a degree of understanding and wariness that might be viewed (incorrectly) as cynicism by some, but is perhaps more accurately viewed as a realistic understanding of past injustices and current mistreatments. Jan McKenley's life history research with Black 40-something fathers, for example, reveals the vital but complex place that education holds within their lives as parents and as ex-students:

> When I sat my maths exam at school, one look at the paper told me that I was not equipped to do it, to pass it so I left after a few minutes. I knew I was going to fail, so I take control. (Owen)

> My kids know that I am in private aggressively pro-black and condemning of white racism and so debates around subjects become quite lively at home … My kids watched me as I did my MBA [Master of Business Administration] and my son, in particular who is good at maths, was roped in to help me with the mathematics in the MBA. They have a sense that there are benefits to be gained. So he knows it's to be strived for. I said to him don't be doing yours at my age, do bits of study but get the bulk of it out of your way while you're young. (Dennis)

> I make my guidance explicit and I insist on homework being done. I make my expectations and goals explicit and encourage my children to do the same. (Devon)[39]

Similarly, Lorna Cork's work with Black parents and students powerfully demonstrates that many parents, especially fathers, are deeply involved in their children's education but sometimes in ways that are not immediately visible to schools, who assume that absence at a parents' evening denotes an absent or uninterested parent and are unaware of the myriad complex constraints that can prevent such overt displays.[40] None of this should come as a surprise: migrant communities frequently look to education as a way of cementing their future. The commitments of 'model minorities' are no more impressive than those of less successful and more maligned groups: Exhibit 7.3, for example, provides the most powerful evidence possible, in this case relating to an 'asylum seeker'; a group defined in current

British popular and political discourses as among the least deserving and most Othered of groups.

Exhibit 7. 3

'I want my son Antonio to stay in the UK to continue his studies'

So read a note found after Manuel Bravo, a 35-year-old asylum seeker, hung himself at the Yarl's Wood Detention Centre, Bedfordshire, the day before he expected to be forcibly repatriated to Angola.

Mr Bravo's son Antonio, aged 13 at the time of his father's death, will now be able to stay in England until he is 18, when he will be able to apply for asylum.

Mr Bravo's parents, who had links to a political opposition group, were murdered in Angola in 2001. Mr Bravo's wife and youngest child had returned briefly to Angola, so that she could care for a recently orphaned niece: they were imprisoned for two months and then fled to a neighbouring country.

At his first tribunal hearing in England Mr Bravo represented himself because his solicitor failed to show. Contemporary newspaper reports suggest that Mr Bravo and his son were taken into custody at 6am when police broke into their house. At that point there had still been no official result from his earlier asylum hearing, making his removal to the detention centre illegal.

A year later the inquest heard that a note left for Antonio read: 'Be a good son and do well at school.'

Sources: BBC News Online (2006m); Herbert (2005); Pallister (2006).

Damaged models: the costs of 'success'

The presence of high-achieving supposedly 'model minorities' is clearly a good thing for those who would argue that racism in education is a marginal issue or perhaps even a wholly phantom concern. Although the assertion is patently wrong, as we have seen previously, it is a regular and well loved staple of British educational commentators. It might also be assumed that the model minority stereotype is pretty good news for the students concerned; after all, the exceptionally high teacher expectations generally translate into additional educational resources and high achievement. As Asian American scholars have pointed out, however, being a 'model' is not a uniformly positive experience; unfortunately, the same patterns of racist abuse and social exclusion have been documented in the UK. Chinese and 'Caribbean' people, for example, report similar levels of racial harassment.[41] In the late 1990s research revealed 'a minimum of a quarter of a million racist incidents a year. Nearly a quarter of those who had been racially harassed had been victimised five or more times in the past year.'[42]

As Tariq Modood notes, these statistics are especially sickening because *racist* harassment carries additional important dimensions:

> Racial victimisation ... is not random: victims are chosen on the basis of their group characteristics. The victim cannot console themselves by saying 'it

could have happened to anybody'. You know you were chosen because of what you are, because of a malice directed at a part of yourself. Thus racial attacks are both more deeply personally damaging and frighten not just the individual victims but groups of people.[43]

There has undoubtedly been a significant increase in racist harassment following the events of 9/11 and the 2005 London bombings. Although full official figures have not been released it is known that 'Asian' people have been especially affected.[44] Similarly, within schools, Archer and Francis talk of a 'negative positive' stereotype, which continues the 'exoticising and pathologising' Orientalist discourse that has been current, but constantly developing, for centuries. Alongside these complex exclusions they also note that: '"old" racisms – based on essentialised constructions of bodily differences, and expressed as explicit racist abuse – remain a common and "everyday" experience for British-Chinese pupils in London schools'.[45]

Deborah Youdell's detailed ethnography of young people's school lives goes even further, exploring how an intermeshing set of racist stereotypes and (hetero)sexist practices and beliefs come to construct informal, but incredibly powerful, lines of sanctioned and prohibited social relations between young people in a London school. Her work shows how even the most intimate and apparently personal of relationships are shaped by racism and how, among peers in Taylor Comprehensive, Indian students of both sexes occupied an isolated and denigrated position in the informal 'Hierarchy within the Other'.[46]

The model minority stereotype does not automatically continue into the post-school world. On average Indian and Chinese young people leave the state education system with significantly higher qualifications than other groups but there is evidence that these do not translate into a privileged position in the labour market; here, racism – both overt and indirect – remains a major barrier that is acknowledged even in official reports. Take, for example, the following Cabinet Office quote:

> Even when differences in educational attainment are accounted for, ethnic minorities still experience significant labour market disadvantages.
>
> In general, ethnic minorities, including Indians, do not get the jobs that their qualification levels justify … [There is] strong evidence that discrimination plays a significant role.[47]

It is clear, therefore, that the often cited examples of Indian and Chinese educational success are a lot more complex, and a lot less rosy, than is usually portrayed in politics and the popular media. Before concluding this chapter, however, I want to highlight a further aspect of the model minority issue that is especially unsettling: it concerns the question of the *disposable* nature of model minorities.

Disposable models: the case of the Montserratian diaspora

I have shown that White people draw considerable benefit from the existence of so-called model minorities: the stereotype provides a strong rhetorical counter to accusations of racism and unfairness. In contrast, the minoritized groups themselves are assumed to enjoy a racism-free life despite the reality of racist harassment and labour market exclusion. But there is a case in recent British history which suggests that it does not matter *who* provides the model so long as there is *a* model to point to. So far as popular and political discourses of education and meritocracy are concerned the existence of high-performing minoritized groups is a significant advantage but the position of the particular groups themselves may not be as secure as is often supposed. The case of the Montserratian diaspora provides a tragic example.

On 18 July 1995, after centuries of inactivity, the Soufriere Hills Volcano burst into life, bringing destruction to the Caribbean island of Montserrat (a British dependent territory). Successive eruptions led to considerable internal displacement but a major eruption on 25 June 1997 destroyed seven villages and prompted the British Government to create an assisted passage programme, sparking a major outward migration.[48]

Although many families had initially fled the island for a variety of destinations, including the US and Canada, a large majority relocated to the UK; not only because of the assisted passage scheme but also because, like many of the post-war Caribbean migrants before them, they saw Britain as the 'Mother' country.[49] Based on an analysis of an official Montserrat Government survey, Gertrude Shotte notes that: '[E]ducation was the decisive factor that influenced families to relocate to England … It was a widely held belief among islanders that England's education system was the best.'[50] But the islanders were surprised by the system that greeted them. Many felt that the work was unchallenging and the popular media, hungry for stories critical of educational 'standards', was happy to publicize the situation.

Under the headline 'British schools are second rate say the volcano island refugees', the *Mail on Sunday* used interviews with a small number of parents and students to launch an attack on the UK system that covered many of the perennial complaints beloved of conservative critics, including school discipline, the supposed loss of rigour in examinations and the use of 'mixed ability' teaching rather than academic selection:

> BRITISH schooling was once the envy of the world, a byword for academic excellence adopted by 150 nations as the gold standard of education.
>
> But today that belief has been exposed as a myth by 2,000 school children from Montserrat, who put our schools to shame. … For the parents of Montserrat – a British dependency – are astonished at Britain's poor school standards and lack of discipline …
>
> The people of Montserrat – population 12,000 – have been raised in an educational time-warp with a system modelled on the traditional set of standards which many believe have been destroyed by 'progressive' teaching in Britain.[51]

Alongside a picture of neatly dressed students doing their homework (see Exhibit 7.4), the newspaper presented the Montserratian students as a model of commitment and hard work who were 'horrified' at the low standards they encountered:

The Mail on Sunday, November 30, 1997

British schools are second rate say the volcano island refugees

By Rosie Waterhouse
Education Correspondent

BRITISH schooling was once the envy of the world, a byword for academic excellence adopted by 150 nations as the gold standard of education.

But today that belief has been exposed as a myth by 2,000 schoolchildren from Montserrat, who put our schools to shame.

The tiny Caribbean island, laid waste by volcanic eruptions, is already at the centre of a row over the handling of the crisis, which a Commons committee condemned last week as inept.

Yet the arrival of evacuated children from the island has revealed a far greater worry.

For the parents of Montserrat — a British dependency — are astonished at Britain's poor school standards and lack of discipline, which some of them say should include corporal punishment.

Indeed, many evacuated children are so far ahead of their British classmates — especially in science and maths — that parents in Hackney, East London, where 160 Montserrat families are staying, have organised extra lessons to ensure their children do not fall behind in core subjects.

And former Beatles record producer Sir George Martin, who helped to organise a fund-raising concert, has backed a £3,000 donation for the Saturday schools.

The alien education culture is also hitting evacuated children in Birmingham, Leicester and Preston — for precisely the same reasons.

The people of Montserrat — population 12,000 — have been raised in an educational time-warp with a system modelled on the traditional set of standards which many believe have been destroyed by 'progressive' teaching in Britain.

UNDER FIRE: The Clapton school, above, that Montserrat children attend after fleeing the island's volcano

CLASS ACT: Talented evacuees Denbert and Clairson White, left, and Glynis Meade
Pictures: IAN McILGORM

Horrified

Schools still teach the Three Rs — reading, writing and arithmetic — and maintain high academic achievement. Pupils sit GCE O-level exams set by Cambridge University — exams that were replaced here in 1988 by the GCSE in a move partly blamed for declining exam standards in science and maths than GCSEs.

As a result, the evacuated children can be up to two years ahead of their classmates in British schools. In Montserrat, pupils are in three streams and are urged to compete to be 'top of the class'. Yet here they are frustrated by the lack of drive to excel in mixed-ability classes.

Discipline has also horrified parents, who criticise noisy lessons, scant respect for teachers and smoking outside school by pupils and staff.

Certainly, the evacuees' plight has exposed appalling weaknesses in our schools.

Clarence Greaves and his wife were among 3,500 evacuees who chose a temporary new life in the UK because they thought their teenage daughters, Natasha and Treecia, would be well-educated.

But soon after she started lessons at Clapton School for Girls in Hackney, 14-year-old Natasha was amazed that pupils sitting a GCSE maths exam would be given a sheet of mathematical formulae which she would have had to memorise in Montserrat. In contrast, 18-year-old Treecia, who is studying to be a nurse, said vocational opportunities at a

North-East London college were 'fantastic'.

But Glynis Meade, 14, who attends the Clapton school with Natasha and three other Montserrat children, claimed she was so far ahead of her classmates in maths that her teacher had told her to slow down.

Unruly

Head teacher Cheryl Day defended her provision for the evacuees, saying: 'This school is very experienced at dealing with pupils with a whole range of abilities.

'We had discussions with one of the girls' parents and she has been urged to take up extra-curricular activities via maths and science clubs offered at the school.'

The White brothers from Stoke Newington — Clairson, five,

Denbert 10 and Varez, 13 — have been in British schools for seven weeks and Denbert is already a year ahead of his UK classmates.

But the biggest difference they have noticed is how unruly the lessons are. Varez recalled being hit on his palm with a ruler when he misbehaved in Montserrat — yet he and his brothers saw nothing wrong with this.

Janice Panton, co-ordinator of the voluntary Montserrat Aid Committee — set up to co-ordinate the reception of evacuees in Britain — said: 'I've encountered a lot of concern among Montserratian parents here about education. Their children seem at least a year ahead of those born in the UK in the same class.'

Michael Halstead, chief executive of Cambridge University's Local Examinations Syndicate — which sets exams for 1.8 million candidates in 154 countries —

confirmed that 'the best candidates in maths and science were from countries like Montserrat, Zimbabwe and Singapore.'

And Lazelle Howe, Montserrat's former Education Minister, who has set up an advisory group to investigate education problems around the country, said in London: 'In the Caribbean we believe children need a challenge, but this just isn't happening in UK schools.'

Education Secretary David Blunkett was shocked last night by The Mail on Sunday's findings, saying: 'This just reinforces our drive to raise standards.'

But that will mean little to the Monserrat parents forced to flee a natural disaster, only to walk into a man-made one which could prevent their children rebuilding their lives.

OPINION: Page 32

Source: Waterhouse (1997). Reproduced with permission.

Exhibit 7.4:

[T]he evacuated children can be up to two years ahead of their classmates in British schools. In Montserrat pupils are in three streams and are urged to compete to be 'top of the class'. Yet here they are frustrated by the lack of drive to excel in mixed-ability classes.[52]

Despite such publicity, however, the Montserratian students did not find themselves treated as a model minority inside school. They were classified simply as 'Caribbean'; a symbol of the system's almost total failure to recognize their particular needs arising from the trauma of what had happened on – and to – their homeland and the fact of their enforced passage to England.

Gertrude Shotte was a headteacher on Montserrat who shared the students' passage to England and has become the leading authority on their subsequent experiences in the UK. She notes that:

> They were repeatedly stereotyped into situations with little or no consideration given to their Montserratian and/or individual identity ... [I]t appears that they had automatically acquired all the stereotypes and negative perceptions that teachers have of first wave African Caribbean students. [53]

To make matters worse, both the welfare and education systems seemed to respond in ways that owed much to bureaucracy and ignorance and little to humanity or professionalism. Indeed, it seems that labels such as 'refugee' were inconsistently applied or denied by different organizations but *always* in ways that disadvantaged the Montserratians. Hence, they were denied the usual range of refugee support, including counselling services, because they did not meet the definition of refugees fleeing a war-torn country with a fear of persecution. However, British schools often placed them in classes to focus on 'English as an additional language' (EAL) because that was what they did with 'refugee' children: the fact that English is the official language of Montserrat had, apparently, not been considered. [54]

Ultimately, the educational experiences and achievements of Montserratian youth in the UK have been low, especially among the boys. They have also experienced disproportionate numbers of exclusions from school and involvement with the criminal justice system (like the larger group of African Caribbean students into which they were assumed to fit). [55]

A final heartbreaking measure of the disposable nature of model minorities can be found in a subsequent press story about the students. This story appears in the specialist education press, not the popular press of Exhibit 7.4. Indeed, no further trace of the Montserratian students can be found in the *Mail on Sunday* nor its sister title the *Daily Mail*: having acted as a launch pad for criticisms of the state system it seems their purpose had been served. [56] Several years later, however, the *Times Educational Supplement* included an account of Gertrude Shotte's research: it featured a response by a teachers' representative, which typifies the standard non-engagement with evidence of institutional racism (see Chapter 6):

> Dr Shotte's research, which forms a PhD thesis for London's Institute of Education, is based on a five-year investigation of 40 pupils' experiences in London ... Dr Shotte said the pupils' main problems were institutional racism and teachers' poor expectations.

> Julie Davies, secretary of Haringey National Union of Teachers, said it was understandable the families felt disappointed with schools in a deprived part of London. But she said it was 'absolutely dreadful' to claim teachers were failing the pupils. [57]

Once again, a teachers' representative is quick to feel sympathy for minoritized students but angered by the suggestion that teachers' own actions and assumptions could possibly be implicated.

Conclusion

This chapter has focused on the issue of 'model minorities'; not merely on the groups themselves but on their construction and deployment as a stereotype. The popular image of Indian and Chinese students as hard-working and successful enables the education system to sustain its claim to fairness and impartiality and, in particular, to reject accusations of racism. I have shown how the relevant debates are characterized by a number of myths. At this stage it may be useful briefly to recap some of the facts that have emerged contrary to the 'model minority' stereotype:

MYTH: 'Chinese and Indian children … are just as likely to come from poor backgrounds … as black boys',[58] so their success has nothing to do with social class.

REALITY: Chinese and Indian students have a markedly different socio-economic profile compared with other minoritized groups: they are significantly less likely to experience economic disadvantage and more likely to attend private schools.

MYTH: '[T]raditional family values and hard work are responsible for the outstanding school performance of Young Asians',[59] which suggests that other minoritized groups fail because they lack sufficient drive and ambition.

REALITY: The successful minoritized groups are not alone in having high expectations and commitment to education. Education is frequently valued extremely highly by migrant communities, including those who experience considerable educational and economic disadvantage. Black groups, often disparaged by media commentators, have established thousands of supplementary schools to boost their children's achievement.

MYTH: 'Chinese and Indian children … are just as likely … to face racism'[60] and so their higher than average performance proves that other groups' underachievement cannot be blamed on racism.

REALITY: White teachers tend to view 'model minorities' with exaggeratedly positive expectations so far as their academic potential is concerned. These expectations translate into tangible advantages in the classroom. However, Chinese and Indian people (adults and children) are frequently subjected to racist harassment in school and wider society.

In addition, I have suggested that the current success of certain minoritized groups may be less secure than is often assumed. The attainment of all ethnic groups, including the White majority, is subject to fluctuations as the education system responds to outside pressures to 'raise standards'. Indian students, in particular, appear to have benefited from recent changes that have placed a premium on students that schools believe are capable of reaching the benchmark levels in public measures of standards and accountability. In marked contrast, Montserratian students, once held up as a model of good discipline and hard work, appear to have been treated in school as part of the wider group of Black Caribbean children – with all the attendant negative attributions – and have suffered a spectacular slump in their attainments as a result.

The message of this chapter, therefore, is clear: White powerholders are the only group to draw unquestioned advantage from the continued stereotype of Indian and Chinese model minorities. Other less highly achieving groups are demonized by comparison; accusations of racism are dismissed out of hand; and even the 'model' students themselves experience the negative side of stereotyping and racism at the hands of their teachers and peers. The racism that characterizes education, therefore, runs so deep that even the very groups that are held up as proof of an equitable and prejudice-free system are themselves subject to racist violence and exclusions.

This chapter, like so many of the previous chapters, has revealed how the official image of education hides a system of racial exclusion and oppression where the most consistent beneficiaries are White people. The following chapter, therefore, takes White people – and the construction of 'Whiteness' – as its focus.

8 WhiteWorld

Whiteness and the performance of racial domination

> What has become clear to me is my parents have a disdain towards 'white-world'. They came here to earn money. They came for no other reason. They don't trust white people, they don't engage with them more than they have to and certainly school was a white institution.
>
> Dennis, a Black Londoner
> whose parents migrated to England in the 1950s[1]

Introduction

Most White people would probably be surprised by the idea of 'WhiteWorld': they see only the world; its Whiteness is invisible to them because the racialized nature of politics, policing, education and every other sphere of public life is so deeply ingrained that it has become normalized; unremarked and taken for granted. As I argued in Chapters 1 and 2, this is an exercise of power that goes beyond notions of 'White *privilege*' and can only be adequately understood through a language of power and domination. Privilege is too soft a word; this is about *supremacy*. But it is a form of supremacy that is multifaceted: at one moment harsh and aggressive (seen at its most obvious in relation to the so-called 'War on Terror') but at the next moment, subtle and hidden – written through the fabric of what counts as 'normality' in what Dennis describes as 'WhiteWorld'.

This chapter addresses two key issues that are fundamental to understanding the workings of racism in the education system. First, I look at how critical scholars have theorized Whiteness: in other words, what is the nature of Whiteness? How is it best understood? What processes produce and enforce it? The second part of the chapter applies this understanding to an empirical example of Whiteness in action; in this case, a national radio phone-in devoted to the discussion of race and intelligence. The analysis shows how supposedly 'free speech' is highly structured in ways that constantly foreground the perspectives and interests of White people, while euphemisms and pseudo-science construct an image of Black people as irrational and inherently less intelligent. The episode highlights the continued discursive power of racist beliefs about the nature of ability and the role of the media in recycling and respecting arguments that have long been discredited.

Theorizing Whiteness

The sound of silence

> 'Some of your other work – on under-achievement – that was quite good. My students really like that thing you did for Ofsted; that was useful. But all this talk about White Supremacy? I think you've gone mad.'

This is how a White professor responded to a conference presentation that I made in late 2003. It was the first time I had presented my ideas about CRT and White Supremacy in public and the event had already proven to be a memorable one. I made my comments as part of a symposium; each speaker presented for around ten minutes and then fielded questions for a further five minutes. My talk looked at how Black students had been disadvantaged historically by educational reforms that were presented as in the interests of 'everyone' but where the most significant and consistent beneficiaries were always White students.[2] In conclusion, I linked the empirical data to a CRT analysis of White Supremacy as a hidden but ever-present aspect of the political mainstream rather than the fringe neo-Nazi manifestations that usually spring to mind when the phrase is used (see Chapter 2).

My presentation was met with total silence.

Admittedly, my talk may not have been the most stimulating ten minutes the audience had ever experienced but it was far from the worst presentation of the session. Nevertheless, no-one in the overwhelmingly White audience had a question. No-one wanted to challenge my statistics; no-one wanted to hear more about this thing 'Critical Race Theory'. In short, everyone had heard more than enough. This was the first time that I'd experienced such a reaction: even as an undergraduate my presentations would always generate a few challenges or queries.

Afterwards I spoke to one of my graduate students, one of the few people of color in the audience. She said that there were two White people in front of her who, as I spoke, got lower and lower in their seats: 'It was as if they were trying to disappear,' she observed.

This experience often comes to my mind. I have presented data on the extensive and deepening race inequities in schools to extremely varied audiences, from senior policymakers and teachers' leaders, to parents and community groups working for grass-roots change. When I talk about the scale of race inequality an intense and interesting discussion usually follows. But when I talk to mostly-White audiences about how White people are actively implicated in the situation (as teachers, policymakers, media commentators) then the reaction changes; as at the earlier conference, I am sometimes met with complete silence. The audience stares at the PowerPoint slide on display behind me; some audience members shuffle papers; others look at the table in front of them. Soon the chairperson takes the hint and thanks me for my time. Silence. Goodbye. Next item of business.

Charles Mills has said:

> [T]here will be characteristic and pervasive patterns of not seeing and not knowing – structured white ignorance, motivated inattention, self-deception, historical amnesia, and moral rationalization – that people of color, for their

own survival, have to learn to become familiar with and overcome in making their case for racial equality.[3]

Charles Mills is one of the most important contemporary race theorists. Currently a Distinguished Professor in the Department of Philosophy at the University of Illinois at Chicago, Mills captures brilliantly the many contours of White Supremacy as it saturates the everyday reality of the US. The silence that so often descends around questions of White complicity is part of the 'motivated inattention' and 'self-deception' that Mills describes. However, it would be foolish to imagine that White Supremacy is always so low key.

Whiteness, property and 'Other' people's bodies

> To understand the long, bloody history of police brutality against blacks in the United States, for example, one has to recognize it not as excesses by individual racists but as an organic part of this political enterprise.
>
> Charles W. Mills[4]

Mills argues that threats to White racial domination are typically met with disproportionate brutality as a means of restating and reinforcing the unequal distribution of power. He notes, for example, that slave revolts were 'punished in an exemplary way … with torture and retaliatory mass killings far exceeding the number of white victims'.[5] He sees such action in contemporary police brutality and in the state-sanctioned racist application of the death penalty where, of the thousands executed, 'only very rarely has a white been executed for killing a black'.[6]

A report on the USA by Amnesty International indicates that:

> The race of the murder victim appears to be a major factor in determining who is sentenced to death. Blacks and whites in the USA are the victims of murder in almost equal numbers, yet 82 per cent of prisoners executed since 1977 were convicted of the murder of a white person … The race of the defendant is also a factor. A recent study, made public in June 1998, found that in Philadelphia the likelihood of receiving a death sentence is nearly four times higher if the defendant is black, after taking into account aggravating factors. In effect, the study found that being black could in itself act as an aggravating factor in determining a sentence.[7]

In Chapter 2, I described how Jean Charles de Menezes, an innocent man, was shot dead by police who had followed him as he caught a bus, entered a train station, calmly swiped his ticket and then boarded a train. Race played a key role in the events that led to his death and racism found further expression in the subsequent media reaction as right-wing commentators sought to praise his killers, defend them from possible prosecution and ensure that they would act in the same way under similar circumstances in the future. It seems reasonable to suggest that this utter disregard for the potential threat of more innocent victims of police shootings cannot be completely unrelated to the racial identification of the media commentators (overwhelmingly White) and the potential victims (overwhelmingly people of color). Put simply, the White commentators *know* – though they may not admit it, even to themselves – that they will never be mistaken for a terrorist and killed on their way to work. Consequently, the argument that such mistakes are a price worth paying trades on the tacit awareness that the price will be paid by Other people. Such brutal acts are, thankfully, rare but lower level racist harassment is a fact of life in the so-called 'War on Terror'.

Racial profiling: restoring White 'normality'

> [A]n *ontological shudder* has been sent through the system of the white polity, calling forth what could be called *the white terror* to make sure that the foundations of the moral and political universe stay in place.
>
> Charles W. Mills[8]

Mills's quote relates to earlier perceived threats to White Supremacy but the scale of the anger, fear and desire for retribution that has sprung from 9/11 and subsequent events is neatly captured by the notion of an 'ontological shudder' passing through the system. In Chapter 4, I described the tremendous anger and 'retaliatory confidence' that found expression in political discourse and policy after 9/11. A further example of these forces can be found in the discussion, and practice, of racial profiling.[9]

The police's power to 'stop and search' has a long history of disproportionately targeting Black Britons.[10] Following the 2005 London bombings, however, those powers swung to target the latest perceived threat. People of color knew that racial profiling was in operation immediately after the 7 July bombings. The underground rail network opened for business the following day but heightened security included the use of stop and search at station entrances and the people selected for questioning appeared anything but random. Nevertheless, it was several weeks before the policy was officially acknowledged. At the end of July 2005 a Sunday paper carried an interview with Ian Johnston, the chief constable of the British Transport Police. The article stated the following:

> Mr Johnston made it clear he would not shy away from targeting those groups likely to present the greatest threat – most obviously young Asian men.
>
> He said: 'Intelligence-led stop-and-searches have got to be the way,' adding that there were 'challenges for us in managing diversity as an issue' but that 'we should not bottle out over this. We should not waste time searching old white ladies.' … Technological solutions such as scanners to check people entering the stations were dismissed by Mr Johnston. 'You could do one in a hundred or one in 200, but if you tried to do any more, people trying to get into Oxford Circus station would back up to Bond Street. You would just be doing the terrorists' job for them,' he said.
>
> Keeping the Tube and the national railway system operating normally is now a police priority.[11]

This is an important development, which was supported by a Government minister. Note the particular view of 'normality' that is assumed in the final sentence of the quotation. The use of racial profiling to justify the routine harassment and humiliation of people of color, 'most obviously young Asian men', is by no means normal – at least not in relation to anything in living memory. However, the quotation reveals a definition of normality that takes for granted a White subject. The policy priority here is to return White lives to normal as quickly as possible: distress and inconvenience for people of color is not a threat to this particular version of normality. The interview generated considerable debate and Hazel Blears MP (then a minister in the Home Office, later promoted to communities secretary by Prime Minister Gordon Brown) issued a statement supporting the policy. She was quoted as follows:

> What it means is if your intelligence in a particular area tells you that you're looking for somebody of a particular description, perhaps with particular clothing on, then clearly you're going to exercise that power in that way … I think most ordinary decent people will entirely accept that in terms of their own safety and security.[12]

Interestingly, the minister chose to illustrate her point by referring to clothing, rather than race/ethnicity – an illustration of a tendency to avoid naming race as an issue even when it is entirely obvious that race (or rather state racism) is the point at issue. Note also how the minister's de-racialized talk ends by asserting that 'most ordinary decent people' will agree with the policy, implicitly placing outside the mainstream all people who object to racial profiling on any grounds: such people simply fail this test of decency.

The issue of officially sanctioned racial profiling once again erupted in August 2006, following police announcements that they had foiled an attempt to destroy up to ten airliners on route between London and the US.[13] The episode proved to be a revealing example of how economic interests and racism combine powerfully to argue for additional racist exclusion and harassment. The British Government initially reacted by forbidding all hand luggage on planes. This was extremely inconvenient for passengers but the loudest complaints (and persistent threats of legal action) came from so-called 'budget' airlines, which repeatedly called for a return to the 'normality' established in the wake of the London bombs. The chief executive of Ryanair (one of Britain's most profitable budget airlines) was quoted as follows:

> What the government should then have done was return air travel to normality in much the same way as it successfully restored normal operations to the London underground within two days of the 7/7 attacks. It is the government's failure that is allowing these terrorists to alter Britain's normal way of life.[14]

One of the reasons for the budget airlines' anger was that restrictions on hand luggage threatened their key money-making strategy. As an aviation analyst explained at the time: 'They have developed a business model based on a 30-minute turnaround and are moving to hand luggage.'[15] The airlines themselves did not explicitly call for racial profiling. That role was taken by right-wing commentators and think-tanks.[16] Speaking on one of the highest profile TV news programmes in the UK, Susan MacDonald of the Manhattan Institute[17] argued:

> We're talking about *Islamic* terrorists and it is not just statistically overwhelmingly true that the vast majority of Islamic terrorists have been young men from South Asian, North Africa or Middle Eastern countries, it is also a logical tautology ... It is only logical and necessary for the police to look at Islamic people.[18]

When it was pointed out that one of the 2005 London bombers (the only one not born in Britain) was not Asian and that the so-called 'shoe bomber' (in an earlier attempt to blow up a transatlantic airliner) was White, MacDonald replied:

> Those are the outliers and you have to use generalisations in law enforcement ... I would say 95 to 97 per cent of successful and intending Islamic terrorists have fit the profile of young Muslim men of a certain origin in the world.[19]

The fervour with which commentators such as MacDonald assert the necessity of racial profiling is every bit as powerful as the campaign waged in the British media to defend the officers who killed Jean Charles de Menezes (see Chapter 2). Once again a particular and racist version of 'normality' and 'necessity' is asserted, one driven by White interests and White subject positions. It might be suggested, by the defenders of the Menezes shooters, for example, that these are exceptional responses born of exceptional times but critical race scholars have argued that *this drive to classify, control and exclude is not merely an unfortunate by-product of events; it is actually a defining characteristic of Whiteness.*

The absolute right to exclude: Whiteness as property

> Whiteness at various times signifies and is deployed as identity, status, and property, sometimes singularly, sometimes in tandem ... Whiteness has been characterized, not by an inherent unifying characteristic, but by the exclusion of others deemed 'not white'.
>
> Cheryl I. Harris[20]

I have already shown how racial identifications can change over time and, under certain circumstances, be defined by external forces with extreme consequences for social justice (Chapter 2). It would be wrong, however, to imagine that Whiteness is an ethereal, endlessly malleable identity. The borders of Whiteness are policed very actively and, as several of the preceding chapters demonstrate, the interests of White people are always placed centre stage.[21]

Several critical race theorists have documented how White identity has been constituted historically by the law – where (even after the formal abolition of slavery) being defined as legally White meant access to a wide range of freedoms and rights that were withheld from other races.[22] In one of the most important contributions Cheryl Harris examines the legal definition of Whiteness and argues that it is a form of property – where property is understood to include rights as well as physical 'things':

> Although by popular usage property describes 'things' owned by persons, or the rights of persons with respect to a thing … property may 'consist of rights in "things" that are intangible, or whose existence is a matter of legal definition.' … Thus, the fact that whiteness is not a 'physical' entity does not remove it from the realm of property.[23]

Harris goes on to examine the different characteristics and functions of Whiteness, concluding that the most important characteristic is *'the absolute right to exclude'*:[24] 'Whiteness and property share a common premise – a conceptual nucleus – of a right to exclude. This conceptual nucleus has proven to be a powerful center around which whiteness as property has taken shape.'[25]

This absolute right to exclude can be seen vividly in the reactions after 9/11 and the 2005 London bombings. The mobilization of discourses about the need to return to 'normality' (by fundamentally changing the daily reality of life for people of color) masks an almost visceral reaction among White policymakers, commentators and media alike, who felt able to embark on the aggressive majoritarianism that I described in Chapter 4: this is the attitude that gives licence to attack veils; to attack Islam; to attack difference merely because certain actions offend Whites. Elsewhere I have commented on the complex interplay of race and class,[26] but at this point it is necessary to note clearly that at key points – like the discourses surrounding the War on Terror – Whiteness operates to position White people (*all* White people) as more important, that is, as *superior*. Cheryl Harris argues:

> 'White' was defined and constructed in ways that increased its value by reinforcing its exclusivity … The wages of whiteness are available to all whites regardless of class position, even to those whites who are without power, money, or influence. Whiteness, the characteristic that distinguishes them from Blacks, serves as compensation even to those who lack material wealth … as Kimberlé Crenshaw points out, whites have an actual stake in racism.[27]

These benefits (the 'wages of whiteness') are particularly clear in the examples of racial profiling and other post-9/11 elements of White mobilization against aspects of the Other that are labelled as un-British or contrary to 'British' (that is, White British) sensitivities. But how does Whiteness operate on a mundane, day-to-day level? Is Whiteness generally dormant, only coming into action when threatened? Recent work on the nature of identity in general, and Whiteness in particular, suggests that Whiteness is an ever-present regime of control and classification that saturates society; it is present in the moment-to-moment, seemingly random and intensely personal interactions and thoughts that shape our lives.

Whiteness in practice

Building on a range of work, in particular the scholarship of Ruth Frankenberg[28] and David Roediger,[29] Zeus Leonardo discusses some of the defining characteristics of Whiteness.[30] For example:

- 'An unwillingness to name the contours of racism': inequality (in employment, education, wealth etc.) is explained by reference to any number of alternative factors rather than being attributable to the actions of Whites.
- 'The avoidance of identifying with a racial experience or group': Whiteness draws much of its power from 'Othering' the very idea of ethnicity. A central characteristic of Whiteness is a process of 'naturalisation' such that White becomes the norm from which other 'races' stand apart and in relation to which they are defined. When White-identified groups *do* make a claim for a White *ethnic* identity alongside other officially recognized ethnic groups (e.g. as has been tried by the Ku Klux Klan in the US and the British National Party in England) it is the very exceptionality of such claims that points to the common-sense naturalization of Whiteness at the heart of contemporary politics.[31]
- 'The minimization of racist legacy': seeking to 'draw a line' under past atrocities as if that would negate their continued importance as historic, economic and cultural factors.

These are some of the broad contours of racism and Whiteness, but an even more powerful understanding of Whiteness is offered through detailed research on the constant interplay of identities at the individual level.

Whiteness as 'performatively constituted'

In critical scholarship it is not uncommon to hear Whiteness described as a 'performance'. This can operate as a short-hand means of drawing attention to the importance of actions and constructed identities – rejecting the simplistic assumption that 'Whiteness' and White-identified people are one and the same thing. Henry Giroux argues:

> [T]he critical project that largely informs the new scholarship on 'whiteness' rests on a singular assumption. Its primary aim is to unveil the rhetorical, political, cultural, and social mechanisms through which 'whiteness' is both invented and used to mask its power and privilege.[32]

However, at risk of seeming pedantic, there is an important distinction to be made here between performance and 'performativity': it is a distinction that directly addresses the power of Whiteness and the problems that critical scholars and activists face in trying to de-centre it.

The idea of likening social 'actors' to performers on a stage is far from novel. One of the most insightful analyses remains that associated with the so-called 'Chicago School' of symbolic interaction, especially in the work of Howard Becker and Erving Goffman. The latter took the analogy as far as describing an entire dramaturgical analysis of social interaction; where he talked of 'performers', 'communication out of character' and 'front-' and 'back' regions, where actors allow different (often contradictory) faces to be seen by particular audiences.[33] However, one of the problems with such an analysis is the degree to which performers are *aware* of the performance they are giving. Even the most dedicated method-actor retains a knowledge that they are an actor giving an invented performance. One of the most powerful and dangerous aspects of Whiteness is that many (possibly the majority) of White people have no awareness of Whiteness as a construction, let alone their own role in sustaining and playing out the inequities at the heart of Whiteness. In this sense, the dramaturgical overtones of the analysis actually *under-estimate* the size of the task facing critical antiracists. As Deborah Youdell argues: 'The terms "perform" and "performance" imply a volitional subject, even a self-conscious, choosing performer, behind the "act" which is performed.'[34]

Drawing on theorists such as Michel Foucault and Judith Butler,[35] Youdell argues for a particular understanding of how power operates on and through the creation of different subject identities. Through a meticulously documented and highly sensitive analysis of teenage identity-work in school, Youdell takes seriously the spaces and possibilities for resistance and subversion. Crucially, however, her analysis also demonstrates the numerous ways in which *certain identities are strengthened and legitimized through countless acts of reiteration and reinforcement*.[36] These processes are not foolproof – there is always some scope for resistance – but their power is enormous, extending even into the most intimate and apparently idiosyncratic of actions and relationships, including, for example, the particular constellations of heterosexual desire that are deemed 'possible' across race lines in school.[37] Youdell terms this the *performative constitution of identity* and it points to the ways in which race and racism are constantly re-inscribed in the endless mundane yet powerful matrix of raced talk and actions:

> Butler suggests that '[b]eing called a name is … one of the conditions by which a subject is constituted in language' … This does not infer that the address conveys a 'truth' about the one addressed. Such interpellations are not understood as being descriptive; rather they are understood as being 'inaugurative': '[i]t seeks to introduce a reality rather than reporting an existing one'.[38]

It is this performative constitution of particular identities and roles that lends Whiteness its deep-rooted, almost invisible status. This may sound highly theoretical but what it points to is the fact that Whiteness exists forcefully and is constantly re-enacted and reinforced; through endless, overlapping racialized and racist actions and discourses – from the assumptions and actions of a White teacher making decisions about tracking and setting 'by ability' (Chapter 5) to policymakers' assumptions about the appropriate means of enforcing 'community cohesion' and safeguarding 'security' (Chapter 4). In the next section I examine a particularly important arena for the performative constitution of Whiteness: public talk about race, education and intelligence that *appears* open and democratic but where White voices come to dominate through the mobilization of particular ideas and strategies that render minoritized voices as illegitimate and untrustworthy; a case where talk of racism (presented as an opportunity to freely debate controversial ideas) functions to remake and reinforce White racial domination.

Free speech as hate speech: racism, Whiteness and phone-in democracy

Phone-ins, fairness and trust

Radio phone-in shows are big business. In the US the format has proven especially fruitful for right-wing commentators whose brash attacks on 'liberal' campaigners and issues command a nation-wide audience. Richard Delgado and Jean Stefancic note, for example, that the *Rush Limbaugh Show* alone plays five days a week on more than 600 radio stations to an audience in excess of 20 million a week.[39] Many of the most successful 'shock jocks' – as they are sometimes known – make a career out of attacks that tread a thin line between what is considered provocative and downright offensive. The following examples are quoted by Delgado and Stefancic:

> Rush Limbaugh to a black caller: 'Take that bone out of your nose and call me back.'

> Rush Limbaugh on immigrants: 'Taxpaying citizens are not being given access to these welfare and health services that they deserve and desire, but if you're an illegal immigrant and cross the border, you get everything you want.'

> Bob Grant following a gay pride march: 'Ideally, it would have been nice to have a few phalanxes of policemen with machine guns and mow them down.'

> Michael Savage in response to protesters: 'I wonder how many of those people outside the radio station are American citizens? I wonder how many of them are front groups for the very terrorists that John Ashcroft is looking for?'[40]

Radio stations in the US are at liberty to air as much of this material as they wish because of the repeal, in 1987, of the Fairness Doctrine, which had previously obliged stations 'to afford reasonable opportunity for discussion of contrasting points of view on controversial issues of public importance'.[41] During the pursuit of de-regulation, under the Reagan presidency, the requirements were withdrawn and successive attempts to restore the doctrine have failed in the face of media campaigns that claim the doctrine would limit 'free speech'.

In contrast, UK broadcasters continue to face a much wider range of regulations. The British Broadcasting Corporation (BBC) has a particularly stringent set of requirements, reflecting its unique status as a major global broadcaster funded in large part through public money.[42] The BBC describes itself as follows:

BBC purpose
To enrich people's lives with programmes and services that inform, educate and entertain.

Our vision
To be the most creative organisation in the world.

Our values
- Trust is the foundation of the BBC: we are independent, impartial and honest.
- Audiences are at the heart of everything we do.
- We take pride in delivering quality and value for money.
- Creativity is the lifeblood of our organisation.
- We respect each other and celebrate our diversity so that everyone can give their best.
- We are one BBC: great things happen when we work together.[43]

Note the emphasis on public service and the combined goal of educating and informing, whilst entertaining. A concern with honesty, impartiality, quality and diversity is also prominent. Research suggests that the BBC is extraordinarily successful in creating trust in its audience. A survey for the *Press Gazette* found that, despite strong Government criticism over the way the corporation handled the build-up to the 2003 invasion of Iraq, 'the BBC is still the first place most of the public turn to when they want to find news reports they can trust … [the BBC] polled more than five times its nearest rivals'.[44]

In addition to 'trust', the BBC also has an historical commitment to *involving* its audience, represented in the assertion that 'Audiences are at the heart of everything we do'. Charles Tolson has commented on the BBC's 'long-held belief' in 'active listening' as opposed to 'uncommitted hearing'.[45] In the earliest days of BBC radio, for example, schedulers would frequently move programmes in order to require listeners actively to seek them out and make a deliberate decision to listen. Scheduling principles have altered over the years but a commitment to audience interactivity has grown. Nowhere is this more in evidence than on Radio 5 Live, the BBC's fifth national radio station.

Radio 5 Live launched in 1990 and, after an uncertain start, was rebranded as a dedicated news and sport channel in 1994. Since then the station has become 'one of the success stories in the recent history of British broadcasting' and boasts at least 5 per cent of the national audience (over six million listeners weekly).[46] The station makes a priority of offering what it calls 'interactive opportunities for listeners' by using 'phone-ins, live debates and on-air requests for emails and text messages'.[47] I have already quoted from one of the station's most successful shows, where the presenter calmly relayed the views of a listener who was pleased that 'Muslims, Arabs and Asians are having it rough here' and was content if 'the odd one got shot' in error by the police (see Chapter 2). This focus on 'interactivity' has become a hallmark of the station, so much so that it has been described as 'the BBC's national radio talk show'.[48]

Significantly, the BBC proclaims the focus on interactivity as an important part of its *social* duty. This reflects a common assumption among media professionals that interactivity *by definition* represents a kind of democratizing of the airwaves. Radio 5 Live's programme policy, for example, includes a section entitled 'Sustaining citizenship and civil society', which states that:

> Programmes such as *Victoria Derbyshire* and *Simon Mayo* give people the opportunity to join in the debate that arises from the news. Five Live will continue to use interactive technologies to involve listeners *as much as possible*.[49]

The following section looks at how interactivity works in relation to a controversial issue concerning race and education, i.e. the supposed intellectual inferiority of Black people. Far from guaranteeing an open, enlightening and democratic exchange that (in the words of the corporation's charter) informs, educates and entertains, the programme presents an object lesson in the operation of Whiteness.

Media interactivity and Whiteness's absolute right to exclude

Radio 5 Live's success is not measured in audience ratings alone. The station has a healthy record of awards, many of which highlight the interactivity that it cherishes so much. The Sony Radio Academy Awards recently honoured the station's breakfast programme as the country's best 'news and current affairs' show:

> This programme cleverly weaves the serious with the humorous and involves its listeners on so many levels that they are an integral part of it. It has a great sense of movement and being 'out there' and is the perfect antidote to the normal studio bound fare at that time of day.[50]

The breakfast show is followed in the weekday schedule by the three-hour-long *Morning Programme*. The first hour of the show is given over to a phone-in on a single topic, which changes daily. The remaining two hours feature a mix of current affairs items and, throughout, listeners are invited to share their experiences and opinions via telephone, email, fax and mobile phone texting. The show that I focus on here was broadcast on 8 March 2006. The presenter, Victoria Derbyshire, is a past nominee for the Sony Radio Academy Award for 'interactive programme' and drew the following praise from the judges:

> Victoria Derbyshire demonstrates an outstanding ability to involve her audience in the fabric of her programming. *The audience is allowed to play a full part in generating content and determining editorial direction,* while the presenter's personality and professionalism assures that continuity is retained throughout.[51]

It is clear, therefore, that the programme I am about to analyse is a very mainstream example of public talk about race. It is on a commercially and artistically successful radio station, famed for its interactivity, which places a premium on audience participation as part of its social mission in relation to 'sustaining citizenship and civil society'. The programme airs at a premium time (9am till noon) and features an experienced and admired host. If talk radio can really offer a context for enlivened and educative debate, as its advocates claim, this should be the place for it to happen. As I show, however, the programme merely provided another, very powerful, conduit for the performative constitution of Whiteness.

The interview

The *Morning Programme* usually begins with a brief introduction by the host outlining the topic for the day's phone-in. Often there will be studio guests (usually two people from opposite sides of the discussion) who, after short opening statements, are then able to contribute throughout the next hour's debate as callers are put on air and the presenter reads out listeners' emails and texts. The programme in question, however, took a different approach; it began with a pre-recorded (and apparently edited) interview with Dr Frank Ellis, a lecturer in Russian and Slavonic Studies at Leeds University, who was in the news because students had called for his dismissal. Ellis had been quoted in the Leeds student newspaper expressing his view that Black people, as a group, are substantially less intelligent than Whites and that this inequality is genetically based and, therefore, resistant to ameliorative action through education and other social programmes (see Chapter 5 for a discussion of this strand of pseudo-science).

The use of a pre-recorded interview meant that while Ellis was free to give vent to his assertions only the presenter was able to interrogate him: Ellis was not present in the phone-in studio to field calls. Despite the fact that this process broke with the programme's established format, no explanation was offered. It may have been that Ellis was not able to set aside sufficient time to be involved in the phone-in; alternatively, he may have set a precondition on his involvement (as Government ministers often do) so that he could have a platform for his opinions but not be challenged by anyone except the host. In the following discussion I use 'host' to denote Victoria Derbyshire and 'Ellis' to denote Dr Frank Ellis.

The programme began as follows:

HOST: Welcome to the phone in. Today, should a lecturer be sacked for offending some of his students? [52]

The Leeds students' union, subsequently backed by the National Union of Students, called for Ellis's dismissal on the grounds of *racism*, not merely causing offence.[53] The host's introduction could, therefore, be thought to trivialize the issue but was repeated verbatim half an hour later when returning from a news break. The interview segment began as follows:

ELLIS: Calling somebody a racist or accusations of racism is, in effect, as far as I can see, an attempt to – it's an *ad hominem* attack, and it's an attempt to close down any discussion.[54]

The broadcast interview segment, therefore, did not begin with Ellis explaining his views and being challenged to defend them. Rather it started with him presenting himself as a victim of critics who wish to silence him; what he later called 'the free speech issue'. So, within minutes of the interview (between two White people) beginning, the inherent racism of Ellis's claims had slipped down the agenda. The discussion was framed in terms of the 'offence' he had caused and the first topic of debate was his own perception of victimization and a threat to free speech.

In total almost 12 minutes of the interview with Ellis was broadcast. Before considering the interview further, it is worth asking whether the balance of the discussion had already swung in Ellis's favour through the decision to pre-record the interview. This meant that he was free to confidently repeat his pseudo-scientific assertions without fear of any specialist interrogation: his only questioner was the programme host.

The BBC's editorial guidelines are clear on the dangers of dealing with controversial issues. In relation to impartiality and controversial issues, the guidance states:

- we will sometimes need to report on or interview people whose views may cause serious offence to many in our audiences. We must be convinced, after appropriate referral, that a clear public interest outweighs the possible offence.

- *we must rigorously test contributors expressing contentious views during an interview* whilst giving them a fair chance to set out their full response to our questions.[55]

The host was persistent, later in the interview, in trying to pin Ellis down on his views about different racial groups but, of course, she was not an expert on eugenic theories and so was poorly placed to offer any critical response when faced with his confident assertion of scientific truth and rigour:

ELLIS: [T]he process has been *refined* over the last hundred years so it's *extremely* effective; [it] shows a persistent, erm, er, one standard deviation between average – *average* – Black IQ and average White IQ. … I'm afraid we *have* to accept, I believe, that there are these differences, that they're not, erm, fundamentally amenable to, er, to vast amounts of money being spent on them.[56]

Throughout the interview Ellis had free reign to state and re-state his belief in the scientific merit and absolute accuracy of IQ tests. At one stage the host offered a faint challenge (noting that some people question whether IQ tests are 'a reliable measure of intelligence') but at no stage was the *concept* of intelligence itself questioned. Both the host and the interviewee (like most of the subsequent callers) apparently shared the incorrect assumption (common to many teachers and policymakers – see Chapter 5) that intelligence is a generalized academic potential that remains relatively fixed throughout life. Ellis responded to the challenge by restating his total belief in IQ tests and their significance:

ELLIS: There is no doubt at all that IQ still has, has astonishing validity.[57]

Despite editorial guidance that requires 'contributors expressing contentious views' to be interrogated 'rigorously', therefore, when IQists like Ellis put themselves forward as 'mainstream' and 'scientific' the media are simply not equipped to offer meaningful critique. The IQist position is incredibly powerful because it *asserts* its complete scientific validity over and over again. The claim of 'astonishing validity' leaves no room for uncertainty and the position is free to trade on an incorrect – but widely held – view of intelligence as generalized and fixed. Worst of all, it gains strength from reinforcing, and itself being strengthened by, a range of strategies that embody Whiteness's absolute right to exclude.

At one stage the host tried a different approach, directly asking Ellis whether he was racist:

ELLIS: Well I don't know a ra– what you mean? What is *a racist*?
HOST: You don't know what racism means?
ELLIS: Well I'm asking you, I mean, what is a racist? I mean, these days a racist is anything that you don't like … racist basically means anything they don't like. It's a *hate* word, calling somebody a racist or a fascist or a neo-Nazi or whatever has become a kind of a racist slur in its own right.[58]

The important element in this exchange was Ellis's attempt (as at the start of the interview) to deny legitimacy to the word 'racist'. First he evacuated the term of any significance by asserting that it can mean 'anything'. Then he sought to turn the tables by labelling it a '*hate* word'. The effect of these discursive strategies is to refuse racism any legitimacy as an accusation. This was a theme that several callers echoed in the subsequent discussion.

Ellis's interview ended with him returning to the theme of White victimization and included an impassioned defence of White people and a denial of Britain's central role in the transatlantic slave trade:

ELLIS: We've only had Blacks in any significant numbers in this country since about 1948. So we don't have a history – we have – White people in this country have absolutely *nothing* to apologize for or to debase themselves about. We don't *have* a history of slavery or, er erm, or *racism*. … White people are expected to take this sort of stuff on the chin whereas the *slightest* offence, erm, given to Blacks or the slightest *possibility* of giving offence to Blacks leads to all kinds of excruciating, erm, rewriting of comedy, sit-coms, remarks on the radio and so on.[59]

And so the interview segment ended, as it began, with Ellis claiming the status of White race victim and his racist views recast as a debate about 'Blacks' taking offence. As we will see, the notion of White victimization and one-sided concessions to minoritized groups was to be repeated during the rest of the programme as callers phoned, emailed and texted their views.

The discussion

In this section I examine some of the strands of argument that emerged as callers' views were aired. The first caller to be put on air was a fan of Dr Ellis but I want to start with 'Benjamin' – one of the few Black callers to the show.[60]

HATE SPEECH AS SYMBOLIC VIOLENCE

The reason for beginning with Benjamin is that his call addressed one of the fundamental problems with the idea that 'free speech' is in everyone's interests because it magically guarantees equal opportunity to state your case.[61] Quite apart from the fact that certain groups and individuals are granted, or can demand, disproportionate time and status, Benjamin's call pointed to the personal distress and anguish caused by IQist rhetoric which, despite its protagonists' claim to scientific respectability, operates as symbolic violence: that is, as an aggressive form of hate speech.

BENJAMIN: [A]s I was driving I started listening to 5 Live and, erm, my children were asking me questions, that … 'Dad, what do you think about this?' And afterwards I had to explain to them that, I mean, comparing your class – even though you *are* Black – you are still one of the top performers in your class, both children.[62]

Ian Hutchby has noted that talk radio has a particular immediacy, a kind of *intimacy*, that derives from its production and consumption in 'the domestic sphere': 'the voices of ordinary citizens are carried from the domestic sphere into the institutional space of the studio, and then projected back again'.[63] This degree of intimacy heightens the sense of violent invasion created by Ellis's words, putting Benjamin in a situation where, driving his children to school, he was confronted by their reaction to being told (by a university lecturer on the radio – an apparently authoritative person) that as Black people they are less likely to be intelligent. Benjamin and his children have been assaulted by Ellis's words: Benjamin had to explain to his children that they are *not* inferior 'even though you *are* Black'. This throws into relief the crass absurdity of White callers who stated that Black people were simply over-reacting:

CHARLES: [S]ome of the minorities are starting to take all these comments far too offensively.[64]

RATIONALITY AS A PRIZED (WHITE) CHARACTERISTIC

A theme that emerged in several calls concerned the view that Ellis's arguments and/or delivery were 'rational' and, therefore, somehow more likely to be valid. The host read out the following email from a listener:

HOST: Everything Dr Ellis says is rational, well-founded and true. … It was refreshing to hear him speak his mind. Researched, reasoned and well put. I found myself standing in my kitchen making a cup of tea and cheering him on.[65]

Several callers made reference to Dr Ellis's 'expert' status:

MARTIN: We've got to assume that Professor Ellis is – has done an amount of study and he's come to the *rational* conclusion and he hasn't just thought it up.[66]

The prized status of 'rationality' is clear here but, in fact, there is little that is rational about these contributions. Note, for example, that the host reads out a message from someone who says they are 'standing in my kitchen making a cup of tea and cheering him on': this emotional reaction, turning the discussion into a kind of gladiatorial competition, hardly seems rational. Similarly, Martin assumes that Dr Ellis (whom he incorrectly promotes to the status of professor) has reached his 'rational' conclusions after a process of research. But Ellis is a lecturer in Russian and Slavonic Studies, not a field known for its focus on the question of IQ and race differences in education: again, the rationality of the assumption is questionable.

We can see here the premium placed on an *assertion* of rationality. These respondents either failed to register Ellis's concluding slavery-denying rant or they share his interpretation of history. What is certain is that for all the kudos that some callers attached to Ellis's supposed 'rationality', there was an opposite reaction to what they labelled as emotional responses by Ellis's critics.

ANGER AND EMOTION AS IRRATIONAL RESPONSES

Henry, a caller with a pronounced African accent, was the first respondent to directly name Ellis as a racist:

HENRY: You just asked that gentleman, erm, er, Dr Ellis, a simple question, *if he is a racist?* The man could not even bring himself to answer the question. ... *A university should be a place where there is new perspectives to help mankind – not somebody coming up and, and, and – if the man was a politician, he's not a politician – he's a racist, a – a tool for the far right.*

SUSAN: I think this gentleman has just made my point: it's irrational. You have to be allowed to make your point, in public, and defend your view.[67]

Susan (also a caller) was no less dismissive a few minutes later when Joseph, a caller who identified himself as a person of color, made the point – *very calmly* – that Britain already operates considerable barriers to 'free speech' for certain communities. Despite Joseph's direct appeal to 'logic and reason', Susan simply rejected his view. Her reaction suggests that Susan's verdict on Henry was as much a reflection of the speaker as the manner or content of his opinion:

JOSEPH: [T]here are problems with other ethnic groups, still exercising this freedom of speech; they're igniting *terrorism* if you like. This has many aspects to it. The same way we apply logic and reason and reasoning on what *should* apply to freedom of speech for the Muslims, equally that should apply to White people.

SUSAN: I don't think that's happened. I think it's skewed the other way and I think a lot of people in our society feel that they are *not* allowed to speak out in a way that people in the multi-cultural society are allowed to. It's one rule for one and one rule for another and I think that's what's *really* at the crux of this problem.[68]

Susan's final statements are enormously significant. Although she adopted euphemisms I think her meaning is clear: 'a lot of people in our society feel that they are *not* allowed to speak out' is a claim that *White* people face censorship while people of color ('people in the multi-cultural society') enjoy additional freedoms. Once again, we have a claim of White victimization – echoing Ellis's own closing words in the interview that began the programme. Although this claim is demonstrably false, Susan is correct in stating that the phone-in was about more than IQ and intelligence. As Benjamin's call demonstrated, and Susan hints, the core of the discussion was about racial domination – about the absolute right of Whites to continue to peddle racist nonsense about Black intellectual inferiority in the name of 'freedom of speech'. To borrow Susan's phrase 'that's what's *really* at the crux of this problem'.

WHITENESS AND THE MORAL HIGH-GROUND

A famous quotation on the value of 'free speech' is often attributed (incorrectly) to the eighteenth-century French writer Voltaire: 'I disapprove of what you say, but I will defend to the death your right to say it.'[69] Several callers quoted this, or a version of it, as if its mere recitation was proof of something; from Ellis's *right* to say whatever he likes, through to an assumption of the *worth* of his views as against the presumed negative motives of anyone who sought to silence him. Remember that Ellis faced calls for his dismissal as a racist but the interview segment of the programme began with arguments about 'free speech' not racism. Similarly, the first caller to be aired after the interview segment stated:

> CHARLES: I agree with *everything* Dr Ellis has said with regard to colonial legacies … I really don't know enough about the *Bell Curve* theory to express an opinion but what I *do* support is that gentleman's right to express his opinion as he sees fit. This is not the Soviet Union; this is a country where free speech has been cherished from time immemorial.[70]

Susan also quoted the 'Voltaire' line and then repeated Ellis's assertion that the word 'racist' was being used to silence free speech: 'If he's just going to be branded a racist, it just *closes down* the discussion.'[71]

Some White callers' commitment to free speech seemed to give them licence to wander wherever they pleased. Charles, for example, euphemistically revisited the familiar stereotype about Black physicality[72] and, despite the fact that 'coloured' is widely held to be a racist term in the UK, the comment went unremarked by the host.

> CHARLES: People *are* different … I was a very good runner but when I came up against, erm, the coloured guys that I used to run with at school [pause] you know, as soon as we started to develop and get into manhood, they were *far* stronger and *far* more superior to me.[73]

According to press reports, four months after the phone-in was broadcast, Frank Ellis took early retirement and Leeds University 'agreed to pay him a year's salary and to make a contribution towards his legal costs'.[74]

No such thing as 'free' speech

My point in analysing the radio phone-in is to illustrate some of the mundane, taken-for-granted and yet extremely powerful ways in which Whiteness operates. The programme was produced by the UK's 'most trusted' broadcaster; it was hosted by an experienced presenter; and the whole thing is bound by a series of apparently stringent editorial guidelines meant to guarantee fairness whilst contributing to the wellbeing of 'citizenship and civil society'. And yet the broadcast provided an open platform for racism: Ellis's assertions about race and IQ were broadcast without a single challenge from a suitably knowledgeable source and a crude and regressive notion of 'intelligence' (as generalized, measurable and fixed) was taken for granted throughout.

Black people were subject to a prolonged and repeated slur (that as a group they are considerably less 'intelligent' than Whites) while White people simultaneously projected a vision of themselves as unfairly victimized. Ellis's pseudo-scientific racism was repeatedly praised as 'rational' while any accusation of racism was effectively ruled out of bounds by Ellis and by White callers, who presented the term as an under-handed attempt to close down discussion and force illiberal views on the world.

Perhaps the most disturbing aspect of the episode is that whatever strategy people of color adopted, in their criticism of Ellis, the approach was denied legitimacy. In this open and supposedly democratic exchange of views, Black voices were marginalized as too sensitive ('starting to take all these comments far too offensively'); too emotional ('it's irrational'); too aggressive and lacking in an understanding of proper debate ('this is not the Soviet Union').

Critical race theorists have written a good deal on the issue of 'free speech'. They have shown how the supposed neutrality and liberalism of free speech doctrines actually work in favour of the already powerful. Richard Delgado and Jean Stefancic, two of the foundational CRT scholars, warn against any simplistic answers to the complex web of issues that are involved in these questions but identify a number of fatal weaknesses in the arguments that are usually marshalled in defence of absolute free speech.[75] The limits of space prevent a thorough review of all the various debates but it is worth noting, in conclusion, that *there is simply no such thing as entirely free speech*. The law already operates considerable controls over speech. The prohibitions on libel, defamation, copyright and incitement to 'terrorism', for example, all prevent citizens from saying and writing whatever they wish free from control. This argument was made in the phone-in by Joseph, who proposed that restrictions that 'apply to freedom of speech for the Muslims, equally that should apply to White people'. His argument was summarily dismissed by the White caller, Susan.

It is quite remarkable how frequently one hears the argument that *any* restriction on free speech would start a chain of ever greater restrictions (a domino effect, or the 'thin end of the wedge') so that, regrettably, 'Toleration of a few wounded feelings on the part of minorities and gays is the "price we pay" for living in a free society'.[76] In fact, it is a price that minoritized groups pay for the freedom of Whites to parade their prejudices and enforce their interests on others.

Conclusion

> I sit on a man's back, choking him and making him carry me, and yet assure myself and others that I am very sorry for him and wish to ease his lot by all possible means – except by getting off his back.
>
> Leo Tolstoy[77]

Every chapter of this book has added a new element to a cumulative analysis of Whiteness and its role in constructing and reinforcing racial inequality in education. In this chapter I placed Whiteness centre-stage to explore its constant construction and enforcement. The radio phone-in provides a novel, but revealing, case study in how Whiteness operates to define the boundaries of acceptability and normality. The rules of the game are defined by, and for, White people. Like a game of chance played with loaded dice, the phone-in (like the education system) presents itself superficially as open and fair. But the reality is a situation where the perspectives and interests of White people are constantly enforced over those of minoritized groups. In the following chapter I consider how these processes mesh together in the education system and discuss their consequences for racism and inequality now and in the future.

9   Conclusion
Understanding race inequality
in education

To use the word *conspiracy* to describe certain aspects of our society is a strong indictment against the social fabric of this country. I have been challenged hundreds of times in debates and by the media with the use of this word *conspiracy*. Many of the challengers want me to document who were the plotters of this conspiracy, where was the meeting and when did it take place? I smile and listen to their barrage and remain confident in knowing as Neely Fuller stated 'until you understand White supremacy, everything else will confuse you'.

Jawanza Kunjufu[1]

Being in a minority, even a minority of one, did not make you mad. There was truth and there was untruth, and if you clung to the truth even against the whole world, you were not mad.

George Orwell[2]

Introduction

In this chapter I pull together the key ideas and findings that have shaped the previous chapters and consider the wider conclusions that can be drawn from the evidence. Once again I use the narrative technique of a CRT chronicle to provide an unusual and, hopefully, engaging context within which to debate the significance of the issues that have arisen.[3] My fictional characters, the Professor and Stephen Freeman, his activist protégé, return to discuss the chapters and to reveal what they have discovered about the nature of conspiracy.

The two men reflect on the speed of societal change and the resilient nature of White Supremacy. They briefly review the evidence assembled in the book[4] and then consider the utility of viewing racism as a sophisticated and highly successful form of conspiracy. The Professor explains that there is a scholarly literature about conspiracy theories, especially in the African American community, where a number of officially sanctioned and deadly conspiracies are now a matter of public record. Despite this long history, he notes that the language of conspiracy is usually ridiculed in both the academy and the popular media. Determined to reclaim the idea, Steve offers a legal perspective that advances the analysis in important ways, especially concerning how conspiracies are to be judged by their overall impacts, not their constituent parts. He also shows how a legal approach can move the discussion away from the stereotype of illicit meetings and secret pacts. Finally, the protagonists discuss the form that the White racist conspiracy in education takes and review the ways in which the analysis offers a positive way ahead.

Chronicle II: Racism and education – judging the evidence

The Professor flicked through the sheaf of conference papers and stretched. Thirty minutes earlier the room had been a hive of activity but now the conference on the education of Muslim children was over and he was alone. Fortunately, the chairs were comfortable. Ken Livingstone, mayor of London and vociferous campaigner on equity issues, had made available the main auditorium of City Hall, one of the capital's newest and most striking landmarks. The design afforded the conference audience, banked in several rows of plush blue seats, an excellent view of the chamber floor, where a succession of speakers had addressed the rise in anti-Islamic violence in Britain and debated the way ahead for Muslim children in a society that increasingly views them not merely with disdain but with open hostility.[5]

'Hey, Prof – fancy meeting you here!' The Professor turned to see his friend Stephen Freeman – part-time law student and full-time antiracist – bursting through the outer doors, waving his greeting. 'Sorry I'm late,' he said, panting. 'Long story.'

'No problem.' The Professor reached out a welcoming hand. 'You okay?' Steve nodded and smiled but didn't speak while he caught his breath. 'Congratulations on your exam results,' said the Professor, 'I knew you'd be fine! Second in your class. By the way, I have to show you this.'

He gathered his papers, swung his bag over his shoulder, and led Steve down towards the centre of the chamber where the speakers had stood. Steve looked at him quizzically.

'Look up,' the Professor suggested.

Steve raised his eyes and stood open-mouthed at the sight that met him. Above him a spiral walkway circled into the sky, the glass walls illuminated by light reflecting from the surface of the River Thames outside. Most striking of all was the effect caused by the building's pinnacle being placed off-centre, meaning that the spiral seemed to disappear into itself above them.

Steve finally spoke: 'Wow.'

'Very profound,' the Professor joked. 'Thought you'd like it! Now, come with me.'

Stasis and flux

A few minutes later the two men entered City Hall's viewing platform, high above the Thames. They stood silently for a moment, enjoying the beauty of London's iconic skyline. Steve was the first to speak: 'Good conference?'

'Yeah, very interesting,' the Professor enthused. 'Did you know that 1 in 12 of London's population is Muslim? There's been a Muslim presence here for centuries and it's growing fast. Half of London's Muslims are under 24.'[6]

'Interesting! I guess the city's in for some changes?'

The Professor looked troubled. 'Well, on one hand, London has always been home to a very diverse population. It's constantly changing … ' His voice trailed off.

'On the other hand,' Steve completed the thought, 'the same folks tend to stay in control?'

The Professor nodded. 'Take a look across the river,' he suggested, 'off to the right –'

'Geographers call it "the east",' Steve joked.

'Off to the *east*,' the Professor continued, 'you can see the skyscrapers of Canary Wharf. A centre for global capital that's almost entirely disconnected from the community that lives in its shadow.[7] To the left – *west* – there's HMS *Belfast*: a Second World War battleship now moored as a monument to British military power. And finally, on the opposite bank of the river, the Tower of London – a symbol of the ultimate power of the state to imprison, and even to kill, its own citizens: the tower in the middle has been there for over 900 years.'

'You sound like a tour guide,' Steve teased.

'Sorry – I didn't mean to be pompous,' the Professor apologized. 'It's just that power has a remarkable way of sustaining itself. This city has seen so much change superficially, but how much *really* changes? The Muslim population is already subject to the full force of the War on Terror: stop-and-search, racial profiling … Who knows what the future will bring?[8] Jean Charles de Menezes took seven bullets to the head because White officers thought he looked suspicious and had the same "Mongolian eyes" as a suspect they'd seen a picture of. And although he was later found to be entirely innocent, no-one has been prosecuted and the chief of police says "things just happen that way".'[9]

'Steady on, Prof,' Steve turned to face his friend. 'You're beginning to sound like a conspiracy theorist.'

Racism and education: weighing the evidence

Soon the two friends emerged from City Hall and onto the riverside walkway which was busy with tourists enjoying the late afternoon sights. As they weaved their way through the crowds, in search of a vacant bench, the conversation turned to the Professor's new book on racism in the English education system.

'Thanks for sending me your detailed notes,' Steve said. 'It gave me a nice feel for how the issues develop over the different chapters.'

'No problem – I'm grateful for your offer to look at them so quickly,' the Professor replied. 'Did you think that starting the CRT chapter with the Menezes killing was a bit too strong?'

'Well, it certainly got my attention,' Steve remembered. 'Starting with that *is* shocking but I thought it was justified. It really brings home how quickly White people's ideas about race and the protection of *their* normality can escalate into violence.'

The Professor nodded. 'With *lethal* consequences.'

'That's true,' Steve agreed. 'But looking at the different chapters as a whole, what I found *most* disturbing was the mundane banality of the racism that operates across the entire educational system. I mean, I have a pretty jaundiced view of politicians but I was shocked by the repeated use of Gap Talk to give a false impression of improvement. Obviously, we expect politicians to put a positive spin on things, but repeating the same old lines year after year after year? And the press lap it up.'[10]

'Or worse still,' the Professor observed, 'they start to say that too much attention is focusing on minorities and that White kids are suffering.'[11]

'Meanwhile, you say that official statistics show that the scale of the Black/White gap is so big that it'll *never* close because Whites will hit 100 per cent long before Black kids catch them?' Steve asked.

'That's what would happen based on past events,' the Professor clarified. 'But realistically we know that the system will introduce new measures before that happens – they've already done it with different categories in the school league tables – and each one tends to widen the Black/White gap again.'[12]

The two men walked in silence for a few minutes, lost in their thoughts. They were surprised to come across a series of brightly painted guitar-shaped statues: each one over six feet high and decorated in a different style. The figures were part of a new exhibition showing nearby, which used the terrace as an extended gallery space. Both men liked music, though of markedly different styles, but they were in no mood to discuss the joyful shapes in front of them. The Professor broke the silence. 'It's so difficult to deconstruct the illusion that school assessments are a scientific and neutral way of identifying ability.'

'Yeah. Everyone goes through the same system so it *must* be fair,' Steve said, mimicking the usual argument.

'But the assessments *create* inequality by dividing students along arbitrary lines,' the Professor continued. 'Then the results are used as if they have an independent existence and look into the kids' souls to tell you what they're capable of.'

'*Could you design a system any better to destroy Black educational chances?*' Steve's voice was raised in anger and several passers-by looked at him with apprehension. 'I mean, lets start with five-year-olds: the Foundation Stage Profile puts White kids top of the class and relegates Black kids from "above average" in the old system, to "below average" in the new one. Then let's use those scores as the basis for selecting kids for different types of teaching – call it "personalised learning" or "individualization" – and let's measure their progress against those early scores. What happens? Black kids continue to leave school with worse exam results than most White kids but hey – don't worry – they did quite well when you look at how far they've *progressed* from their terrible starting points.'[13]

The Professor nodded wearily and walked towards the side of the river terrace, where they could lean against the rail and look out over the Thames. 'But it's not *inevitable*,' he said. 'There are some schools that do a superb job with raising minoritized youth to truly excellent levels of achievement – by whatever measure you like.'

'There are precious few schools like that,' Steve argued.

'There was a Muslim headteacher at the conference today,' the Professor continued. 'She's run a state school for more than a decade: 90 per cent of her kids are from a minoritized background, mostly Pakistani and Bangladeshi; 40 per cent receive free school meals; but she's getting nearly 70 per cent leaving with at least five higher passes *including* English and maths – that compares to a national rate of about 44 per cent!'

Steve looked suitably impressed but noted, 'We *know* that minority kids can excel. The problem is that there aren't enough teachers in enough schools willing to tackle the issues and take race seriously.'[14] Steve's voice was quieter now but no less angry. 'And what do we see in this brave new world of a single equality body and a single equality law? We see the mandatory legal duties for race equality, that were created in the name of Stephen Lawrence, diluted and reduced to an optional extra in the name of "modernization". *It's obscene.*'[15]

'Meanwhile,' the Professor added, 'education policy is getting more and more regressive. Talk of *integration* and *cohesion* can be used to attack anything – even how kids dress – and politicians, commentators and union leaders line up to pronounce that multiculturalism is dead and we need to "move on".'[16]

The two men stared out across the river. 'So anyway,' the Professor asked eventually, 'how come you missed the conference?'

Steve turned to him and smiled. 'I've been researching conspiracy laws! And I found a few things that might surprise you.'

'Really?' exclaimed the Professor, brightening. 'I've been doing a bit of that myself.'

Conspiracy theories and theorizing conspiracy

'I think there's a park near Tower Bridge,' Steve remembered. 'Let's see if we can find somewhere to sit.'

As they headed towards the bridge, the Professor turned to his friend. 'I'm afraid I owe you an apology.' Steve looked surprised. 'Last month, when you first challenged me about my use of the term conspiracy –'

'– I wouldn't say I *challenged* you,' Steve protested.

'Well, okay, you *prodded* me quite hard,' the older man laughed. 'You pushed me to take the idea seriously and I'm sorry to say that I was quite dismissive.'

'Initially, yes,' Steve corrected, 'but I think I got you interested eventually.'

As they entered the park, they could see a free bench ahead of them. 'Well, now I'm more than interested,' the Professor said as he sat down. 'I've been looking into academic work on conspiracy and there's quite a literature on it – especially among African-American writers.'[17] He delved inside his leather bag, then handed his friend a battered copy of a large paperback with a striking cover in red, gold and black.

Steve read the details aloud as he turned the book over in his hands and then flipped through its pages, 'Patricia Turner, *I Heard it Through the Grapevine – Rumor in African American Culture.*[18] Hmm, looks fascinating.'

'The more I looked into the subject the more I started to think that conspiracy might be a useful way of thinking about some of the issues,' the Professor explained.

'Great,' Steve encouraged.

'Originally, I fell into the trap of assuming that conspiracy meant some fanciful *X-Files* type scenario where aliens have taken over or the world is about to end. But actually there's a serious tradition of scholarship on African-American beliefs about conspiracies and their link to *racism* as a form of systematic oppression.'

'I assume this is one of the major works in the field?' Steve asked as he handed the book back to the Professor.

'Yes. Turner does a great job of tracing the development of different versions of conspiracy thinking and she shows how these "rumours" of coordinated White hostility and oppression often reflect elements of actual racial oppression in the past and the present.'

'Sounds good,' Steve commented. 'I'm surprised I haven't heard of it before.'

'Well,' the Professor continued, 'she was attacked by other writers on conspiracy for failing to condemn what they called "the virus of paranoia". I think they found her work too challenging.'[19]

'*Paranoia*,' repeated Steve. 'Interesting word. It takes for granted that any talk of a conspiracy must, *by definition*, be completely groundless.'

'Exactly,' agreed the Professor. 'But, it's not paranoia if they're really out to get you.'

Steve looked at the Professor quizzically. 'I've heard that before. Remind me.'

It's not paranoia if they're really out to get you

'It's usually attributed to Huey Newton, a co-founder of the Black Panther Party in the 1960s,' the Professor explained.[20] 'But the thing is, they really *were* out to get him. It's now known that the FBI ran a concerted campaign to discredit the Panthers and disrupt their activities. And not just the Panthers: the FBI ran systematic operations against *all* the major civil rights figures.'[21]

'*Cointelpro*,' Steve said.

'You've heard of it?'

'Yeah. A counterintelligence programme. FBI agents were told to do whatever they could to weaken support for civil rights campaigns and get different groups at each other's throats.'

'That's right. They even planted newspaper stories and distributed disinformation to undermine the civil rights leaders and provoke violence.'[22] The Professor looked inside his bag and found a scrap of paper with a quote he'd scribbled down. 'A Senate investigation described it as "a sophisticated vigilante operation".[23] I'd never heard of it until I started digging in the conspiracy literature.'

'Malcolm X? Martin Luther King?' Steve added. 'You didn't think that inspirational Black leaders just *happened* to get killed did you?'

The Professor looked a little defensive. 'I remember hearing that the local police who should have been guarding King were called away just before his assassination.'[24]

Steve nodded. 'Official involvement in the killings has never been proven, but it's known that the FBI tried to blackmail King into committing suicide.[25] King's family brought a civil action in 1999 –'

'– I saw that on the net,' the Professor added. 'The jury unanimously returned a verdict that he had been killed as part of a "conspiracy" that included "governmental agencies".'[26]

'That's right,' Steve continued. 'No wonder African Americans believe in conspiracies!'

'I was reading a study,' the Professor recalled, 'which commented that these kinds of thing are dismissed as overblown *conspiracy theories* until they're proven. And then they're re-designated as *history* or sound *investigative journalism*.'[27]

The problem with conspiracies

The Professor stood and stretched. 'It's getting a little chilly; shall we get a drink?'

'Sure,' Steve replied. 'There's a nice fair trade coffee place north of the river, okay?'

The two men left the bench and made their way up the steep stone steps that took them to Tower Bridge's south entrance. 'It sounds like you're coming around to the idea of using conspiracy in the new book?' Steve commented.

The Professor looked uncertain. 'The problem is that any mention of the word conspiracy and most readers – most *White* readers,' he corrected himself, '– will leap to those old assumptions about cults and UFOs. We hear *conspiracy* and we're conditioned to scoff.'

'I can see the problem,' Steve agreed. 'But maybe the word can be reclaimed? Especially since there's so much evidence of real conspiracies to protect the racist status quo?'

'I agree,' the Professor stated firmly. They had barely reached the bridge entrance when they had to stop. A crowd of people in front of them signalled that the bridge was about to be raised to allow a ship to cross beneath. 'How's that for timing – they hardly ever raise the bridge these days.'

Steve glanced around. 'It's nice for the tourists,' he joked.

'What would you say,' the Professor asked, 'if I told you that in one study almost 90 per cent of African Americans were categorized as agreeing with conspiracy theories?'

Steve looked at him suspiciously. 'I'd say, "That sounds like a lot of people." Then I'd say, "When was the study conducted? What was the sample? and What do you mean by conspiracy theory?"'

'Good reply.' The Professor smiled. 'It claimed to be the first extensive quantitative study of Black views on conspiracy theories about the US government. It was carried out in the late 1990s with just over 1,000 African Americans in Louisiana.'[28]

'And the conspiracies?' Steve asked.

'That's the whole point,' the Professor explained. 'They included some rumours that get a lot of publicity when the US media want to portray African Americans as obsessed with conspiracies; like AIDS being a man-made genocidal tool. But that one didn't generate much support.'[29]

'And the other *conspiracies*?' Steve asked.

'Almost nine out of ten agreed that "African Americans are harassed by police because of their race and that the criminal justice system is not fair to Blacks".'[30]

Steve looked surprised. 'In view of the US prison statistics, and things like the Rodney King case, I'm shocked that it wasn't *ten* out of ten.'[31]

'That's my point,' the Professor continued. 'Those things are not at all strange allegations in view of the real-world experiences of African Americans. And yet the article calls them "conspiracy theories", describes the findings as "alarming" and worries about the need to restore trust in the government.'[32]

'Reform of the criminal justice system might be a good place to start,' Steve suggested.

Conspiracy theories and pessimism

A large container ship passed slowly beneath them as the two men continued their discussion. 'And here's why I'm so worried about using the term,' the Professor confided. 'The moment you attach the word conspiracy, conservatives come along and do their usual blame-the-victim routine by saying that African Americans are using racism as an excuse to avoid standing on their own two feet. Both Shelby Steele and Dinesh D'Souza are prominent people of color who have climbed on board that particular bandwagon.'[33]

'Yeah, but that happens on both sides of the Atlantic, Prof,' Steve replied. 'And they don't need the language of conspiracy to pull that trick: they just argue that it's no good blaming racism all the time. Then they usually launch into an attack on Black men, Black parents and Black culture and always, of course, with a nice big picture of the author so that the White readership feels okay about agreeing – after all, they think, it can't be racist if it's a Black man saying it.'[34]

'That's true,' the Professor conceded. 'And in any case, those claims about pessimism don't stand up. There are solid examples where belief in an orchestrated campaign of racist oppression has clearly spurred people on to *greater* resistance.'[35]

'Isn't that what Derrick Bell argues about CRT?' asked Steve. 'That far from breeding hopelessness, its analysis of the scale of White racism offers the strongest possible motive for ever greater action to oppose it?'[36]

Finally, the ship cleared Tower Bridge and the central sections began to descend slowly back into place across the river. The Professor looked at his friend. 'Well, it's a risk. If I use a term like conspiracy I could be playing right into the hands of conservatives who'll rubbish me just by saying that I'm a conspiracy theorist. I bet they accuse me of believing that the Earth is flat,' he joked.

As the crowd began to move forward across the bridge, Steve laughed. 'They think you're mad already! Besides, commentators, policymakers and the media are not your main audience. If you want to connect with real people – students, parents, teachers, headteachers and the like – I think that conspiracy is a very powerful concept. Don't forget, you're not the only one who's been researching the idea.'

Concerted practices: conspiracies without meetings

The warmth of the coffee house was a welcome relief from the growing chill of the London night air. Steve placed two cups of coffee on the table and opened his backpack, which was so much smaller than the Professor's bag that the older man wondered whether it was even worth carrying such a lightweight article. With a flourish, Steve produced a very small, ultra slim laptop and explained, 'I bought myself a present – a sort of pat on the back after the exams.'

The Professor sipped his coffee and sat back in his chair. 'Very nice. I hope your research is as impressive as the machinery.'

Steve winked and, as the computer whirred into life, began to explain what he had discovered about conspiracy from a legal standpoint. 'Earlier today, down by the river, you mentioned our first conversation about conspiracy – in The Dog and Duck in Soho.'[37]

'I wish we were there now,' joked the Professor as he looked at his coffee.

'Well, one of the reasons you disliked the idea of conspiracy was because it made you think of a small group of conspirators huddled together in a smoke-filled room, working on some grand plot.'

'I'm not sure those were my *exact* words,' the Professor smiled. 'But it sounds about right.'

'You can relax, Prof.' Steve smiled reassuringly. 'I'm not qualified yet; we're not in court; and this isn't a properly worked out case presentation.' Steve pressed a few keys and, happy that he'd found the right document, began his explanation: 'Okay. The first thing to note is that conspiracies are judged, legally, by their overall impact. According to the US Supreme Court ...' His voice trailed off while he located a particular paragraph in the document.

> It hardly needs statement that the character and effect of a conspiracy is not to be judged by dismembering it and viewing its separate parts, but only by looking at it as a whole.
>
> *United States v. Patten*, 226 U.S. 525.

'That's from a 1913 judgement,' Steve explained. 'Let me give it in more contemporary language:

> [A] conspiracy has to be viewed as a whole, the component parts – which may be unobjectionable by themselves or taken individually – are not to be weeded out and enquired into separately.'[38]

'That's really important,' the Professor said, leaning forward earnestly. 'A lot of the institutional racism in education happens through mundane little actions that have an enormous *cumulative* weight: you know, which kids are called to answer teachers' questions; who's singled out as the *ringleader* when the whole class is misbehaving; who's expression is read as contempt regardless of whether the kid is averting their eyes or staring straight at the teacher.'[39]

Steve nodded; at school he had been on the wrong end of every one of the processes that the Professor had listed. 'So conspiracy is a big word – for a big crime – that can be made up of lots and lots of smaller actions. And your concern about meetings in smoke-filled rooms?' Steve paused theatrically.

'Come on, yes?' the Professor asked impatiently.

'*No need for it*,' Steve announced. The Professor stared at him blankly. 'Conspiracies – or "concerted practices" as they're called in relation to cartels between big businesses – can be *inferred* by the behaviour of the conspirators. If they're working to a common purpose, that's enough. No need for a meeting; no need for an agreement. Their actions alone are enough to establish a conspiracy.' He drew breath and once again read aloud from the computer screen:

> [N]o formal agreement is required, it may be express or implied, and it is not even necessary to prove the terms of any particular agreement or plan. Conspiracy may be demonstrated by concert of action between the partici-pants all working together for a common purpose.[40]

'*Concert of action for a common purpose*,' the Professor repeated slowly.

'I'd say that the chapters in your book describe *exactly* that kind of concerted practice,' continued Steve, gulping down his now lukewarm coffee. 'And always to the benefit of the racist status quo. It's a web of actions by teachers, policymakers, right-wing commentators, uncritical academics and the media – all working in one direction, day after day and to incredibly powerful effect.'

There was silence. It was as if the other people in the coffee house had ceased to exist.

The Professor struggled to find the right words. 'Wow,' he said eventually.

Steve grinned. 'Wow? *Very* profound.'

The Professor smiled as his earlier comment was returned with interest. 'That's very important,' he continued. 'It will really strengthen my analysis if I can show that the law works with a notion of conspiracy that's sensitive enough to fit the case of racism in education. The law is pretty conservative and so if conspiracy works legally, then educationists have no excuse for ignoring it.' He expected Steve to close his computer but instead he noted even more frantic keyboard work.

Steve hit the return key, opening a new document, and looked at the Professor. 'That's not the best bit,' he said. 'Do you want to know what *kind* of conspiracy it is?'

Whiteness as a hub-and-spoke conspiracy

With fresh coffees in front of them, the two men lent forward, peering at the screen: the teacher was now the student.

Steve sipped his steaming coffee and tried to decide how best to present his arguments. 'This is why I was late for the conference today,' he began. 'I started doing some online searches, using the University of London legal gateway: they've got an incredible collection –' He stopped as he realized that the Professor couldn't care less about the University's legal facilities, excellent though they might be. 'Sorry. Er, anyway.' He gathered his thoughts. 'So there I am at breakfast, playing with my new computer, and I decide to try some different searches. As I look at the different listings for "conspiracy" I start to find lots of references to something called "a chain conspiracy".'

The Professor raised a quizzical eyebrow but remained silent. Steve read from his screen:

> [A] *chain conspiracy* involves several parties as links in one long criminal chain. Defendants in chain conspiracies are responsible for the actions of all partici-pants in the chain, even if they never met some of the other participants in the chain.[41]

The Professor lent back in his chair. 'Hmm, I like the idea,' he said thoughtfully, 'but it's not *quite* right.' Steve started to speak but the Professor continued, 'Whiteness isn't sequential – that's part of its strength. It doesn't *begin* with an individual classroom teacher any more than it *begins* with the prime minister. They're both deeply implicated but it's a dialectical situation: the classroom and school dynamics feed off, and reinforce, the wider societal oppressions and assumptions.'

'That's right,' Steve agreed.

'And there's the old cliché about a chain only being as strong as its weakest link,' the Professor continued. 'But Whiteness is incredibly strong. There are lots of broken links – antiracist campaigners, public victories like the Stephen Lawrence and David Bennett inquiries – they have an important impact but overall Whiteness seems to go on more or less unchanged; it's incredibly resilient.'

'Yes,' Steve agreed, 'that's why I *rejected* the idea of a chain conspiracy. I suggest you use the hub-and-spoke model.' He moved the cursor to highlight the relevant part of the computer screen: 'In a *hub-and-spoke conspiracy*, many parties (the spokes), conspire with one person (the hub), but not with other defendants.'[42]

The Professor crossed his arms as he weighed the definition in his mind.

'I think it captures the essence of what's happening quite accurately,' Steve suggested. 'Individual people and different agencies (like education, the economy, media) are all spokes connected through the central hub of Whiteness.'

'You're suggesting that White people are linked together – in a *de facto* conspiracy – by the shared "common-sense" assumptions and actions that charac-terize them and support their cultural and economic dominance?'

'Hub-and-spoke conspiracy,' Steve repeated.

'It's a very *big* wheel,' the Professor observed, 'with *a lot* of spokes.'

'*Millions*,' Steve corrected. 'And, obviously, some spokes are more important than others: the criminal justice system, the economy, education. I picture those as really big struts, you know, doing a lot of work supporting the structure, but surrounded by millions of smaller spokes: the individual teachers, politicians, doctors, police officers, journalists … all you White people busily going about your business-as-usual, unaware for the most part that you're not only *benefiting* from institutional racism, you're actively *supporting* it.'

The Professor nodded. 'Are you sure you're okay with me using this? It's a powerful idea: maybe we should write it up together?'

'Put me in your acknowledgements.' Steve laughed and held up his empty coffee cup: 'Another?'

The Professor shook his head. 'I'd better be getting home. I promised I'd be back before the kids went to bed.'

The usefulness of a conspiracy analysis

As they retraced their steps across Tower Bridge and towards the nearest train station, Steve turned to the Professor. 'You okay?' he asked. 'I thought you'd be excited at my legal discoveries.'

'Yeah, sorry!' the older man exclaimed. 'I was just trying to work through all the opposing arguments in my head.'

The two men stopped by a crossing and waited for the traffic to slow down.

'I'm really *very* grateful,' the Professor explained. 'I think the legal dimension is vitally important: being able to show that conspiracies don't have to involve conscious plots, that they can consist of a multitude of inter-related actions all having a combined effect of truly awful consequences.'

'So why the long face?' Steve asked as they crossed the road.

'Partly it's because the metaphor works *so* well,' the Professor explained. 'The idea of racism working like a hub-and-spoke conspiracy makes you look at the world rather differently.'

'Makes *you* look at the world differently,' Steve corrected. 'You're White. You're on the *inside*. But for me it's a familiar feeling to be wary of how I'm going to be treated; the assumptions Whites make about me. That's how it is.'

'Hopefully,' the Professor replied, 'it'll help more people grasp how Whiteness operates.'

'Exactly!' agreed Steve. '*Every individual is important and implicated*, but each individual can hide in the mass of other spokes and deny their involvement.'

'That's part of the strength of institutional racism,' the Professor added. 'No single person or agency can be held up as wholly responsible, but to some extent the power and force of the edifice relies on them *all*; from Whitehall and Parliament all the way down to the newest first-year teacher. I'm not saying that they have equal weight but they are all important; they are all spokes. The concept of a hub-and-spoke conspiracy highlights the dialectic between the wider structures and individual agency: they feed off and reinforce each other.'

'It doesn't just describe the mechanism,' Steve added. 'It also conveys *the sheer scale of the task facing us as antiracists*. Every white person we meet is more likely than not to share a whole series of basic assumptions that we need to deconstruct: assumptions about everything from criminality to ability and motivation. The problem is everywhere and the *mundane* aspects are incredibly dangerous because they provide the basis for the *extraordinary* aspects. Racial profiling wouldn't be discussed if it meant targeting Whites; pulling *them* out of lines and humiliating *them* as they go about their daily business.'

The Professor nodded. 'I wonder how long Gifted and Talented schemes would have lasted if the stats showed White kids *five times* less likely to be selected than Black Africans?'[43]

As the two men passed by a now deserted City Hall, they looked up at the illuminated windows.

'In fact, the Gifted and Talented scheme highlights another reason why the idea of a hub-and-spoke conspiracy is so powerful,' the Professor continued excitedly. 'It suggests that *every single action and policy is potentially implicated*. Because of the existing race inequalities in society, and because of the racist assumptions that most Whites bring into school, every single education policy is likely to impact on minoritized groups *differently*; and it's likely to have a disproportionately *negative* impact on particular groups, such as Black kids and their Muslim peers.'

'*Every* policy?' Steve queried.

'*Every* policy,' the Professor confirmed. 'Think about it. It doesn't matter what the explicit focus of the policy is – it could be academic, pastoral, financial; it could be about management styles, behavioural policies, curriculum reform – *anything*. Because racist assumptions saturate the system, and we're not starting from a level playing field in terms of existing inequalities, unless they're consciously interrogated for race equality impacts, the chances are that *every policy* will become another spoke in the conspiracy.'

The two friends reached London Bridge railway station just as the first drops of a late evening shower started to fall. They entered through the large archway and walked up the inclined corridor towards the main ticket hall.

'That shows another reason why the hub-and-spoke conspiracy is a useful idea,' Steve suggested. 'If every policy and action is potentially implicated, *it shows how vital it is to get actively involved in antiracist struggles*.'

The Professor smiled. 'Trust you to end on a note of resistance.'

'Thank you.' Steve accepted the compliment. 'Whiteness is like a vast conspiracy that pulls most White people in without them even realizing they're involved. We can stand back and look at the evidence and it's damning: concerted practices that maintain White Supremacy and systematically disadvantage particular minoritized groups.'

'Yes,' the Professor agreed. 'There's no need for a conscious plot. As you explained, we can *see* the conspiracy in the evidence of the education system itself – who wins, who loses.'

'*Correct*,' Steve continued. 'And the conspiracy is so deeply entrenched in White assumptions and actions that resistance can't be left to other people. Unless you are actively resisting, the chances are you're just another spoke who routinely reinforces the situation – whether you realize it or not.'

They passed through the ticket barrier and entered the throng of people, all rushing to get to different destinations as quickly as possible. The friends stood to one side, keen to finish their conversation before heading to their separate platforms.

Steve turned to his White friend and mentor. 'I know the conspiracy idea might offend some people, but if Whites don't like being implicated in a conspiracy to ensure that minoritized groups are constantly thwarted, demonized and denied a fair chance, then merely opting out isn't good enough.'

'You're right – as usual,' the Professor agreed. 'And the more that racism in education is named and challenged, the more chance we have of defeating it.'

'*Right*,' Steve said excitedly. 'As your chapter on the Stephen Lawrence case shows, there are people willing to fight and they can win important victories. Hell, there won't be any progress *unless* we fight: your analysis of education policy says that every advance – no matter how small – has been won through social action.'[44]

'Derrick Bell thinks we'll never eradicate racism completely,' the older man noted.

'That's as maybe,' Steve continued, 'but he's definitely right when he says that we have no alternative but to *oppose* it every step of the way.'[45]

The two men stood close to the wall, pulling themselves as far back as possible to avoid a group of young sightseers intent on walking four abreast the length of the corridor.

The Professor noticed that Steve was grinning. 'So,' the younger man enquired, 'I guess you're going to make the conspiracy argument in your book?'

'Definitely,' the Professor replied. 'I think the idea of Whiteness as a hub-and-spoke conspiracy is too strong to ignore. The evidence is overwhelming and the idea not only describes how things work across the system, through every policy and implicating us all, it also highlights the need for widespread resistance.'

Steve straightened the shoulder straps on his backpack, preparing to leave.

'Thanks again, Steve.' The Professor shook his friend's hand. 'I owe you one for all that research.'

'No problem. Just don't blame *me* when White people stop talking to you,' Steve smiled. 'I doubt many teachers, policymakers and journalists are going to enjoy being told they're part of a conspiracy to protect White Supremacy in education.'

The Professor nodded. 'If the past is anything to go by I'll get some positive responses too. Especially among community activists, students and teachers who want to make a difference and *really* pursue race equality.'

'Fingers crossed,' Steve smiled. 'We'd better get moving: it's later than we think.'

Appendix: notes from the author

Some thoughts on Whiteness, critical scholarship and political struggle

I have frequently been encouraged to write about my own positioning and experiences as a White person engaged in antiracist work but, until now, I have resisted these invitations. My hesitance reflected a number of concerns: first, on a very practical level, my time for writing is finite and always pressured; consequently I prefer to use the time and space available to examine issues that I think are more important. Second, I have always been worried that too much introspection can quickly cross the line between necessary critical reflection on one hand, and egotistical posturing on the other hand.[1] Mindful of these risks, however, numerous friends and colleagues have argued that I should say something directly about these issues, not least because Whiteness has become such a key topic for my analysis.

This appendix is also a response to an incident that happened recently when, after delivering a keynote address on the central, hidden but immensely powerful forces of White Supremacy at the heart of education policy, the first question came from a member of the audience who ignored all of my arguments and data and complained 'You haven't said anything about yourself ...'. I can understand the significance of the issues that the questioner was probing but I do not see them as a necessary aspect of every talk I give or article I write. Addressing them here, as part of a longer work, seems a sensible solution.

In this appendix, therefore, I reflect on some aspects of my work as a White antiracist that may be of further interest. In particular, I offer some thoughts in relation to several key questions. Do White researchers have a legitimate role in antiracism in general, and Critical Race Theory in particular? How does my being identified as White affect my research? What is the role of Critical Race Theory and social action in the struggle for race equality? These are complex issues and my thoughts here are neither authoritative nor final: they are works in progress.

The rules of racial standing

> True awareness requires an understanding of the Rules of Racial Standing. As an individual's understanding of these rules increases, there will be more and more instances where one can discern their working.
>
> Derrick Bell[2]

One of the key arguments suggested by the data in this book is that individual experiences, no matter how intimate and apparently random, can rarely be fully understood without reference to wider structures of power and oppression that are historically rooted and racially patterned. Although highly personal, therefore, these appendix notes must be seen within the wider context of race and racism, especially in relation to what Derrick Bell has termed 'the rules of racial standing', i.e. five statements about the relationship between race/racism and how people's views are shaped, received and (mis)represented. As with so much of Bell's work, the analysis is at once clear and immediately striking, and yet draws together numerous complex strands that suggest further issues and problems; in this case, concerning the particular nexus between research, politics, the academy and individual actions:

FIRST RULE
No matter their experience or expertise, blacks' statements involving race are deemed 'special pleading' and thus not entitled to serious consideration.[3]

SECOND RULE
Not only are blacks' complaints discounted, but black victims of racism are less effective witnesses than are whites, who are members of the oppressor class. This phenomenon reflects a widespread assumption that blacks, unlike whites, cannot be objective on racial issues.[4]

THIRD RULE
The usual exception … is the black person who publicly disparages or criticizes other blacks who are speaking or acting in ways that upset whites. Instantly, such statements are granted 'enhanced standing' even when the speaker has no special expertise or experience in the subject he or she is criticizing.[5]

Bell makes clear that he is concerned with the *effects* of actions and makes no assumptions about writers' personal motivations, regardless of their race or pro-/anti-civil rights positions. Black writers who gain enhanced status by denying racism, like White antiracists who gain greater exposure than minoritized peers saying much the same thing, may be entirely genuine in their commitments: whether genuine or opportunist, what matters for Derrick Bell is how the different positions play out in relation to struggles for race equality. This, of course, is highly uncomfortable reading for White antiracists who must realize that, whatever their own commitments and actions, the chances are that they are personally benefiting quite substantially from the racist structures and assumptions that they are seeking to destroy. In view of this, *is the only ethical line for Whites to withdraw from the field?* My answer, and the answer of many critical race theorists, is *no*.

First, the idea that antiracist politics is served by anyone vacating the field is somewhat perverse and actually invites Whites to salve their race consciences by doing nothing; thereby leaving White Supremacy untouched. For example, I have met several well qualified and highly motivated people of color who find it difficult to secure post-graduate supervision because universities have told them that the absence of suitably qualified minoritized staff means that they cannot accept them as students. Notwithstanding the pressing need for more diverse faculty in all university departments, this reaction has all the hallmarks of empty liberal gestural politics; it allows White liberals to feel good about their race politics whilst doing absolutely nothing to challenge the status quo and thereby *maintaining* the exclusion of minoritized people.

Richard Delgado has written extensively about the problem of false-empathy:

> False-empathy is worse than none at all, worse than indifference. It makes you overconfident, so that you can easily harm the intended beneficiary. You are apt to be paternalistic, thinking you know what the other really wants or needs … You can end up thinking that race is no different from class – that blacks are just whites who happen not to have any money right now.
>
> Empathy – the shallow, chic kind – is always more attractive than *responsibility*, which is hard work.[6]

This is a vitally important observation that highlights the need for tangible action rather than eloquent speeches and empty gestures. This points to a further compelling reason for Whites to be fundamentally engaged in antiracist scholarship: Bell's rules of racial standing note that radical analyses by Whites play an important role in challenging the assumption of 'special pleading' and bias that greets Black radicalism (the first rule). Because of the very racism that it challenges, critical race scholarship by White-identified people is less easily dismissed and provides an opportunity to use Whiteness against itself. This does not mean, of course, that radical scholarship by Whites is any more important than that by minoritized scholars; rather, the two can come together in complementary ways so that the whole is greater than the sum of the parts. I want to emphasize, however, that I believe that White people working with CRT must be prepared to take a back seat when necessary and, although they have a genuine contribution to make, they should remember Zeus Leonardo's observation that 'whenever whiteness, as an imagined racial collective, inserts itself into history, material and discursive violence accompanies it'.[7]

Conceptually this means there can never be 'White CRT' in a shallow imitation of the branches developed by scholars in the traditions of Latino/a, Native American and Asian American Studies (sometimes called LatCrit, TribalCrit and

AsianCrit).[8] Although there is a strong tradition of critical White studies in CRT (see Chapter 2) this takes Whiteness and White people as its focus. It does not draw inspiration or strength from a shared White identity or history; rather, it seeks to critique and dismantle those very illusions. Whiteness is a problem that critical educators must combat; it is *not* part of the solution.

This adds further weight to the position stated by David Stovall[9] that the experiential knowledge of Whites places a particular responsibility on them to use their insider-understandings of White racism to expose and challenge Whiteness (see Chapter 2). Recognizing the political value of having White-identified people working in the antiracist struggle, however, is only a part of the issue. In the next section I consider some different aspects of the same dynamic.

Whiteness and antiracist struggles

'Are you White?'

After a lecture to first-year teachers (where I'd focused very largely on White racism in the teaching and policy contexts) a student approached me (not in the public plenary) and asked if she could ask me 'a personal question'. Her hesitant demeanour suggested that the question was of an extremely sensitive and possibly intrusive nature. I said she could ask but I might choose not to answer. She looked around nervously and then asked in a quiet voice, 'Are you White?'

I said something about my family coming from varied backgrounds in England, Scotland and Eire but yes, I was pretty sure that everyone in my family would describe themselves as White. She said, 'Oh, I wasn't sure.' The student (who looked White to me) was clearly uncomfortable; she smiled and moved away.

I'm fairly certain that the student was checking whether or not I was of mixed race/dual heritage;[10] many people of mixed background, of course, are not distinctively 'raced' in terms of the usual stereotypical markers (such as skin tone and hair texture).

I am often asked how I came to be working on race, but this was the first time I had heard the question 'Are you White?' The question is a vital one because I suspect that by placing the 'blame' for race inequality so squarely on the shoulders of White people during my talk, I had temporarily stepped outside of – or at least troubled – the boundaries of 'Whiteness' as a regime of truth; so much so that my credentials as a White person were now in jeopardy. Put simply, the act of challenging White Supremacy was calling into question the possibility of me *being* White. At this fundamental level, White people *embody* White Supremacy.

I should add that when the student asked the question a series of possible answers flashed before me. The most obvious reply, a simple 'Yes', could have reinforced the dangerous idea that races are real and clearly demarcated *entities* but the alternative – a long explanation about the nature of Whiteness as a psychological, social, historical, economic and political construct – also seemed out of place. It would be interesting to talk with the student about the reason for the question and how she would have reacted to a range of different answers. What if I had said 'No'? Would my talk have had greater authority (because I could have been drawing on personal experience of racism) or would its validity have been called into doubt, as a form of 'special pleading'? Perhaps this illustrates the most significant aspect of the incident: *whatever* answer I had given, the student could easily have decided that my response *decreased* the significance of what I had said – regardless of the fact that at no time had I invoked personal experience as a part of my data or analysis. Once again, Whiteness is highlighted as both powerful and incredibly flexible: the question potentially puts me (and every other antiracist scholar) in a lose–lose situation. This sounds a further warning about the potential threats of individualized identity-politics within the academy.

'What do your people think about the work you do?'

In 2002 Dianne Abbott MP, one of the first ever Black members of the British Parliament, organized a cross-London event that focused on the education of Black children. It generated national interest and the famous QEII conference centre had to close its doors when more than 2,000 Black parents, teachers and students turned up for the first session. Alongside Gus John, I spoke as part of a 'workshop' (addressing around 1,000 people). I set out some of the ways that schools fail Black students, not least through placement in the lowest teaching groups where the level of exam entry can mean that a failing 'D' grade is the very best a child can possibly attain.[11] I discussed how the system works and strategies parents can use to challenge it.

After the conference I spoke with many people, including an elderly African Caribbean woman. She approached me and thanked me for the session, adding, 'What do *your* people think about the work you do?'

Clearly, for this woman (who's likely had a lifetime of experiencing and resisting racism) there was no doubting my race, unlike the White student described previously. We spoke about White people's reactions to antiracism and the kind of letters and emails that this work can attract from 'my people': I have a number of colleagues who have received death threats. She thanked me again for my work and, with great warmth and concern, asked me to 'Be careful.'

What do these incidents suggest? Well, first, that no matter how radically one attempts to question and destabilize racial categories (abolish Whiteness)[12] other people's assumptions are *always* in play. However, Whiteness as a practice of power *can* be disrupted, even to the extent that one's location within the category White is actually called into question. But these are uncertain and unstable categories which, despite our consciously progressive intent, can easily be reconstructed in regressive ways. The elderly Black woman had no doubt that many of 'my people' would not welcome my work, and that assessment is certainly correct. I am hopeful, however, that the White teacher's expectations and assumptions had been sufficiently troubled that she began to rethink her ideas about minoritized students in her school.

We must struggle where we are

In terms of antiracist praxis, I continually return to a simple but powerful idea suggested more than 20 years ago by Stuart Hall, Britain's foremost Black sociologist. The statement came in a video recording where Hall was being interviewed as part of the work of a small Black-run education resource centre, which produced posters, guides and other curricular materials to aid antiracist teachers in London. The interview began with Professor Hall being invited to explain something about the nature of racism. He gave a typically eloquent, highly accessible answer that highlighted the extensive, normalized but incredibly damaging effects of racism. The interviewer looked somewhat crestfallen and asked, in view of the scale of racism, what was the point of a small self-help project like theirs. In reply Stuart Hall made a deceptively simple observation: '[Racism] is inside the schools and outside the schools, but we must struggle where we are.'[13]

I repeatedly come back to Hall's entreaty to 'struggle where we are', especially when I am asked about solutions and the scale of the antiracist struggle. I have already addressed the problem of perceived hopelessness that can come from a misreading of CRT (see Chapters 2, 6 and 9). To suggest that critical race analyses breed hopelessness and disempowerment is a cruel distortion of an approach that, more than any other conceptual framework of which I'm aware, places genuine social action at the heart of its enterprise.

Hall's advice speaks to everyone who wants to contribute to antiracist change: regardless of our institutional location (in a school, university, school district, factory, community group or political party) and irrespective of our positioning at the intersection of numerous identity categories (raced, classed, gendered, dis/abled) we all can – and must – struggle where we are.

For what it's worth, I try to engage in this struggle in numerous ways: in addition to my research and teaching, I also work with a variety of groups that make or seek to influence policy (including governmental and non-governmental organizations) and a range of community advocacy and campaigning groups. I try to use the media to disseminate antiracist research and challenge the stereotypes that dominate so much of the airwaves. I work with colleagues internationally, and edit a journal publishing critical education scholarship, to take forward antiracist and critical scholarship more widely. I do not offer these notes as in any way a declaration of an antiracist transcendence of Whiteness – of the sort critiqued by Sara Ahmed[14] – rather, they are meant to show that (as a critical race theorist) I take seriously the need for an engaged critical race praxis (as highlighted by David Stovall)[15] and do not imagine for a second that an analysis of racism alone is a sufficient contribution to the struggle for race equality.

The need to stay critical

I have argued elsewhere that critical research must always remain reflexive and self-critical.[16] In many ways the issues I have addressed in this appendix, although prompted by my identity as a White researcher, pose questions for everyone engaged in critical scholarship. We are all captured, to some degree, by the very machinery of racism and White Supremacy that we seek to criticize in our work. Despite our best efforts our work, indeed our very presence in the system, may have unintended consequences. An honest awareness of this danger is the first step in resisting it:

> [W]e all legitimate an unfair system, merely by agreeing to teach in institutions that have terrible records on matters of race.
>
> Richard Delgado[17]

> [G]enuine service requires humility. We must first recognize and acknowledge (at least to ourselves) that our actions are not likely to lead to transcendent change and may indeed, despite our best efforts, be of more help to the system we despise than to the victims of that system whom we are trying to help. Then, and only then, can that realization and the dedication based on it lead to policy positions and campaigns that are less likely to worsen conditions for those we are trying to help and more likely to remind the powers that be that out there are persons like us who are not only not on their side but determined to stand in their way.
>
> Derrick Bell[18]

Notes

1 Introduction

1 A limited form of devolution within the United Kingdom means that although a single British Parliament resides in Westminster, certain powers (including those to determine the school curriculum) are now held separately in England, Wales, Scotland and Northern Ireland.

2 Bickerton (1971).

3 Unfortunately, I have been unable to identify an authoritative first source for this usage.

4 See Mason (2000); Omi and Winant (1993); Ratcliffe, P. (1994).

5 See Entine (2000); Herrnstein and Murray (1994).

6 See Back and Solomos (2000); Mac an Ghaill (1999).

7 Carmichael and Hamilton (1967).

8 Gillborn (2006a).

9 My acknowledgements name the friends and colleagues who particularly helped me with these issues; in addition, I was prompted, questioned and supported by conference-goers in Barcelona, Buffalo, Chicago, Copenhagen, London, Madison, Manchester, Melbourne, San Francisco, Seattle and Toronto.

10 Bell (1985).

11 See Delgado (1989); Williams (1987).

12 See Bell (1987, 1992); Delgado (1995, 2003).

13 Ladson-Billings (2006a).

14 Burke and Jackson (2007); Delamont (2001, 2003).

15 Stephen Freeman is an entirely fictitious character and bears no relation to anyone with a similar name, either alive or dead.

16 The Open University is a distance teaching university established in the late 1960s. It awards recognized degrees but accepts mature students with few or no formal qualifications.

17 Delamont (2003): xiii.

18 The appendix to this book addresses my own positioning more directly.

19 Orwell (1949).

20 See Whitty (2006).

21 See Chapters 4 and 5.

22 Oxford English Dictionary (1989).

23 Coard (1971).

24 Gillborn (2005c).

25 There is a common myth that Black girls excel in school: despite its superficial positivity this myth hides inequalities experienced by Black girls and simultane-

ously demonizes Black boys as victims of their own hyper-masculinity: see Rollock (2007); see also Chapters 3, 4 and 5.

26   For an extended version of this argument see Gillborn (2006a, 2006b).
27   McIntosh (1992).
28   Leonardo (2004): 138.
29   See Chapter 8 for detail on White people's characteristic refusal to engage in critical discussion of Whiteness.
30   Mills (2003): 190.
31   See Chapters 3 and 5.
32   See Chapter 8 for an analysis of how 'free speech' and the popular media promote White interests and perspectives.
33   Delgado and Stefancic (2000): xvi.
34   See Chapter 4 for a detailed analysis of different policy phases and their under-lying commonalities.
35   Bourdieu and Wacquant (1999). For critical discussions see Bonnett (2006) and Werbner (2000).
36   See Delamont (2001).
37   London is reported to be the world's third most popular film location after New York and Los Angeles. In 2005 there were an average of 35 different crews at work every day in the city. Source: *Observer* (2007): 42.
38   Roithmayr (2003).
39   Compare Gillborn and Gipps (1996) and Gorard (1999): see Chapter 3.
40   Beratan (2008).
41   Gillborn (2005b).
42   Gillborn (2005a).
43   (Harris 1993).

2   Critical Race Theory

1   Calmore (1992): 145.
2   Ladson-Billings and Tate (1995).
3   See Cole and Maisuria (2007); Darder and Torres (2004).
4   The exact events that took place over the following hour are the source of huge controversy and an entirely undisputed account is unlikely ever to be established. The following version is based on the best available evidence from a tapestry of sources, including news services, online information and leaked evidence from an official independent inquiry.
5   Changes in US immigration rules were one of the key factors behind the waves of migration to the UK from the Caribbean in the post-war years: see Lawrence (1974).
6   Jean Charles de Menezes Family Campaign (2006).
7   BBC News Online (2006a). The officer's leaked statement is quoted at greater length in Jamieson and Brown (2005).
8   Williams and Wright (2005). The use of pseudo-scientific racialized language is highly significant. The 'Mongolian eyes' comment is confirmed by leaked parts of an independent inquiry, published in several additional places: see Jamieson and Brown (2005); *The Independent* (2005); Twomey and Pilditch (2005).
9   Source: BBC News Online (2006b).
10   In September 2006 Commander Cressida Dick was made deputy assistant commissioner: BBC News Online (2006c).
11   BBC News Online (2005e); *The Guardian* (2006a).
12   Vandenberghe (2006).
13   Twomey and Pilditch (2005).

14 BBC News Online (2006d).
15 BBC TV (2006a).
16 Transcribed from a broadcast interview with Sir Ian Blair on *The Simon Mayo Show*, BBC Radio 5 Live, 20 September 2006. All transcripts of radio broadcasts in this book are my own. With the exception of the hosts and public figures, such as Sir Ian Blair, all names of people and places have been changed.
17 Twomey and Pilditch (2005).
18 Littlejohn (2005).
19 Stevens (2006). Following Gordon Brown's appointment as prime minister, in June 2007, Stevens was made an official government adviser. Source: BBC News Online (2007a).
20 Her website describes Melanie Phillips as follows: 'Styled a conservative by her opponents, she prefers to think of herself as defending authentic liberal values against the attempt to destroy western culture from within.' http://www.melaniephillips.com/biography (accessed 28 December 2007).
21 Phillips, M. (2005), original emphasis.
22 In the three weeks following 7 July, the number of reported 'religious hate crimes' in London rose more than 600 per cent: from 40 in the same period in 2004 to 269. Source: BBC News Online (2005a).
23 Bhatia (no date).
24 West (1995): xi–xii.
25 Ibid.: xi.
26 Bell (1980a); Crenshaw (1988); Delgado (1989); Matsuda *et al.* (1993).
27 Bell (1995): 898; Delgado and Stefancic (2001): 6.
28 Crenshaw *et al.* (1995): xiii.
29 See Delgado and Stefancic (2001); Yosso (2005); Wing (1997).
30 See Delgado and Stefancic (2001): 6.
31 Ladson-Billings and Tate (1995).
32 Ladson-Billings (1998, 1999, 2005); Tate (1997, 1999, 2005).
33 See Dixson and Rousseau (2006); Parker (1998); Taylor (1999); Villenas *et al.* (1999).
34 Crenshaw *et al.* (1995): xiii.
35 Tate (1997): 235.
36 Eric Yamamoto quoted in Stovall (2006): 245.
37 See Gillborn (2006c).
38 See Bonnett (2000); Gillborn (1995); Sivanandan (1990).
39 Indeed, the picture I present here is a little different to the one I sketched just a year or so ago: Gillborn (2006c).
40 Delgado and Stefancic (2000): xvi.
41 Tate (1997): 234.
42 See Chapter 6.
43 Carmichael and Hamilton (1967): 112, original emphasis.
44 Delgado and Stefancic (2001): 7.
45 See Chapter 1.
46 See Mason (2000): 8.
47 See Barrett and Roediger (1997); Mason (2000); Omi and Winant (1993); Roediger (1994); Sacks (1997).
48 See Stovall's (2006) call for constructive work on race and class.
49 Tate (1997): 234.
50 Ibid.: 235.
51 Ibid.: 234.
52 Yosso *et al.* (2004).
53 Delgado and Stefancic (2000): xvi.

54 Crenshaw *et al.* (1995): xiv.

55 Delgado and Stefancic (2000): xvi.

56 Crenshaw *et al.* (1995): xiv.

57 The debate about antiracist research in the UK is frequently conducted in the language of 'methodology' but actually focuses attention on questions of power, privilege and politics. For examples of the 'standards' approach see Foster *et al.* (1996); Hammersley (1995, 2000); Tooley with Darby (1998). For critical commentaries and replies see Blair (2004); Connolly (1998a); Gillborn (1998a).

58 For an excellent discussion of these debates in the US see Levit (1999).

59 Tate (1997): 235.

60 This is an extract from an interview with Howard Becker conducted by J.C. Verhoeven (personal communication): see Verhoeven (1989).

61 See Brandt (1986); Sivanandan (1990).

62 Dlamini (2002); Leonardo (2002); Rich and Cargile (2004).

63 Delgado and Stefancic (2000).

64 Tate (1997).

65 See Cixous and Clément (1996); Sellers (1994).

66 One of the most outstanding examples of this work is the development of characters and plot lines that run through successive chronicles written by Richard Delgado: see Delgado (1995, 1996, 2003).

67 Ladson-Billings (2006a): xi.

68 Bell (1980b).

69 Delgado and Stefancic (2000): xvii.

70 Ladson-Billings (1998): 12.

71 Bell (1980b); Dudziak (2000).

72 This is one of the factors identified in the brief by the University of Michigan that defends its admissions policies. The support of then US Secretary of State, the Republican former General Colin Powell, was also seen as a key factor in contemporary news coverage: see CNN.com (2003). For background on the Michigan case, see Ethridge (2003).

73 Bell (1985): 32.

74 Delgado (1998a): 445

75 Delgado and Stefancic (2001): 33.

76 Hare (2002): 7–8.

77 Sheets (2000, 2003). See also Howard (2004).

78 See Bush (2004); Delgado and Stefancic (1997); Fine *et al.* (1997); Leonardo (2002).

79 Leonardo (2002): 31.

80 See Ladson-Billings and Tate (1995): 58–60.

81 Bonnett (1997): 189, emphasis added.

82 Ignatiev (1994).

83 See 'The rules of racial standing' in Bell (1992).

84 Stovall (2006): 251–2.

85 Newitz and Wray (1997).

86 Howard (2004): 69. Howard's paper is presented as a critique of 'critical whiteness studies' but it actually focuses on quite a small range of work and does not directly address CRT. The critique itself is well grounded but is more specific than the paper, and especially its title, suggests.

87 Crenshaw *et al.* (1995): xiii.

88 McIntosh (1992): 291.

89 Leonardo (2004): 138.

90 Apple (1998): xi.

91 Ansley (1997): 592.

92   See Mills (2003): 182; Stovall (2006): 247.
93   See Crenshaw (1995); Wing (1997); Youdell (2006).
94   Brah and Phoenix (2004).
95   See Darder and Torres (2004): 104.
96   Troyna (1994).
97   Darder and Torres (2004): 97.
98   Ibid.: 99–100.
99   Stovall (2006): 252.
100 Cole and Maisuria (2007).
101 Allen (2006): 5 and 9.
102 Mills (2003): xvii.
103 Although the Slave Trade Abolition Bill was passed by the British Parliament in 1807 it was another 30 years before slavery was abolished throughout the Empire. Slavery was abolished in US territories in 1865. Source: Directgov (2007).
104 Crenshaw (1995): 377.
105 Stovall (2006): 257.
106 Mills (1997): 137.
107 Delgado and Stefancic (1998): xvii.
108 Snipp (2004): 322. See also Hare (2007); Tippeconnic and Saunders (2007).
109 See Modood (1989, 2005, 2007); Gillborn (1995), especially Chapter 4.
110 See BBC News Online (2005b); BBC News Online (2007b).
111 Delgado and Stefancic (2001): 13.
112 Bell (1987, 1992).
113 Bell (1992): 92.
114 See Dixson and Rousseau (2005); Stovall (2006).
115 Taylor (1998): 124.
116 First published as Bell (1990) and subsequently reprinted numerous times, including as a chapter in Bell (1992).
117 DV Republic (2005); Internet Movie Database (no date).
118 Bell (1992): 13.
119 See Chapter 8 for further analysis of this type of 'interactive' programme.
120 Transcript of a broadcast on Radio 5 Live, 14 June 2006, original emphasis.

3   Inequality, Inequality, Inequality

1   Ladson-Billings (2006b): 3
2   Compulsory education in England covers the ages 5 to 16. The government has announced its intention to legislate 'so that from 2015 all young people will remain in some form of education or training until their 18th birthday': DfES (2007a).
3   After Roithmayr (2000, 2003, 2004).
4   Gillborn and Mirza (2000).
5   The main government department dealing with education has changed its name many times in the last decade or so. It's most recent incarnations are the Department for Education and Employment (DfEE), the Department for Education and Skills (DfES) and, from mid-2007, the Department for Children, Schools and Families (DCSF). These changes are largely superficial and so, for the sake of clarity, I simply use the term 'Education Department' throughout the text.
6   Gillborn and Mirza (2000): 27–9.
7   The GCSE (General Certificate of Secondary Education) was introduced in 1988 and is the most common form of high-stakes test taken by students at the end of

their compulsory schooling. Separate subjects have their own GCSE examinations and good results are a vital part of the competition for places in further and higher education. GCSE results are graded A*, A, B, C, D, E, F and G, with U (ungraded) as a failing result. Although the other grades are officially counted as 'pass' grades, a common distinction is the greater status accorded the 'higher grade passes' from A* to C inclusive.

8   Personal communication, November 2000.
9   The percentage point method was common in the early research that drew attention to race inequalities, and made the case for multicultural education in the 1970s and 1980s: e.g. Drew and Gray (1990); Kysel (1988); Mabey (1986); Maughan and Rutter (1986). The approach was also at the heart of the statistical analyses produced for the landmark public inquiries chaired by Anthony Rampton and Lord Swann: Rampton (1981); Swann (1985).
10 Gorard (1999).
11 Ibid.: 236.
12 Ibid.
13 Gorard *et al.* (1999).
14 Gorard (1999): 243.
15 Ibid.: 236.
16 Gorard and Smith (2003). Interestingly, although criticism of the percentage point approach is included in his evidence to the politicians, Gorard chose not to repeat the actual phrase 'politician's error'.
17 See Connolly (2006a, 2006b).
18 Gorard (1999).
19 Gillborn and Gipps (1996).
20 First, Gorard reports the data as referring to the proportion of students gaining at least five higher grade GCSE passes and he repeats this error several times: e.g. Gorard (1999): 242; Gorard and White (nd): 17; White and Gorard (1999). In fact, the figures he quotes are for changes in the *average exam score*: a completely different measure. Second, I have omitted from the table the row giving 'overall' values because, again, Gorard has misread the original. He says that 'there appears to be a misprint in the overall improvement figures cited … it would be difficult for all subgroups to improve by less than the overall improvement' (Gorard 1999: 241–2). In fact, he fails to note that the overall figures given by Gillborn and Gipps (1996: 20) are reported for a longer timespan, 1990 to 1994, rather than the period reported for separate ethnic groups, 1991 to 1993 (Gillborn and Gipps 1996: 21). As Caroline Gipps and I explained, this was because ethnic breakdowns were not available for the longer time period (Gillborn and Gipps 1996: footnote 38, pp. 20 and 32). The errors appear to have crept in because Gorard chose to construct a table from a range of data that we reported in text form. It is not clear why he preferred this to any of the existing tables in our report.
21 Gillborn and Gipps (1996): 21, original emphasis.
22 Gorard (1999): 241.
23 White and Gorard (1999); Gorard and White (nd): 17.
24 Gorard (2000a: 393, 2000b: 310); Gorard and Smith (2003).
25 Hammersley (2001): 293 and 294.
26 Gorard (1999): 241, emphasis added.
27 Figures before adjustments for tax and benefits: National Statistics (2007).
28 For a discussion see Ball (2003), especially Chapter 2.
29 DfES (2005a): Table B.
30 Gorard and White (nd): 17.
31 See Archer and Francis (2007): 10.

32   For more on the discourse of male under-achievement see Epstein *et al.* (1998); Francis (2000); Raphael Reed (1999); Skelton (2001); Yates (1997).
33   *Daily Mail* (2007a).
34   A discourse that constructs Whites as race victims is increasingly common on both sides of the Atlantic: see Apple (1998).
35   Cassen and Kingdon (2007).
36   Blair (2007).
37   *Daily Mail* (2007b).
38   Paton (2007).
39   *Daily Express* (2007).
40   Garner (2007).
41   Meikle (2007).
42   The exceptions are students of Chinese, Indian and Dual Heritage (White/Asian) backgrounds.
43   *The Times Educational Supplement* ran an article that made no reference to the non-FSM data but included several quotes from people arguing that White students' poor performance was 'a gift' to far right parties like the British National Party: see Abrams and Stewart (2007).
44   See DfES (2006a): 64–68.
45   See Apple (2001); Ball (2003); Gewirtz *et al.* (1995); Whitty *et al.* (1998).
46   For an account of how these changes have impacted on every aspect of secondary school life see Gillborn and Youdell (2000).
47   Data for 1988 are available in DfES (2005a). The figure for 2006 is from DfES (2007b).
48   See Gillborn and Youdell (2000).
49   See Chapter 7 for more detail on Indian students.
50   For example, see Dei *et al.* (1997).
51   Equalities Review (2006): 41.
52   Gillborn (1995): 37.
53   Gillborn (1998b).
54   Gillborn (1998b): 13.
55   Social Exclusion Unit (1998).
56   DfES (2001a); DfES (2003): Table 1.
57   Osler *et al.* (2001).
58   John (2006): 225–38.
59   The only exception to this pattern was in 1996–7 when the percentage of Pakistanis excluded was the same as the White rate (0.18).
60   The only exception was Black African students in 2002–3; when their rate of exclusion was the same as Whites.
61   See Richardson (2005) and GLA (2003): 48–51.
62   Blair (2001); John (2006); Wright *et al.* (2000).
63   Rollock (2006).
64   DfES (2007c); Ofsted (1996, 2001).
65   Quoted in Ratcliffe, S. (1994): 200.
66   I am grateful to Richard Delgado for bringing this concept to my attention.
67   See Roithmayr (1998, 2000, 2003, 2004).
68   Roithmayr (2003): 38.
69   Roithmayr (2004): 197.
70   Roithmayr (2003): 38.
71   Archer and Francis (2007): 13 and 16.
72   See Sleeter (2007).
73   DfES (2006b): Table 32.

74 In some respects these projections are among the more optimistic that the data suggest: looking over the last four years, for example, would project an ever widening gap based on Black students' falling attainment during the period (from 39 per cent in 2000 to 34 per cent in 2004).
75 DfES (2007d): 7.
76 DfES (2007d).

4 Policy

1 Apple (2006): 681.
2 Reproduced in File and Power (1981): 6–7.
3 For more detail on the history of migration to Britain see Pilkington (2003): Chapter 2.
4 See, for example, Ball (2006) and Bowe *et al.* (1992).
5 Hall (1992): 291.
6 Youdell (2006): 35, original emphasis.
7 Tomlinson (1977).
8 The most frequently cited addition to this literature is undoubtedly an essay by Chris Mullard (1982). See Tomlinson (2005) for a wide-ranging and invaluable analysis of wider social policy developments.
9 Figueroa (2004).
10 Gillborn (1999, 2001).
11 *The Observer* (1997).
12 Blair termed his party '*New* Labour' in a conscious break with the socialist history of the Labour Party. This broadened its appeal, especially to middle-class voters, and was meant to signal an end to the in-fighting that had dogged the party during its years in opposition. Blair's victory ended 18 years of Conservative rule and he enjoyed the largest ever Labour majority.
13 The dramatic exception to this description would appear to be the Stephen Lawrence Inquiry. As I note in Chapter 6, however, the episode is not as simple as is often assumed.
14 DfEE (1997).
15 Gillborn (1995): 32.
16 DfEE (1997): 34–5.
17 Social Exclusion Unit (1998).
18 There have been many attempts to formulate definitions of equality of opportunity in education. Briefly, 'weak' versions tend to stress questions of *access* (concerning the existence of formal conditions that restrict access) rather than *substantive* differences in attainment and experience, which are central to 'strong' versions of the concept: Gillborn and Youdell (2000); Halsey *et al.* (1980); Valli *et al.* (1997).
19 David Blunkett MP, then Secretary of State for Education, quoted in Lepkowska (1998): 18.
20 See Swann (1985): 514–20; Gillborn (2001).
21 Orwell (1949): 35.
22 By 'public multiculturalism' I mean the liberal rhetorical commitments to diversity and 'mutual respect' that had come to typify political debate during the earlier 'naive' period of Labour rule: see Gillborn (2006d).
23 Quoted in Adams and Burke (2006): 990–1.
24 See Adams and Burke (2006): 991.
25 *Searchlight* (2001): 2.
26 Quoted in *Searchlight* (2001): 3.
27 Personal communication (2002).
28 *Independent on Sunday* (2001): 4.

29 Home Office (2002).
30 Cantle (2001).
31 BBC News Online (2004).
32 BBC News Online (2003).
33 Margaret Thatcher, January 1978, quoted in Barker (1981): 15.
34 *The Sun* (2003): 14–15.
35 *Daily Mail* (2003): 18–19.
36 Trevor Phillips quoted in Baldwin (2004).
37 Ibid..
38 Baldwin and Rozenberg (2004).
39 Alan Duncan speaking on the BBC Radio 4 *Today Programme*, 5 April 2004.
40 Phillips (2004).
41 Ibid.: 2.
42 In his interviews with education policy advisers and civil servants, Dan Gibton reports that *every* respondent from a political and/or official role described the middle class with a reference to '*Daily Mail* readers': Gibton (2006).
43 For a detailed account of the 'Honeyford affair' see Demaine (1993) and Halstead (1988).
44 Honeyford (2004): 10.
45 Phillips (2004).
46 Kilroy-Silk (2004).
47 Blair (2006).
48 BBC News Online (2005c).
49 Phillips, T. (2005).
50 *Sunday Times* (2005a): 1.
51 *Sunday Times* (2005b): 14–15.
52 Circular 7/65 quoted in Swann (1985): 194.
53 Younge (2005).
54 Quoted by Holloway (2006). Herman – now Lord – Ouseley was Trevor Phillips's predecessor as chair of the CRE.
55 Beratan (2008) develops this concept in relation to the ways in which disabled students are robbed of their rights through the mobilization of alternative discourses, especially around race and class.
56 For a critical race feminist account of key issues in relation to veiling see Wing and Smith (2005).
57 BBC News Online (2006e).
58 See BBC News (2006e).
59 Phillips (2006).
60 BBC News Online (2006f).
61 BBC News Online (2006g).
62 Barney (2006).
63 BBC News Online (2006h).
64 BBC News Online(2006i).
65 Blair (2006). An uncorrected text was published on the 10 Downing Street website: http://www.pm.gov.uk/output/Page10563.asp£content (accessed 10 December 2006). All quotes here are taken from the text *as delivered*, which I confirmed against video of the entire speech broadcast on BBC News Online at http://news.bbc.co.uk/1/hi/uk_politics/6219626.stm (accessed 28 December 2007).
66 Chouhan (2006).
67 Blair (2006).
68 Derrick Bell (1992) has written powerfully about the strategic use of people of color where they can be positioned as defending White interests.
69 Blair (2006).

70 Ibid.
71 Ibid.
72 Quoted by Wilson (2007): 8.
73 Quoted in BBC News Online (2007c).
74 DfES (2007e), emphasis added.
75 DfES (2007e).
76 BBC News Online (2007d).
77 *The Sun* (2007a): 1.
78 *The Sun* (2007b): 2 and 3.
79 Morris (2007).
80 See, for example, Raffe and Spours (2007).
81 Ministry of Education (1954) in Figueroa (2004): 1,002.
82 Blair (2006).
83 DfES (2007e).
84 For a detailed account see Gillborn (2005c).
85 Quoted in Barker (1981): 15.
86 Major (1997): 7.
87 Blair (2006).

5   Assessment

1   Hursh (2007): 299.
2   See Gipps and Murphy (1994): 87.
3   Arnot *et al.* (1998): 36.
4   Ladson-Billings (2004): 60.
5   See Foster (1993); Foster *et al.* (1996); Hammersley (1995). For a reply see Gillborn (1998a).
6   Macpherson (1999): 57, original emphasis.
7   See Chapter 2.
8   Braddock and Dawkins (1993); Oakes (1990); Oakes *et al.* (2004).
9   Oakes *et al.* (2004): 77–8; Talbert and Ennis (1990).
10 'Setting' differs from 'tracking' because, in theory, an individual student might be in the top set for one subject but a much lower set for another subject. In practice, however, students tend to be placed in similar sets across different lessons. See Gillborn and Youdell (2000); Hallam (2002).
11 Labour Party (1997): 7.
12 See Hallam (2002).
13 BBC News Online (2007e).
14 Araujo (2007); CRE (1992); Gillborn and Gipps (1996); Hallam and Toutounji (1996); Hallam (2002); Sukhnandan and Lee (1998).
15 The 'Aiming High' initiative, funded by the Department for Education and Skills (DfES), ran between 2003 and 2006. The project included 30 secondary schools and aimed to raise the achievement of African Caribbean students through targeted additional support and resources to each school (including extra funding, dedicated training and specialist advice). The data reported here are averages for 2004 and 2005 (as in the original evaluation) and only significant population groups are reported (where they account for at least 3 per cent of the overall sample): Tikly *et al.* (2006): Table 1.
16 Tikly *et al.* (2006): 22 and 26.
17 Araujo (2007); CRE (1992); Gillborn and Gipps (1996); Oakes (1990); Slavin (1996); Sukhnandan and Lee (1998).
18 'Comparing students with the same Key Stage 3 scores, students placed in top sets averaged nearly half a GCSE grade higher than those in the other upper sets,

who in turn averaged a third of a grade higher than those in lower sets, who in turn averaged around a third of a grade higher than those students placed in bottom sets': Wiliam and Bartholomew (2004).

19   Tikly *et al.* (2006): 21.
20   Gillborn and Youdell (2000).
21   Gillborn and Mirza (2000).
22   On the understanding that they would not be identified by name in the report 118 LEAs granted permission to use their data.
23   Gillborn and Mirza (2000): 8–11.
24   Ibid.: 16–17.
25   Richardson and Wood (1999).
26   Gillborn and Mirza (2000) is a prominent source in many introductory texts, including Browne (2002: 239–45) where the report is one of three principal sources used to introduce the section on race and educational attainment. See also Haralambos and Holborn (2004: 774–5, 777, 778–9); Holborn and Langley (2004: 164–5).
27   *The Guardian* (2005): 7.
28   Abbott (2005): 12.
29   Despite the common term, the 'Foundation Stage' for primary school students and 'Foundation Tiers' in GCSE examinations should not be confused – they are entirely separate.
30   QCA (2003): 1.
31   DfES (2004b): 1, original emphasis.
32   Ibid.: 1.
33   DfES (2005d).
34   Ibid.: 8.
35   Ibid.: 8.
36   Atkinson (2005); Halpin (2005); Vevers (2005).
37   Quoted in Vevers (2005): 10–11.
38   DfES (2004b): 1.
39   'Since 2003 improvements have been made in the training of teachers to assess children's performance, in the moderation of assessments and to the quality of the data': DfES (2006a): 32.
40   DfES (2006a): Figure 17.
41   DCLG (2006): 13.
42   I am grateful to David Bartlett for sharing his knowledge of the FSP with me (personal communication).
43   See Gipps (1994); Kornhaber (2004).
44   Connolly (1998b); Gillborn (2004a, 2004b); Oakes (1990); Oakes *et al.* (2004); QCA (2000).
45   Maeroff (1991) quoted in Sanders and Horn (1995).
46   I am grateful to numerous antiracist practitioners who have taken the time to discuss these issues with me.
47   Neisser *et al.* (1995).
48   DfES (2005e): 20.
49   Goldstein (1986).
50   Gipps and Murphy (1994): 88–9.
51   DfES (2005e): 20.
52   Although there have been attempts to revive Burt's reputation he was devastatingly exposed by several writers, including his official biographer. For accounts see Kamin (1974, 1981): 98–105.
53   Norwood Report (1943): 1–6, emphasis added.
54   Rushton (1997): xiii.

55 Pioneer Fund 1937 charter quoted by Lane (1999): 411.
56 Pioneer Fund (2007).
57 Jensen (1969, 1998); Eysenck (1971); Rushton (1997). For a fuller critique see Gillborn and Youdell (2000, 2001); Gillborn (2004b).
58 Herrnstein and Murray (1994).
59 Delgado (1998b): 1,932. See Stefancic and Delgado (1996).
60 Herrnstein and Murray (1994): 91 and 269: original emphases.
61 For critical discussions see Fraser (1995); Gillborn and Youdell (2000); Kamin (1999); Kincheloe *et al.* (1996).
62 *Wall Street Journal* (1994): A18.
63 Ibid..
64 See Kamin (1999) for a critical account of the distortions and misrepresentations behind such secondary analyses.
65 *The Bell Curve* is reported to have sold more than 400,000 copies in the first six months of publication. Source: *Journal of Blacks in Higher Education* (2000–1), 30: 32.
66 The term 'IQism' is adapted from Bowles and Gintis (1976). See Gillborn and Youdell (2000, 2001).
67 Sternberg (1998): 18.
68 Cleary Committee of the American Psychological Association, Board of Scientific Affairs quoted in Kamin (1981): 94, emphasis added.
69 Sternberg (2001).
70 DfEE (1999).
71 This rebuttal was reported as part of press coverage of a public lecture I gave on institutional racism in education in 2002. See Smithers (2002); BBC News Online (2002).
72 DfES (2005d): 36.
73 Baker (2002): 663.
74 See Allen (2001); Kaplan (2000); Lowe (1997), especially chapter 6.
75 Pyke (2003).
76 Ibid.
77 NAGTY (2007).
78 Ofsted (2005): 4. This is an almost identical statement to that made a year earlier: 'There were few of Pakistani, Black African and Black Caribbean heritages' Ofsted (2004: 6). Incredibly, no further details nor statistical break-downs are offered in either document and so it is impossible to say what 'few' means precisely.
79 Delgado (1998b): 1,940–1.

6 The Stephen Lawrence Case

1 Lawrence (2006): 91. Two weeks after Stephen's murder, his parents met with Nelson Mandela. The event raised the profile of the case and drew attention to the Conservative Government's refusal to get involved.
2 Lawrence (2006): 179.
3 Bell (1980b): 523, original emphasis.
4 Bell (1985): 32.
5 Delgado (1998a): 445.
6 Delgado and Stefancic (2001): 33.
7 Macpherson (1999): 1, original emphasis.
8 In a case with striking similarities to the Lawrence murder, Black teenager Anthony Walker was killed by White racists in Liverpool in 2005.
9 See Lawrence (2006).

10   No charges have been brought but a BBC TV documentary has alleged that a key officer received money from the father of one of the prime murder suspects: BBC TV (2006b).

11   Macpherson (1999): 15.

12   Ibid.: 16.

13   Ibid.: 11.

14   Lawrence (2006): 121.

15   Macpherson (1999): 197.

16   Jamie Acourt quoted from police surveillance video: see transcript of evidence for day 50, Monday 29 June 1998, p. P-9742, at Black Information Link (2002).

17   Lawrence (2006): 161.

18   See Macpherson (1999): 4–5.

19   Ibid.: 324.

20   Ibid.: 334–5.

21   Ibid.: 321.

22   Ibid.: 328–9, original emphasis.

23   For a longer discussion of how racism operates through the invocation of the 'average' member of the public, and particular notions of 'normality', see Chapter 8.

24   Sir Paul Condon, evidence to the Stephen Lawrence Inquiry, Part 2 Hearings, 1 October 1998, p. 290, at Black Information Link (2002).

25   *Hansard* (1999a): column 380–381.

26   *Hansard* (1999b): column 390.

27   Macpherson (1999): 334–5.

28   *Daily Mail* (1999b): 9.

29   *Daily Telegraph* (1999): 29.

30   *Daily Mail* (1999a): 1.

31   *The Guardian* (1999): 1.

32   *The Independent* (1999a): 1.

33   *Daily Mirror* (1999): 1 and 6.

34   *The Sun*'s editorial praised Jack Straw and went further: 'Straw was right to demand an end to racism. *But, by God, this country has a long way to go before we reach that aim*': *The Sun* (1999): 8, original emphasis.

35   *The Independent* (1999b): 11.

36   Steven (1999): 35.

37   Quoted in Ghouri (1999): 1. When subsequently challenged on this statement Smith sought to clarify his position in a letter to the paper: he stated, 'Having had an Irish mother I know quite a lot about racism. Stereotyping is a risk all of us run.' Source: Smith (1999).

38   Quoted in Ghouri (1999): 1.

39   Quoted in Smithers and Carvel (1999): 4.

40   Dean (1999).

41   Magowan (1999).

42   Green (2000): 41.

43   Dennis *et al.* (2000).

44   Smithers and Carvel (1999): 4.

45   Macpherson (1999): 334.

46   Home Office (1999): 33.

47   DfEE(1999).

48   For a detailed critique of citizenship education in England see Gillborn (2006e).

49   Schneider-Ross (2003).

50   Ibid.: 11.

51   Ibid.: 8.

52   Ibid.: 13.
53   Macpherson (1999): 335.
54   Home Office (1999): 37.
55   Osler and Morrison (2000).
56   Parsons *et al.* (2004): 1.
57   Ibid.: 50.
58   DfES (2007c): 29.
59   DfES (2004c).
60   Macpherson (1999): 31
61   *The Guardian* (2003).
62   Inquest (2004).
63   Blofeld (2003): 67.
64   The review was eventually published the following year: DfES (2007c).
65   *Independent on Sunday* (2006). The leaked quotes are indeed present in the published version: DfES (2007c): 13.
66   *Independent on Sunday* (2006): 8. Also DfES (2007c): 26.
67   BBC News Online (2006l).
68   Knight (2007). Knight's statement claims that Black students improved their GCSE achievement at 'around three times the national average increase'. In fact, he quoted data that was already out of date and, in any case, miscalculated the improvement (which was really *twice*, not *three* times, the national figure). The statement, issued in 2007, used figures from 2005: more recent data, for 2006, were already in the public domain but showed a much smaller improvement. The 2005 figures allowed Knight to cite a rate of improvement over the national average that was almost *four times* that recorded in the 2006 data.
69   BBC Radio 4 (2007).
70   Labour Party (2005): 112.
71   In October 2007 the Commission on Equality and Human Rights (CEHR) replaced the three pre-existing bodies: the Commission for Racial Equality (CRE), Disability Rights Commission (DRC) and the Equal Opportunities Commission (EOC).
72   CRE (2007): 4 and 8.
73   DCLG (2007b): 13.
74   Under the proposals only the new Commission on Equality and Human Rights would be able to bring prosecutions for breaches of the Act.
75   DCLG (2007b): 89.
76   Ibid.: 90.
77   Delgado (1995): 80.
78   Delgado (2006): 31.
79   See Crenshaw *et al.* (1995): xiii–xxxii.
80   See Lawrence (2006). The Stephen Lawrence Charitable Trust is at http://www.stephenlawrence.org.uk.
81   Delgado (2006): 62.
82   Zoric (2007): 246–7.
83   Spann (1990): 1992.
84   Bell (1992): 198, original emphasis.
85   Lawrence (2006): 91.
86   Ibid.: 91.
87   Ibid.: 120
88   Ibid.: 121.
89   Macpherson (1999): 197.
90   Mullin (1994).
91   Black Information Link (2002).

 92 Lawrence (2006): 171.
 93 Ibid.: 172.
 94 Macpherson (1999): 310.
 95 *Hansard* (1999a).
 96 *Hansard* (1999b).
 97 Home Office (1999).
 98 *Daily Mail* (2000): 9.
 99 Inquest (2004).
100 *The Guardian* (2006b).
101 *The Guardian* (2003).
102 John (2003).
103 Blofeld (2003): 25.
104 Ibid.: 67.
105 DfES (2004c).
106 Department of Health (2005): 21.
107 Ibid.: 22.
108 BBC News Online (2005f).
109 Black Information Link (2005).
110 Ibid.
111 Ibid.
112 Mathiason (2005): 9.
113 Home Office (2005): 3.
114 *Independent on Sunday* (2006).
115 Ibid.
116 BBC Radio 4 (2007).
117 CRE (2007).
118 Ibid.
119 House of Commons (2006); see also BBC News Online (2006j).
120 Inquest (2006): 1.
121 BBC News Online (2006k).

7   Model Minorities

 1 A local politician quoted in Gillborn (1990): 72, original emphasis.
 2 Bridges (1999).
 3 Cabinet Office (2003): 14–15.
 4 Runnymede Trust (2000): 35.
 5 Cabinet Office (2003): 32.
 6 Ibid.: 38.
 7 DfES (2006a): Fig. 9, p. 16.
 8 Ten per cent of Indian 16-year-olds attend independent schools compared with 5 per cent of Whites and 2 per cent of their Black peers (DfES 2005a: Table D).
 9 Fernandez (2005): 21.
10 Clark (2003): 23, emphasis added.
11 Mansell (2007): emphasis added.
12 See Connolly and Troyna (1998).
13 Wilson *et al.* (2005): 2.
14 Ibid.: 27.
15 Gillborn and Youdell (2000).
16 See Apple (2001), especially Chapter 3; Booher-Jennings (2005); Cornbleth *et al.* (2007); Saltmarsh and Youdell (2004).
17 See Gillborn (2005a); Gillborn and Youdell (2000); Rollock (2006); Youdell (2003).

18 Youdell (2004a, 2004b, 2004c, 2006).
19 Becker (1952).
20 Youdell (2006): 97, original emphasis.
21 Ibid.: 143.
22 Ibid. See also Said (1978).
23 Runnymede Trust (1997, 2000).
24 Bhatti (1999); Shain (2003).
25 Shain (2003): ix.
26 Archer and Francis (2007); Chau and Yu (2001); Parker (1995); Song (1999).
27 Archer and Francis (2007): 44–5.
28 Ibid.: 44.
29 Ibid.: 58.
30 Min (2004): 332.
31 See Chang (2000); Gould (1988); Hu (1989); Hurh and Kim (1989); Kiang (2006); Lee (2006); Ngo (2006); Osajima (1988); Takagi (1992); Takaki (1993).
32 O'Hear (1999).
33 Phillips (1999).
34 Liddle (2005).
35 Brah (1992); Delgado and Stefancic (2001).
36 Blair *et al.* (1999): 10, emphasis added.
37 Alibhai-Brown (2000): 4, emphasis added.
38 John (2006); Mirza and Reay (2000); Reay and Mirza (1997); Richardson (2005).
39 McKenley (2005): 112–14.
40 Cork (2005).
41 Nazroo (1997).
42 Modood (1997): 353.
43 Ibid.
44 BBC News Online (2005a).
45 Archer and Francis (2007): 169.
46 Youdell (2000), especially Chapter 5; Youdell (2003).
47 Cabinet Office (2003): 6–7.
48 Shotte (2003).
49 Ibid.: 2. See also Lawrence (1974).
50 Shotte (2003): 2.
51 Waterhouse (1997): 5.
52 Ibid.
53 Shotte (2003): 5.
54 Ibid.: 6.
55 Shotte (2006).
56 The website for the *Daily Mail* and the *Mail on Sunday* includes a searchable archive that extends back to 2000. At the time of writing, mid-2007, the site includes no stories at all about Montserratian school students or the social costs of the evacuation to the people involved. See www.dailymail.co.uk.
57 Shaw (2003).
58 Fernandez (2005): 21.
59 Clark (2003): 23.
60 Fernandez (2005): 21.

8 WhiteWorld

1 Quoted in McKenley (2005): 16.
2 See Gillborn (2005c).

3   Mills (2003): 190.
4   Mills (1997): 84–5.
5   Ibid.: 85.
6   Ibid.
7   Amnesty International (1998).
8   Mills (1997): 86, original emphasis.
9   Broadly, 'racial profiling' refers to the use of race-group markers as a means of targeting people assumed to be more likely to be involved in certain criminal activities. There is a considerable body of work on the nature and problems of racial profiling. For a discussion of legal issues raised by anti-terrorist moves see Banks (2003).
10   FitzGerald (1993).
11   Wolmar (2005).
12   BBC News Online (2005d).
13   For background to the events see BBC News Online (2006n).
14   *The Observer* (2006): 38.
15   Gehan Talwatte, managing director, Ascend (aviation analysts), quoted in *Observer* (2006): 38.
16   For a devastating analysis of the power of right-wing think-tanks in the US see Stefancic and Delgado (1996).
17   The Manhattan Institute for Policy Research describes itself as 'a think tank whose mission is to develop and disseminate new ideas that foster greater economic choice and individual responsibility': http://manhattan-institute.org (last accessed 28 December 2007).
18   These quotations are taken verbatim from a recording of the *Newsnight* programme (BBC TV 2006c).
19   Ibid.
20   Harris (1993): 1,725 and 1,736.
21   See Chapters 4 and 5.
22   See Delgado and Stefancic (2001); Harris (1993); Ladson-Billings (2006a).
23   Harris (1993): 1,724–5.
24   Ibid.: 1,736, original emphasis.
25   Ibid.: 1,714.
26   See especially Chapters 2 and 3.
27   Harris (1993): 1,737 and 1,759.
28   Frankenberg (1993).
29   Roediger (1992).
30   Leonardo (2002).
31   See Ratcliffe (2004): 115–17; Swain and Nieli (2003).
32   Giroux (1997): 102.
33   Goffman (1959).
34   Youdell (2000): 64.
35   Butler (1990, 1993, 1997); Foucault (1980, 1990, 1991).
36   See Chapter 7.
37   See Youdell (2003, 2006).
38   Youdell (2006): 44; quoting Butler (1997): 2 and 33.
39   Delgado and Stefancic (2004): 159.
40   Quoted in Delgado and Stefancic (2004): 162.
41   Limburg (nd).
42   The BBC is established by Royal Charter and funded in part by a license fee required of every UK citizen who owns a TV – regardless of whether they ever tune in to any BBC productions.
43   BBC (2007a).

44 YouGov (2005).
45 Tolson (2006): 9, emphasis added.
46 Tolson (2006): 94.
47 BBC (2007b).
48 Tolson (2006): 94.
49 BBC (2007b).
50 Sony Radio Academy Awards (2007).
51 Ibid.
52 BBC Radio 5 Live (2006). All quotations from the *Morning Programme* are my own verbatim transcriptions from an audio recording of the programme. I use standard transcription notations:
    … denotes that speech has been edited out;
    italicized text denotes that the speaker stressed this word/phrase.
53 See Black Information Link (2006).
54 BBC Radio 5 Live (2006).
55 BBC (2007c), emphasis added.
56 BBC Radio 5 Live (2006).
57 Ibid.
58 Ibid.
59 Ibid.
60 Callers' names have been changed. It is, of course, impossible to know how all callers would identify their race/ethnicity: where I give a designation it is based on references in the callers' own descriptions/words.
61 For a detailed and powerful critique of absolutist 'free speech' arguments see Delgado and Stefancic (2004).
62 BBC Radio 5 Live (2006).
63 Hutchby (1996): 8.
64 BBC Radio 5 Live (2006).
65 Ibid.
66 Ibid.
67 Ibid.
68 Ibid.
69 Actually a summary of Voltaire's position by S.G. Tallentyre. Source: Ratcliffe, S. (1994): 49.
70 BBC Radio 5 Live (2006).
71 Ibid.
72 For a discussion of how this stereotype is woven through the pseudo-scientific IQist theory see Gillborn and Youdell (2000). For an example of this stereotype presented as pioneering journalism see Entine (2000).
73 BBC Radio 5 Live (2006).
74 Smith (2006).
75 Delgado and Stefancic (2004).
76 Ibid.: 220.
77 Leo Tolstoy (1886) *What Then Must We Do?*, quoted in Ratcliffe, S. (1994): 169.

9 Conclusion

1 Kunjufu (2005): 1, original emphasis.
2 Orwell (1949): 185.
3 See Chapter 1 for an introduction to the style of CRT chronicles and some background on my main characters.
4 See Chapter 1 for a more detailed exposition of each chapter's content.

5 See Chapter 4 for details on Islamophobia and public policy discourse.
6 GLA (2006): 1–3.
7 For critical analyses of the relationship between Whiteness, race and space (in London and beyond) see Gulson (2006, 2007).
8 See Chapters 4 and 8.
9 Sir Ian Blair quoted in Chapter 2. In November 2007 the Metropolitan Police were found guilty of endangering the public under health and safety regulations and fined £175,000 (with £385,000 costs). No individual officer has ever been prosecuted for the killing.
10 See Chapter 3.
11 See Chapters 3 and 8 for discussions of White victimology.
12 See Chapter 5 and Gillborn and Youdell (2000).
13 See Chapters 3 and 5 for discussion of the difference between progress and achievement. Chapter 7 explores how blame is apportioned in research and press reports.
14 See Tikly *et al.* (2006) for details of a pilot project to support higher achievement by Black students – its successes and the barriers encountered.
15 See Chapter 6.
16 See Chapter 4.
17 See Knight (2000); Weissinger (2002, 2007).
18 Turner (1993).
19 Robins and Post (1997) quoted in Knight (2000): 13.
20 Delgado (2006).
21 See Churchill and Vander Wall (1990); Hoover (1967); Knight (2000): 150.
22 See Churchill and Vander Wall (1990).
23 See United States Senate (1976).
24 Ramsay (2006): 133.
25 Churchill and Vander Wall (1990): 97–9.
26 The trial transcript and background information are available on the King Center website: www.thekingcenter.org/news/trial.html (accessed 31 December 2007). The verdict was returned on 8 December 1999. See www.theking center.org/news/trial/Volume14.html (accessed 31 December 2007).
27 See Knight (2000): 10.
28 Parsons *et al.* (1999).
29 In the study 27.4 per cent of respondents agreed that AIDS was part of a genocidal conspiracy against African Americans. Source: Parsons *et al.* (1999): Table 1, p. 212.
30 In the study 89.4 per cent agreed with the item on police harassment; 87.5 per cent agreed on the criminal justice system. Source: Parsons *et al.* (1999): Table 1, p. 211–12.
31 See Amnesty International (1998).
32 Parsons *et al.* (1999): 211 and 218.
33 D'Souza (1995). For details on Shelby Steele's comments see Ruffins (1998).
34 See Matthews (2004); Sewell (2004). For a discussion of these processes in the US see Bell (1992): Chapter 6.
35 Knight (2000): 153; Sassoon (1995).
36 Bell (1992); see also Chapter 2.
37 See Chronicle I in Chapter 1.
38 Joshua and Jordan (2003): 655.
39 See Gillborn (1990, 1995); Gillborn and Mirza (2000); Gillborn and Youdell (2000).
40 Joshua and Jordan (2003): 655.
41 Guide to California Law (no date), original emphasis.
42 Ibid., original emphasis.

43 See Chapter 5.
44 See Chapters 4 and 6.
45 See Chapters 2 and 6.

Appendix

1   In my experience White people are the worst offenders, especially men.
2   Bell (1992): 125.
3   Ibid.: 111.
4   Ibid.: 113.
5   Ibid.: 114.
6   Delgado (1996): 31 and 35–6, original emphasis.
7   Leonardo (2002): 32.
8   Delgado and Stefancic (2001); Yosso (2005).
9   Stovall (2006).
10 In a very real sense, of course, every human being is of 'mixed race' (see Chapter 1). In current academic debates the term is mostly used in relation to people whose birth parents are of different racial backgrounds.
11 See Chapter 5.
12 Roediger (1994).
13 Afro-Caribbean Education Resource (ACER) Project (1985).
14 Ahmed (2004).
15 Stovall (2006).
16 Gillborn (2005d).
17 Delgado (2006): 61.
18 Bell (1992): 198–9.

Bibliography

Abbott, D. (2005) 'Black boys continue to fail but segregation is not the solution', *Daily Express*, 8 March, p. 12.

Abrams, F. and Stewart, W. (2007) 'Low grades "a gift to BNP"', *Times Educational Supplement* magazine, p. 14, http://www.tes.co.uk/2327203 (last accessed 2 February 2007).

Adams, M. and Burke, P.J. (2006) 'Recollections of September 11 in three English villages: identifications and self-narrations', *Journal of Ethnic and Migration Studies*, 32(6): 983–1,003.

Afro-Caribbean Education Resource (ACER) Project (1985) 'Anti-racism in practice: Professor Stuart Hall assesses the implications of ACER materials', Video Cassette VC SH, London: Inner London Education Authority.

Ahmed, S. (2004) 'Declarations of Whiteness: the non-performativity of anti-racism', *Borderlands E-Journal*, 3(2), http://www.borderlandsejournal.adelaide.edu.au/vol3no2_2004/ahmed_declarations.htm (last accessed 8 August 2007).

Alibhai-Brown, Y. (2000) 'At last, someone has confronted the truth about young black men', *The Independent*, 23 August 2000, p. 4.

Allen, G.E. (2001) 'Is a new eugenics afoot?', *Science*, 294: 59–61.

Allen, R.L. (2006) 'The race problem in the critical pedagogy community', in C.A. Rossatto, R.L. Allen and M. Pruyn (eds) *Reinventing Critical Pedagogy: Widening the Circle of Anti-oppressive Education*, Lanham, MD: Rowman & Littlefield, pp. 3–20.

Amnesty International (1998) 'United States: rights for all', London: Amnesty International, http://www.rightsforall.amnesty.org/info/report/r06.htm# (last accessed 9 July 2007).

Ansley, F.L. (1997) 'White supremacy (and what we should do about it)', in R. Delgado and J. Stefancic (eds) (1997) *Critical White Studies: Looking Behind the Mirror*, Philadelphia, PA: Temple University Press, pp. 592–5.

Apple, M.W. (1998) Foreword, in J.L. Kincheloe, S.R. Steinberg, N.M. Rodriguez and R.E. Chennault (eds) *White Reign: Deploying Whiteness in America*, New York: St Martin's Press, pp. ix–xiii.

Apple, M.W. (2001) *Educating the 'Right' Way: Markets, Standards, God, and Inequality*, New York: RoutledgeFalmer.

Apple, M.W. (2006) 'Rhetoric and reality in critical educational studies in the United States', *British Journal of Sociology of Education*, 27(5): 679–87.

Araujo, M. (2007) '"Modernising the Comprehensive principle": selection, setting and the institutionalisation of educational failure', *British Journal of Sociology of Education*, 28(2): 241–57.

Archer, L. and Francis, B. (2007) *Understanding Minority Ethnic Achievement: Race, Gender, Class and 'Success'*, London: Routledge.

Arnot, M., Gray, J., James, M. and Rudduck, J. with Duveen, G. (1998) 'Recent research on gender and educational performance', London: The Stationery Office.

Atkinson, S. (2005) 'Early tests fail black pupils', *Times Educational Supplement*, 16 September, p. 6.

Back, L. and Solomos, J. (2000) 'Introduction: theorizing race and racism', in L. Back and J. Solomos (eds) *Theories of Race and Racism*, London: Routledge, pp. 1–28.

Baker, B. (2002) 'The hunt for disability: the new eugenics and the normalization of school children', *Teacher's College Record*, 104(4): 663–703.

Baldwin, T. (2004) 'I want an integrated society with a difference', *The Times*, 3 April, http://www.timesonline.co.uk/tol/news/uk/article1055207.ece (last accessed 6 March 2007).

Baldwin, T. and Rozenberg, G. (2004) 'Britain "must scrap multiculturalism"', http://www.timesonline.co.uk/tol/news/uk/article1055221.ece (last accessed 6 March 2007).

Ball, S.J. (2003) *Class Strategies and the Education Market: the Middle Classes and Social Advantage*, London: RoutledgeFalmer.

Ball, S.J. (2006) *Education Policy and Social Class: the Selected Works of Stephen J. Ball*, London: Routledge.

Banks, R.R. (2003) 'Racial profiling and antiterrorism efforts', *Cornell Law Review*, 89: 1,201–17.

Barker, M. (1981) *The New Racism: Conservatives and the Ideology of the Tribe*, London: Junction Books.

Barney, K. (2006) 'Surge in racism at schools blamed on 7/7 and veil row', *Evening Standard*, 20 November, p. 20.

Barrett, J.R. and Roediger, D. (1997) 'How white people became white', in R. Delgado and J. Stefancic (eds) *Critical White Studies: Looking Behind the Mirror*, Philadelphia, PA: Temple University Press, pp. 402–6.

BBC (2007a) 'About the BBC: purpose and values', http://www.bbc.co.uk/info/purpose (last accessed 13 July 2007).

BBC (2007b) 'About the BBC: policies, guidelines and reports: BBC statements of programme policy 2006/2007: BBC Radio 5 Live', http://www.bbc.co.uk/info/statements2006/radio/radio5live.shtml (last accessed 13 July 2007).

BBC (2007c) 'Editorial guidelines in full: impartiality and diversity of opinion', http://www.bbc.co.uk/guidelines/editorialguidelines/edguide/impariality (last accessed 13 July 2007).

BBC News Online (1999) 'Stephen Lawrence: chronology of events', http://news.bbc.co.uk/hi/english/static/stephen_lawrence/timeline.htm (last accessed 1 May 2007).

BBC News Online (2002) 'Racism warning over curriculum plans', http://news.bbc.co.uk/1/hi/education/1867639.stm (last accessed 5 November 2005).

BBC News Online (2003) 'Blunkett revels in straight talking image', http://news.bbc.co.uk/1/hi/uk_politics/2240852.stm (last accessed 6 March 2007).

BBC News Online (2004) 'David Blunkett in quotes', http://news.bbc.co.uk/1/hi/uk_politics/4099799.stm (last accessed 6 March 2007)

BBC News Online (2005a) 'Hate crimes soar after bombings', http://news.bbc.co.uk/1/hi/england/london/4740015.stm (last accessed 11 August 2006).

BBC News Online (2005b) 'Stats reveal migrant levels to UK', http://news.bbc.co.uk/1/hi/uk_politics/4075126.stm (last accessed 4 June 2007).

BBC News Online (2005c) '7 July bombings', http://news.bbc.co.uk/1/shared/spl/hi/uk/05/london_blasts/what_happened/html/default.stm (last accessed 4 June 2007).

BBC News Online (2005d) 'Searches to target ethnic groups', http://news.bbc.co.uk/1/hi/england/london/4732465.stm (last accessed 5 September 2006).

BBC News Online (2005e) 'Man shot dead by police on tube', http://news.bbc.co.uk/1/hi/uk/4706787.stm (last accessed 3 October 2007).

BBC News Online (2005f) 'Pledge to end NHS discrimination', http://news.bbc.co.uk/1/hi/health/4161041.stm.

BBC News Online (2006a) 'The Menezes killing: the stakeout', http://news.bbc.co.uk/1/shared/spl/hi/uk/05/london_blasts/tube_shooting/html/stakeout.stm (last accessed 10 August 2006)

BBC News Online (2006b) 'The Menezes killing: the pursuit', http://news.bbc.co.uk/1/shared/spl/hi/uk/05/london_blasts/tube_shooting/html/pursuit.stm (last accessed 10 August 2006).

BBC News Online (2006c) 'Menezes police officer promoted', http://news.bbc.co.uk/1/hi/england/london/5339968.stm (last accessed 15 September 2006).

BBC News Online (2006d) 'The Menezes killing: the shooting', http://news.bbc.co.uk/1/shared/spl/hi/uk/05/london_blasts/tube_shooting/html/shooting.stm (last accessed 11 August 2006).

BBC News Online (2006e) 'In quotes: Jack Straw on the veil', http://news.bbc.co.uk/1/hi/uk_politics/5413470.stm (last accessed 7 March 2007).

BBC News Online (2006f) 'Islam debate continues to bubble', http://news.bbc.co.uk/1/hi/uk/6052350.stm (last accessed 7 March 2007).

BBC News Online (2006g) 'Survey finds support for veil ban', http://news.bbc.co.uk/1/hi/uk/6194032.stm (last accessed 7 March 2007).

BBC News Online (2006h) 'Police chief urges veil row calm', http://news.bbc.co.uk/1/hi/uk/6088684.stm (last accessed 7 March 2007).

BBC News Online (2006i) 'How veil remarks reinforced its support', http://news.bbc.co.uk/1/hi/uk/6117480.stm (last accessed 22 March 2007).

BBC News Online (2006j) 'Timeline: Zahid Mubarek case', http://news.bbc.co.uk/1/hi/uk/4021285.stm (last accessed 1 April 2007).

BBC News Online (2006k) 'Long shadow of a custody death', http://news.bbc.co.uk/1/hi/uk/4849210.stm (last accessed 6 December 2006).

BBC News Online (2006l) 'Expulsions "fuelled by prejudice"', http://news.bbc.co.uk/1/hi/education/6168285.stm (last accessed 10 January 2007).

BBC News Online (2006m) 'Hanged detainee aimed to save son', http://news.bbc.co.uk/1/hi/england/beds/bucks/herts/5361324.stm (last accessed 16 May 2007).

BBC News Online (2006n) 'Timeline: UK "terror plot" investigation', http://news.bbc.co.uk/1/hi/uk/4801183.stm (last accessed 15 September 2006).

BBC News Online (2007a) 'Brown brings in more "outsiders"', http://news.bbc.co.uk/1/hi/uk_politics/6251788.stm (last accessed 29 June 2007).

BBC News Online (2007b) 'Hodge views echo our policy – BNP', http://news.bbc.co.uk/1/hi/uk_politics/6694191.stm (last accessed 4 June 2007).

BBC News Online (2007c) 'Migrants should volunteer – Brown', http://news.bbc.co.uk/1/hi/uk_politics/6399457.stm (last accessed 8 March 2007).

BBC News Online (2007d) 'Schools allowed to ban face veils', http://news. bbc.co.uk/1/hi/education/6466221.stm (last accessed 20 March 2007).

BBC News Online (2007e) 'Brown plans "world class" schools', http://news. bbc.co.uk/1/hi/uk_politics/6224364.stm (last accessed 21 June 2007).

BBC Radio 4 (2004) *Today Programme*, 5 April 2004, http://www.bbc.co.uk/ radio4/today/listenagain/zmonday_20040405.shtml (last accessed 30 October 2007).

BBC Radio 4 (2007) *Today Programme*, 31 March 2007, http://www.bbc.co.uk/ radio4/today/listenagain/zsaturday_20070331.shtml (last accessed 4 April 2007).

BBC Radio 5 Live (2006) *The Morning Programme with Victoria Derbyshire*, 8 March.

BBC TV (2006a) *Newsnight*, 17 July.

BBC TV (2006b) *The Boys Who Killed Stephen Lawrence*, 26 July.

BBC TV (2006c) *Newsnight*, 14 August.

Becker, H.S. (1952) 'Social-class variations in the teacher–pupil relationship', in H.S. Becker (1970) *Sociological Work: Method and Substance*, New Brunswick, NJ: Transaction Books, pp. 137–50.

Bell, D. (1980a) *Race, Racism and American Law*, Boston, MA: Little Brown.

Bell, D. (1980b) 'Brown v. Board of Education and the interest convergence dilemma', *Harvard Law Review*, 93, 518–33.

Bell, D. (1985) 'Foreword: the civil rights chronicles (the Supreme Court, 1984 term)', *Harvard Law Review*, 99: 4–83.

Bell, D. (1987) *And We Are Not Saved: the Elusive Quest for Racial Justice*, New York: Basic Books.

Bell, D. (1990) 'After we're gone: prudent speculations on America in a post-racial epoch' (1989 Sanford E. Sarasohn memorial lecture), *St Louis University Law Journal*, 34: 393–405.

Bell, D. (1992) *Faces at the Bottom of the Well: the Permanence of Racism*, New York: Basic Books.

Bell, D. (1995) 'Who's afraid of critical race theory?', *University of Illinois Law Review*, 1995: 893–910.

Beratan, G. (2008) 'The song remains the same: transposition and the disproportionate representation of minority students in special education', *Race Ethnicity and Education*, 11.

Bhatia, S. (no date) 'The stares in the London underground', http://www.cobrapost. com/documents/Staresshekharbhatia.htm (last accessed 5 September 2006).

Bhatti, G. (1999) *Asian Children at Home and at School: an Ethnographic Study*, London: Routledge.

Bickerton, A. (ed.) (1971) *American English/English American: a Two-way Glossary of Words in Daily Use on Both Sides of the Atlantic*, London: Abson Books.

Black Information Link (2002) 'Stephen Lawrence Inquiry transcripts', http://www. blink.org.uk/sli_transcripts.asp?grp=14 (last accessed 3 May 2007).

Black Information Link (2005) 'Don't axe Stephen Lawrence', http://www.blink.org. uk/pdescription.asp?key=9638andgrp=14 (last accessed 3 May 2007).

Black Information Link (2006) 'NUS condemns racist comments', http://www.blink. org.uk/pdescription.asp?key=10848andgrp=7andcat=31 (last accessed 13 July 2007).

Blair, A. (2007) 'School low achievers and white and British', *The Times*, 22 June, http://www.timesonline.co.uk/tol/news/uk/education/article1969156.ece (last accessed 27 June 2007).

Blair, M. (2001) *Why Pick on Me? School Exclusion and Black Youth*, Stoke-on-Trent: Trentham.

Blair, M. (2004) 'The myth of neutrality in educational research', in G. Ladson-Billings and D. Gillborn (eds) *The RoutledgeFalmer Reader in Multicultural Education*, London: RoutledgeFalmer, pp. 243–51.

Blair, M., Gillborn, D., Kemp, S. and MacDonald, J. (1999) 'Institutional racism, education and the Stephen Lawrence Inquiry', *Education and Social Justice*, 1(3): 6–15.

Blair, T. (2006) 'The duty to integrate: shared British values', http://news.bbc.co.uk/1/hi/uk_politics/6219626.stm (last accessed 16 January 2007).

Blofeld, J. (2003) 'Independent inquiry into the death of David Bennett', http://www.blink.org.uk/docs/David_Bennett_report.pdf.

Bonnett, A. (1997) 'Constructions of whiteness in European and American anti-racism', in P. Werbner and T. Modood (eds) *Debating Cultural Hybridity: Multi-cultural Identities and the Politics of Anti-racism*, London: Zed Books, pp. 173–92.

Bonnett, A. (2000) *Anti-Racism*, London: Routledge.

Bonnett, A. (2006) 'The Americanisation of anti-racism? Global power and hegemony in ethnic equity', *Journal of Ethnic and Migration Studies*, 32(7): 1,083–103.

Booher-Jennings, J. (2005) 'Below the bubble: "Educational triage" and the Texas accountability system', *American Educational Research Journal*, 42(2): 231–68.

Bourdieu, P. and Wacquant, L. (1999) 'On the cunning of imperialist reason', *Theory, Culture & Society*, 16(1): 41–58.

Bowe, R. and Ball, S.J. with Gold, A. (1992) *Reforming Education and Changing Schools: Case Studies in Policy Sociology*, London: Routledge.

Bowles, S. and Gintis, H. (1976) *Schooling in Capitalist America: Educational Reform and the Contradictions of Economic Life*, London: Routledge & Kegan Paul.

Braddock, J.H. and Dawkins, M.P. (1993) 'Ability grouping, aspirations, and attain-ments: evidence from the National Educational Longitudinal Study of 1988', *Journal of Negro Education*, 62(3): 1–13.

Brah, A. (1992) 'Difference, diversity and differentiation', in J. Donald and A. Rattansi (eds) *'Race', Culture and Difference*, London: Sage, pp. 126–45.

Brah, A. and Phoenix, A. (2004) 'Ain't I a woman? Revisiting intersectionality', *Journal of International Women's Studies*, 5(3): 75–86.

Brandt, G.L. (1986) *The Realization of Anti-racist Teaching*, Lewes: Falmer.

Bridges, G. (1999) 'Playgrounds for political correctness: race zealots threaten our children', *The Times*, 12 March.

Browne, K. (2002) *Introducing Sociology for AS Level*, Cambridge: Polity.

Burke, P.J. and Jackson, S. (2007) *Reconceptualising Lifelong Learning: Feminist Interventions*, London: Routledge.

Bush, M.E.L. (2004). 'Race, ethnicity, and Whiteness', *Sage Race Relations Abstracts*, 29 (3–4): 5–48.

Butler, J. (1990) *Gender Trouble: Feminism and the Subversion of Identity*, London: Routledge.

Butler, J. (1993) *Bodies that Matter: on the Discursive Limits of 'Sex'*, London: Routledge.

Butler, J. (1997) *Excitable Speech: a Politics of the Performative*, London: Routledge.

Cabinet Office (2003) 'Ethnic minorities and the labour market: final report', London: Cabinet Office.

Calmore, J.O. (1992) 'Critical race theory, Archie Shepp, and Fire Music: securing an authentic intellectual life in a multicultural world', *Southern California Law Review*, 65(2):129–30.

Cantle, T. (2001) 'Community cohesion: a report of the independent review team', London: Home Office.

Carmichael, S. and Hamilton, C.V. (1967) *Black Power: the Politics of Liberation in America*, New York: Random House. Excerpts reprinted in E. Cashmore and J. Jennings (eds) (2001) *Racism: Essential Readings*, London: Sage.

Cassen, R. and Kingdon, G. (2007) *Tackling low educational achievement*, York: Joseph Rowntree Foundation.

Chang, R.S. (2000) 'Toward an Asian American legal scholarship: critical race theory, post-structuralism, and narrative space', in R. Delgado and J. Stefancic (eds) (2000) *Critical Race Theory: the Cutting Edge*, Philadelphia, PA: Temple University Press, pp. 354–68.

Chau, R. and Yu, S. (2001) 'Social exclusion of Chinese people in Britain', *Critical Social Policy*, 21(1): 103–25.

Chouhan, K. (2006) 'Letter from the Black London Forum & the 1990 Trust', http://www.blink.org.uk/docs/CEHR_priorities.pdf (last accessed 22 January 2007).

Churchill, W. and Vander Wall, J. (1990) *The Cointelpro Papers: Documents from the FBI's Secret Wars Against Dissent in the United States,* 2nd edn, Cambridge, MA: South End Press.

Cixous, H. and Clément, C. (1996) *The Newly Born Woman*, trans. B. Wing, London: I.B. Tauris.

Clark, L. (2003) 'Asian pupils pulling ahead of whites in exam success', *Daily Mail*, 21 February, p. 23.

CNN.com (2003) 'Powell defends affirmative action in college admissions', http://www.cnn.com/2003/ALLPOLITICS/01/19/powell.race (last accessed 1 February 2005).

Coard, B. (1971) *How the West Indian Child is Made Educationally Subnormal in the British School System*, London: New Beacon Books, reprinted in B. Richardson (ed.) (2005) *Tell It Like It Is: How Our Schools Fail Black Children*, London: Bookmarks, pp. 27–59.

Cole, M. and Maisuria, A. (2007) '"Shut the f*** up", "you have no rights here": critical race theory and racialisation in post-7/7 racist Britain', *Journal for Critical Education Policy Studies*, 5(1), http://www.jceps.com/?pageID=articleand articleID=85 (last accessed 4 June 2007).

Commission for Racial Equality (CRE) (1992) 'Set to fail? Setting and banding in secondary schools', London: CRE.

Commission for Racial Equality (CRE) (2007) 'CRE briefings on discrimination law review: equality duties', London: CRE.

Connolly, P. (1998a) '"Dancing to the wrong tune": ethnography, generalization and research on racism in schools', in P. Connolly and B. Troyna (eds) *Researching Racism in Education: Politics, Theory and Practice*, Buckingham: Open University Press, pp. 122–39.

Connolly, P. (1998b) *Racism, Gender Identities and Young Children: Social Relations in a Multi-ethnic, Inner-city Primary School*, London: Routledge.

Connolly, P. (2006a) 'Keeping a sense of proportion but losing all perspective: a critique of Gorard's notion of the "Politician's error"', *British Journal of Educational Studies*, 54(1): 73–88.

Connolly, P. (2006b) 'No new perspectives, just red herrings: a reply to Gorard', *British Journal of Educational Studies*, 54(4): 476–82.

Connolly, P. and Troyna, B. (eds) (1998) *Researching Racism in Education: Politics, Theory and Practice*, Buckingham: Open University Press.

Cork, L. (2005) *Supporting Black Pupils and Parents*, London: Routledge.

Cornbleth, C., Walcott, R., Ovando, C.J. and Zoric, T. (2007) 'Multicultural policies and practices in North America', in R. Joshee and L. Johnson (eds) *Multicultural Education Policies in Canada and the United States*, Vancouver: UBC Press, pp. 241–7.

Crenshaw, K. (1988) 'Race, reform, retrenchment: transformation and legitimation in anti-discrimination law', *Harvard Law Review*, 101: 1,331–87

Crenshaw, K. (1995) 'Mapping the margins: intersectionality, identity politics, and violence against women of color', in K. Crenshaw, N. Gotanda, G. Peller and K. Thomas (eds) (1995) *Critical Race Theory: the Key Writings that Formed the Movement*, New York: New Press, pp. 357–83.

Crenshaw, K., Gotanda, N., Peller, G. and Thomas, K. (eds) (1995) *Critical Race Theory: the Key Writings that Formed the Movement*, New York: New Press.

D'Souza, D. (1995) *The End of Racism: Principles for a Multiracial Society*, New York: The Free Press.

Daily Express (2007) 'Deprived white boys "low achievers"', 22 June, http://www.express.co.uk/posts/view/10834/Deprived+white+boys+'low+achievers (last accessed 27 June 2007).

Daily Mail (1999a) 'The legacy of Stephen: judge's damning report on race murder will change Britain', 25 February, p. 1.

Daily Mail (1999b), 'Lessons against prejudice "should be compulsory"', 25 February, p. 9.

Daily Mail (2000), 'The pupils "let down by black culture"', 5 December, p. 9.

Daily Mail (2003) '"Threat" of asylum pupils', 6 February, pp. 18–19.

Daily Mail (2007a) 'White boys falling behind', 13 January, p. 28.

Daily Mail (2007b) 'White boys "are being left behind" by education system', 22 June, http://www.dailymail.co.uk/pages/live/articles/news/news.html?in_article_id=463614&in_page_id=1770 (last accessed 27 June 2007).

Daily Mirror (1999) 'Nail them: Mirror offers £50,000 to catch Lawrence killers', 25 February, pp. 1 and 6.

Daily Telegraph (1999) 'A misguided and unfair report', 25 February, p. 29.

Darder, A. and Torres, R.D. (2004) *After Race: Racism after Multiculturalism*, New York: New York University Press.

Dean, C. (1999) 'Ethnic monitoring "too scarce"', *Times Educational Supplement*, 26 March, http://www.tes.co.uk/search/story/?story_id=312851 (last accessed 31 October 2007).

Dei, G.J.S., Mazzuca, J., McIsaac, E. and Zine, J. (1997) *Reconstructing 'Dropout': a Critical Ethnography of Black Students' Disengagement from School*, Toronto: University of Toronto Press.

Delamont, S. (2001) 'Review of "Taking sides in social research"', *British Journal of Sociology of Education*, 22(1): 157–60.

Delamont, S. (2003) *Feminist Sociology*, London: Sage.

Delgado, R. (1989) 'Storytelling for oppositionists and others: a plea for narrative', *Michigan Law Review*, 87: 2,411–41.

Delgado, R. (1995) *The Rodrigo Chronicles: Conversations about America and Race*, New York: New York University Press.

Delgado, R. (1996) *The Coming Race War? And Other Apocalyptic Tales of America After Affirmative Action and Welfare*, New York: New York University Press.

Delgado, R. (1998a) 'Rodrigo's committee assignment: a skeptical look at judicial independence', *Southern California Law Review*, 72: 425–54.

Delgado, R. (1998b) 'Rodrigo's bookbag: Brimelow, Bork, Herrnstein, Murray, and D'Souza. Recent conservative thought and the end of equality', *Stanford Law Review*, 50(6): 1,929–57.

Delgado, R. (2003) *Justice at War: Civil Liberties and Civil Rights During Times of Crisis*, New York: New York University Press.

Delgado, R. (2006) 'Rodrigo's roundelay: *Hernandez v. Texas* and the interest-convergence dilemma', *Harvard Civil Rights-Civil Liberties Law Review*, 41: 40–65.

Delgado, R. and Stefancic, J. (eds) (1997) *Critical White Studies: Looking Behind the Mirror*, Philadelphia, PA: Temple University Press.

Delgado, R. and Stefancic, J. (eds) (1998) *The Latino/a Condition: a Critical Reader*, New York: New York University Press.

Delgado, R. and Stefancic, J. (2000) Introduction in R. Delgado and J. Stafancic (eds) *Critical Race Theory: the Cutting edge*, 2nd edn, Philadelphia, PA: Temple University Press.

Delgado, R. and Stefancic, J. (2001) *Critical Race Theory: an Introduction*, New York: New York University Press.

Delgado, R. and Stefancic, J. (2004) *Understanding Words that Wound*, Boulder, CO: Westview Press.

Demaine, J. (1993) 'Racism, ideology and education: the last word on the Honeyford Affair?', *British Journal of Sociology of Education*, 14(4): 409–14.

Dennis, N., Erdos, G. and Al-Shahi, A. (2000) *Racist Murder and Pressure Group Politics: the Macpherson Report and the Police*, London: Institute for the Study of Civil Society.

Department for Communities and Local Government (DCLG) (2006) 'Improving opportunity, strengthening society – One Year On', London: DCLG.

Department for Communities and Local Government (DCLG)(2007a) 'Government Responds to the REACH report', http://www.communities.gov.uk/index.asp?id= 1512220 (last accessed 9 August 2007).

Department for Communities and Local Government (DCLG)(2007b) 'Discrimination law review: a framework for fairness: proposals for a single equality bill for Great Britain: a consultation paper', London: Department for Communities and Local Government.

Department for Education and Employment (DfEE) (1997) 'Excellence in schools', Cm 3681, London: The Stationery Office.

Department for Education and Employment (DfEE) (1999) 'Press release 90/99', 24 February, London: Department for Education and Employment.

Department for Education and Skills (DfES)(2001a) 'New measures will tackle violent pupils and parents and help promote good behaviour: Estelle Morris', Press notice 2001/0300, London: DfES.

Department for Education and Skills (DfES) (2001b) 'Schools achieving success', London: DfES.

Department for Education and Skills (DfES) (2002) 'Statistics of education: permanent exclusions from maintained schools in England', issue no. 09/02, London: DfES.

Department for Education and Skills (DfES)(2003) 'Permanent exclusions from schools and exclusion appeals, England 2001/2002 (provisional)', SFR 16/2003, London: DfES.

Department for Education and Skills (DfES)(2004a) 'Permanent exclusions from maintained schools in England, 2002/2003', SFR 42/2004, London: DfES.

Department for Education and Skills (DfES)(2004b) 'Experimental statistics first release', SFR 25/2004, London: DfES.

Department for Education and Skills (DfES) (2004c) 'Five year strategy for children and learners', London: DfES.

Department for Education and Skills (DfES) (2005a) 'Youth Cohort Study: the activities and experiences of 16 year olds: England and Wales 2004', SFR 04/2005 Revised, London: DfES.

Department for Education and Skills (DfES) (2005b) 'Permanent and fixed period exclusions from schools and exclusion appeals in England, 2003/04', SFR 23/2005, London: DfES.

Department for Education and Skills (DfES) (2005c) 'Minority ethnic pupils make further progress at GCSE', Press release 2005/0027, London: DfES.

Department for Education and Skills (DfES) (2005d) 'Ethnicity and education: the evidence on minority ethnic pupils', London: DfES.

Department for Education and Skills (DfES) (2005e) 'Higher standards, better schools for all: more choice for parents and pupils', CM 6677, London: HMSO.

Department for Education and Skills (DfES) (2006a) 'Ethnicity and education: the evidence on minority ethnic pupils aged 5–16: research topic paper: 2006 edition', London: DfES.

Department for Education and Skills (DfES) (2006b) 'National curriculum assessment, GCSE and equivalent attainment and post-16 attainment by pupil characteristics in England 2005/06 (provisional)', SFR 46/2006, London: DfES.

Department for Education and Skills (DfES) (2006c) 'Permanent and fixed period exclusions from schools and exclusion appeals in England, 2004/05', SFR 24/2006, London: DfES.

Department for Education and Skills (DfES) (2006d) 'Minority ethnic pupils make further progress at GCSE', Press release 2006/0174, London: DfES.

Department for Education and Skills (DfES) (2007a) 'Economic success depends on all young people staying on in education or training until 18 – Johnson,' Press notice 2007/0049, London: DfES.

Department for Education and Skills (DfES) (2007b) 'National curriculum assessment, GCSE and equivalent attainment and post-16 attainment by pupil characteristics in England 2005/06 (revised)', SFR 04/2007, London: DfES.

Department for Education and Skills (DfES) (2007c) 'Getting it. Getting it right. Exclusion of black pupils: priority review', London: DfES.

Department for Education and Skills (DfES) (2007d) '2020 Vision: report of the teaching and learning in 2020 review group', London: DfES.

Department for Education and Skills (DfES) (2007e) 'Guidance to schools on school uniform related policies', 20 March 2007, London: DfES.

Department of Health (2005) 'Delivering race equality in mental health care: an action plan for reform inside and outside services and the Government's response to the independent inquiry into the death of David Bennett', London: Department of Health.

Directgov (2007) 'Abolition of the slave trade', http://www.direct.gov.uk/en/slavery/DG_065859 (last accessed 4 July 2007).

Dixson, A.D. and Rousseau, C.K. (2005) 'And we are still not saved: critical race theory in education ten years later', *Race Ethnicity and Education*, 8(1): 7–27.

Dixson, A.D. and Rousseau, C.K. (eds) (2006) *Critical Race Theory in Education: All God's Children Got a Song*, New York: Routledge.

Dlamini, S.N. (2002) 'From the other side of the desk: notes on teaching about race when racialised', *Race Ethnicity and Education*, 5(1), 51–66.

Drew, D. and Gray, J. (1990) 'The fifth year examination achievements of Black young people in England and Wales', *Educational Research*, 32(3): 107–17.

Dudziak, M.L. (2000) 'Desegregation as a Cold War imperative', in R. Delgado and J. Stefancic (eds) *Critical White Studies: Looking Behind the Mirror*, Philadelphia, PA: Temple University Press, pp. 106–17.

DV Republic (2005) 'Pass the torch: Derrick Bell', http://www.dvrepublic.com/view.php?stid=19 (last accessed 16 September 2006).

Entine, J. (2000) *Taboo: Why Black Athletes Dominate Sports and Why We're Afraid to Talk About It*, New York: PublicAffairs.

Epstein, D., Elwood, J., Hey, V. and Maw, J. (1998) *Failing Boys? Issues in Gender and Achievement*, Buckingham: Open University Press.

Equalities Review (2006) 'The equalities review: interim report for consultation', London: Cabinet Office.

Ethridge, R.W. (2003) 'AAAA Michigan FAQs: Michigan's admissions systems are equitable', http://www.affirmativeaction.org/michigan-FAQs.html (last accessed 1 February 2005).

Eysenck, H.J. (1971) *Race, Intelligence and Education*, London: Maurice Temple Smith.

Fernandez, C. (2005) 'Black boys' failure "not down to racist teachers"', *Daily Mail*, 31 May, p. 21.

Figueroa, P. (2004) 'Multicultural education in the United Kingdom', in J.A. Banks and C.A.M. Banks (eds) *Handbook of Research on Multicultural Education*, 2nd edn, San Francisco, CA: Jossey-Bass, pp. 997–1,026.

File, N. and Power, C. (1981) *Black Settlers in Britain 1555–1958*, London: Heinemann.

Fine, M., Weis, L., Powell, L.C. and Mun Wong, L. (eds) (1997) *Off White: Readings on Race, Power, and Society*, New York: Routledge.

FitzGerald, M. (1993) 'Ethnic minorities and the criminal justice system', Royal Commission on Criminal Justice, research study no 20, London: HMSO.

Foster, P. (1993) '"Methodological purism" or "a defence against hype"? Critical readership in research in "race" and education', *New Community* 19(3): 547–52.

Foster, P., Gomm, R. and Hammersley, M. (1996) *Constructing Educational Inequality*, London: Falmer.

Foucault, M. (1980) *Power/Knowledge: Selected Interviews and Other Writings*, edited by C. Gordon, Hemel Hempstead: Harvester.

Foucault, M. (1990) *Politics Philosophy Culture: Interviews and Other Writings 1977–1984*, edited by L.D. Kritzman, London: Routledge.

Foucault, M. (1991) *Discipline and Punish: the Birth of the Prison*, London: Penguin.

Francis, B. (2000) *Boys, Girls and Achievement,* London: RoutledgeFalmer.

Frankenberg, R. (1993) *White Women, Race Matters: the Social Construction of Whiteness*, Minneapolis, MN: University of Minnesota Press.

Fraser, S. (ed.) (1995) *The Bell Curve Wars: Race, Intelligence, and the Future of America*, New York: Basic Books.

Garner, R. (2007) 'White working-class boys are the worst performers in school', 22 June, http://news.independent.co.uk/education/education_news/article2692502.ece (last accessed 27 June 2007).

Gewirtz, S., Ball, S.J. and Bowe, R. (1995) *Markets, Choice and Equity in Education*, Buckingham: Open University Press.

Ghouri, N. (1999) 'Schools ignore issue of racism', *Times Educational Supplement*, 26 February, p.1.

Gibton, D. (2006) 'New Labour's decade of law-based reform: policy, politics, governance and public education – preliminary findings', seminar presentation at the Institute of Education, University of London, 11 January.

Gillborn, D. (1990) *'Race', Ethnicity and Education: Teaching and Learning in Multiethnic Schools*, London: Unwin Hyman/Routledge.

Gillborn, D. (1995) *Racism and Antiracism in Real Schools: Theory, Policy, Practice*, Buckingham: Open University Press.

Gillborn, D. (1998a) 'Racism and the politics of qualitative research: learning from controversy and critique', in P. Connolly and B. Troyna (eds) *Researching Racism in Education: Politics, Theory and Practice*, Buckingham: Open University Press, pp. 34–54.

Gillborn, D. (1998b) 'Exclusions from school: an overview of the issues', in N. Donovan (ed.) *Second Chances: Exclusion from School and Equality of Opportunity*, London: New Policy Institute.

Gillborn, D. (1999) 'Fifty years of failure: "race" and education policy in Britain', in A. Hayton (ed.) *Tackling Disaffection and Social Exclusion: Education Perspectives and Policies*, London: Kogan Page, pp. 135–55.

Gillborn, D. (2001) 'Racism, policy and the (mis)education of Black children', in R. Majors (ed.) *Educating Our Black Children: New Directions and Radical Approaches*, London: RoutledgeFalmer, pp. 13–27.

Gillborn, D. (2004a) 'Racism, policy and contemporary schooling: current inequities and future possibilities', *Sage Race Relations Abstracts*, 29(2): 5–33.

Gillborn, D. (2004b) 'Ability, selection and institutional racism in schools', in M. Olssen (ed.) *Culture and Learning: Access and Opportunity in the Classroom*, Greenwich, CT: Information Age Publishing.

Gillborn, D. (2005a) 'It takes a nation of millions (and a particular kind of education system) to hold us back', in B. Richardson (ed.) (2005) *Tell It Like It Is: How Our Schools Fail Black Children*, London: Bookmarks, pp. 88–96.

Gillborn, D. (2005b) 'Forget what you *think* you know about race and education: new approaches to racism in policy and practice', Keynote address, BERA Graduate Student Conference, University of Glamorgan, 14 September.

Gillborn, D. (2005c) 'Education policy as an act of White Supremacy: Whiteness, Critical Race Theory and education reform', *Journal of Education Policy*, 20(4): 485–505.

Gillborn, D. (2005d) 'Anti-racism: from policy to praxis', in Zeus Leonardo (ed.) *Critical Pedagogy and Race*, Oxford: Blackwell, pp. 111–26.

Gillborn, D. (2006a) 'Rethinking White Supremacy: who counts in "WhiteWorld"', *Ethnicities*, 6(3): 318–40. *Special Issue: Rethinking Race and Class in a Time of Ethnic*

Nationalism and 'The New Imperialism' (eds) Peter McLaren and Nathalia E. Jaramillo.

Gillborn, D. (2006b) 'Public interest and the interests of White people are not the same: assessment, education policy, and racism', in Gloria Ladson-Billings and William F. Tate (eds) *Education Research in the Public Interest: Social Justice, Action, and Policy*, New York: Teachers College Press, pp. 173–95.

Gillborn, D. (2006c) 'Critical Race Theory and education: racism and anti-racism in educational theory and praxis', *Discourse*, 27(1): 11–32.

Gillborn, D. (2006d) 'Critical Race Theory beyond North America: toward a trans-Atlantic dialogue on racism and antiracism in educational theory and praxis', in A.D. Dixson and C.K. Rousseau (eds) *Critical Race Theory in Education: All God's Children Got a Song*, New York: Routledge, pp. 241–65.

Gillborn, D. (2006e) 'Citizenship education as placebo: "standards", institutional racism and education policy', *Education, Citizenship and Social Justice*, 1(1): 83–104.

Gillborn, D. and Gipps, C. (1996) 'Recent research on the achievements of ethnic minority pupils', report for the Office for Standards in Education, London: HMSO.

Gillborn, D. and Mirza, H.S. (2000) 'Educational inequality: mapping race, class and gender – a synthesis of research evidence', report HMI 232, London: Office for Standards in Education.

Gillborn, D. and Youdell, D. (2000) *Rationing Education: Policy, Practice, Reform and Equity*, Buckingham: Open University Press.

Gillborn, D. and Youdell, D. (2001) 'The new IQism: intelligence, "ability" and the rationing of education', in J. Demaine (ed.) *Sociology of Education Today*, Basingstoke: Palgrave, pp. 65–99.

Gipps, C. (1994) *Beyond Testing: Towards a Theory of Educational Assessment*, London: RoutledgeFalmer.

Gipps, C. and Murphy, P. (1994) *A Fair Test? Assessment, Achievement and Equity*, Buckingham: Open University Press.

Giroux, H. (1997) *Channel Surfing: Racism, the Media, and the Destruction of Today's Youth*, New York: St Martin's Press.

Goffman, E. (1959) *The Presentation of Self in Everyday Life*, London: Penguin.

Goldstein, H. (1986) 'Gender bias and test norms in educational selection', *Research Intelligence*, May, pp. 2–4.

Gorard, S. (1999) 'Keeping a sense of proportion: the "politician's error" in analysing school outcomes', *British Journal of Educational Studies*, 47(3): 235–46.

Gorard, S. (2000a) 'One of us cannot be wrong: the paradox of achievement gaps', *British Journal of Sociology of Education*, 21(3): 391–400.

Gorard, S. (2000b) 'Questioning the crisis account: a review of evidence for increasing polarization in schools', *Educational Research* 42(3): 309–21.

Gorard, S., Rees, G. and Salisbury, J. (1999) 'Reappraising the apparent under-achievement of boys at school', *Gender and Education*, 11(4): 441–54.

Gorard, S. and Smith. E. (2003) 'Written evidence to the Select Committee on Education and Skills', http://www.publications.parliament.uk/pa/cm200203/cmselect/cmeduski/513/513we05.htm (last accessed 3 January 2007).

Gorard, S. and White, P. (no date) 'Ethnicity, education and social justice', in J. Scourfield, J. Evans, R. Fevre, S. Gorard, K. Greenland, P. Gregory, W. Housley, T. Jones, P. Lambert, J. Latimer, M. O'Neill, L. Prior, A. Robinson, E. Smith and P. White (no date) 'Ethnicity: a developing research theme in Cardiff University

School of Social Sciences', http://www.cf.ac.uk/socsi/research/clusters/ethnicity/cluster_research_summary.pdf (last accessed 22 January 2007).

Gould, K.H. (1988) 'Asian and Pacific islanders: myth and reality', *National Association of Social Workers*, 37: 142–7.

Greater London Authority (GLA) (2003) 'Towards a vision of excellence: London schools and the black child 2002 conference report', London: GLA.

Greater London Authority (GLA) (2006) 'Muslims in London', London: GLA.

Green, D.G. (2000) 'Commentary: racial preferences are not the best way to create racial harmony', in D.G. Green (ed.) 'Institutional racism and the police: fact or fiction?', London: Institute for the Study of Civil Society.

The Guardian (1999) 'Stephen Lawrence's legacy: confronting racist Britain', 25 February, p. 1.

The Guardian (2003) 'Blunkett dumps "institutional racism"', http://www.guardian.co.uk/race/story/0,11374,874613,00.html (last accessed 14 January 2003).

The Guardian (2005), 'CRE Chairman defends call for separate classes', 8 March, p. 7.

The Guardian (2006a) 'Met chief to be questioned on Stockwell within days', http://www.guardian.co.uk/menezes/story/0,,1835641,00.html (last accessed 10 August 2006).

The Guardian (2006b) 'They live in the same area, keep in touch, and all but one still has brushes with the law', http://www.guardian.co.uk/lawrence/Story/0,,1831106,00. html (last accessed 7 May 2007).

The Guardian (2007) 'Chronology', http://www.guardian.co.uk/lawrence/Story/0,2763,208309,00.html (last accessed 3 May 2007).

Guide to California Law (no date) 'California criminal law: white collar defense: conspiracy', http://www.weblocator.com/attorney/ca/law/b20.html£cab200700 (last accessed 20 August 2007).

Gulson, K. (2006) 'A white veneer: education policy, space and "race" in the inner city', *Discourse*, 27(2): 259–74.

Gulson, K. (2007) 'With permission: education policy, space and everyday globalisation in London's east end', *Globalisation, Societies and Education*, 5(2): 219–37.

Hall, S. (1992) 'The West and the rest: discourse and power', in S. Hall and B. Gieben (eds) *Formations of Modernity*, Oxford: Polity.

Hallam, S. (2002) *Ability Grouping in Schools: A Literature Review*, London: Institute of Education, University of London.

Hallam, S. and Toutounji, I. (1996) *What Do We Know About the Grouping of Pupils by Ability? A research review*, London: Institute of Education, University of London.

Halpin, T. (2005) 'Racism blamed as black pupils struggle', *The Times*, 19 September, p. 18.

Halsey, A.H., Heath, A.F and Ridge, J.M. (1980) *Origins and Destinations: Family, Class, and Education in Modern Britain*, Oxford: Clarendon Press.

Halstead, M. (1988) *Education, Justice and Cultural Diversity: an Examination of the Honeyford Affair, 1984–85*, London: Falmer Press.

Hammersley, M. (1995) *The Politics of Social Research*, London: Sage.

Hammersley, M. (2000) *Taking Sides in Social Research: Essays on Partisanship and Bias*, London: Routledge.

Hammersley, M. (2001) 'Interpreting achievement gaps: some comments on a dispute', *British Journal of Educational Studies*, 49(3), 285–98.

Hansard (1985), vol. 75, col. 451.

Hansard (1999a) 'Prime minister's questions', 24 February, cols 379–87, http://www.publications.parliament.uk/pa/cm199899/cmhansrd/vo990224/debtext/902 24–20.htm£90224–20_spmin0 (last accessed 3 May 2007).

Hansard (1999b) 'Stephen Lawrence Inquiry', 24 February, cols 389–403, http://www.publications.parliament.uk/pa/cm199899/cmhansrd/vo990224/debtext/902 24–21.htm£90224–21_head0 (last accessed 3 May 2007).

Hansard (1999c) 'The Stephen Lawrence Inquiry debate', 29 March, cols 760–830, http://www.publications.parliament.uk/pa/cm199899/cmhansrd/vo990329/debtext/90329–14.htm£90329–14_head0 (last accessed 3 May 2007).

Haralambos, M. and Holborn, M. (2004) *Sociology: Themes and Perspectives*, London: HarperCollins.

Hare, B.R. (2002) 'Toward cultural pluralism and economic justice', in B. Hare (ed.) *2001 Race Odyssey: African Americans and Sociology*, New York: Syracuse University Press, pp. 3–21.

Hare, J. (2007) 'First Nations education policy in Canada', in R. Joshee and L. Johnson (eds) *Multicultural Education Policies in Canada and the United States*, Vancouver: UBC Press, pp. 51–68.

Harris, C.I. (1993) 'Whiteness as property', *Harvard Law Review*, 106(8): 1,707–91.

Herbert, I. (2005) 'Be good, son, and do well at school', *The Independent*, 17 September, pp. 1–2.

Herrnstein, R.J. and Murray, C. (1994) *The Bell Curve: Intelligence and Class Structure in American Life*, New York: The Free Press.

Holborn, M. and Langley, P. (2004) *Sociology Themes and Perspectives: AS and A-Level Student Handbook*, London: HarperCollins.

Holloway, L. (2006) 'White flight causes segregation', Black Information Link, http://www.blink.org.uk/pdescription.asp?key=13134andgrp=30 (last accessed 7 March 2007).

Home Office (1999) 'Home secretary's action plan', London: Home Office.

Home Office (2002) 'Secure borders, safe haven: integration with diversity in modern Britain', CM 5387, London: TSO.

Home Office (2005) 'Lawrence steering group: 6th annual report', London: Home Office.

Home Office (2007) 'Community policing', http://police.homeoffice.gov.uk/community-policing/race-diversity/stephen-lawrence-inquiry (last accessed 2 May 2007).

Honeyford, R. (2004) 'Is the multicultural madness over? You must be joking ...', *Daily Mail*, 12 April, p. 10.

Hoover. J.E. (1967) 'Counterintelligence program, Black Nationalist-hate groups', in P. Knight (ed.) (2003) *Conspiracy Theories in American History*, Santa Barbara, CA: ABC-Clio, pp. 825–6.

House of Commons (2006) 'Report of the Zahid Mubarek Inquiry', London: The Stationery Office.

Howard, P.S.S. (2004) 'White privilege: for or against? A discussion of ostensibly antiracist discourses in critical whiteness studies', *Race, Gender and Class*, 11(4): 63–79.

Hu, A. (1989) 'Asian Americans: model or double minority?', *Amerasia Journal*, 15(1): 243–57.

Hurh, W.M. and Kim, K.C. (1989) 'The "success" image of Asian Americans: its validity and its practical implications', *Ethnic and Racial Studies*, 12: 512–38.

Hursh, D. (2007) 'Undermining equality: the failed promise of the No Child Left Behind Act', *Race Ethnicity and Education*, 10(3).

Hutchby, I. (1996) *Confrontation Talk: Arguments, Asymmetries, and Power on Talk Radio*, Mahwah, NJ: Lawrence Erlbaum.

Ignatiev, N. (1994) 'How to be a race traitor: six ways to fight being white', in R. Delgado and J. Stefancic (eds) (1997) *Critical White Studies: Looking Behind the Mirror*, Philadelphia, PA: Temple University Press, p. 613.

The Independent (1999a) 'A family tragedy, a police force disgraced and a nation shamed', 25 February, p. 1.

The Independent (1999b) 'Case united every shade of opinion', 25 February, p. 11.

The Independent (2005) 'Doubt over shoot-to-kill policy', 21 August, http://news.independent.co.uk/uk/crime/article307307.ece (last accessed 7 June 2007).

Independent on Sunday (2001) 'Interview with David Blunkett', 9 December, p. 4.

Independent on Sunday (2006) 'Racist: exclusive: a damning report on our schools', 10 December, pp. 1–2, 8–11.

Inquest (2004) 'Inquest briefing: the restraint related death of David "Rocky" Bennett', London: Inquest.

Inquest (2006) 'Damning report on the death of Christopher Alder falls short of family's demand for public inquiry', London: Inquest.

Internet Movie Database (no date) *Cosmic Slop* (1994) (TV), http://www.imdb.com/title/tt0109487 (last accessed 18 September 2006).

Jamieson, A. and Brown, C. (2005) 'Blunders led to police killing of an innocent man', *The Scotsman*, 17 August, http://news.scotsman.com/uk.cfm?id=1794292005 (last accessed 7 June 2007).

Jean Charles de Menezes Family Campaign (2006) 'Who was Jean Charles de Menezes?', http://www.justice4jean.com/about_jeancharles.html (last accessed 28 May 2007).

Jensen, A.R. (1969) 'How much can we boost IQ and scholastic achievement?', *Harvard Educational Review*, 39(1): 1–123.

Jensen, A.R. (1998) *The g Factor: the Science of Mental Ability*, Westport, CT: Praeger.

John, G. (2003) *Review of Race Equality Policies and Action Plans: HEFCE-Funded Higher Education Institutions*, Manchester: Gus John Partnership.

John, G. (2006) *Taking a Stand: Gus John Speaks on Education, Race, Social Action and Civil Unrest 1980–2005*, Manchester: Gus John Partnership.

Joshua, J.M. and Jordan, S. (2003) 'Combinations, concerted practices and cartels: adopting the concept of conspiracy in European Community competition law', *Northwestern Journal of International Law and Business*, 24: 647–81.

Kamin, L.J. (1974) *The Science and Politics of IQ*, London: Penguin.

Kamin, L.J. (1981) 'The Cyril Burt Affair', in H.J. Eysenk versus L. Kamin (1981) *Intelligence: the Battle for the Mind*, London: Pan.

Kamin, L.J. (1999) 'Behind the curve', in A. Montague (ed.) *Race and IQ*, expanded edition, New York: Oxford University Press, pp. 397–407.

Kaplan, G. (2000) 'European respectability, eugenics, and globalization', in M. Crotty, J. Germov and G. Rodwell (eds) *A Race for a Place: Eugenics, Darwinism, and Social Thought and Practice in Australia*, Newcastle: University of Newcastle Press.

Kiang, P.N. (2006) 'Policy challenges for Asian Americans and Pacific Islanders in education', *Race Ethnicity and Education*, 9(1): 103–15.

Kilroy-Silk, R. (2004) 'Thank you very much, Trevor, for giving us your permission to tell the truth about what it means to be a British citizen', *Sunday Express*, 11 April, p. 25.

Kincheloe, J.L., Steinberg, S.R. and Gresson, A. (eds) (1996) *Measured Lies: the Bell Curve Examined*, London: Palgrave.

Knight, J. (2007) *Statement by Jim Knight*, 2 March, http://www.standards.dfes.gov. uk/ethnicminorities (last accessed 8 May 2007).

Knight, P. (2000) *Conspiracy Culture: from the Kennedy Assassination to* The X-Files, London: Routledge.

Kornhaber, M.L. (2004) 'Assessment, standards, and equity', in J.A. Banks and C.A.M. Banks (eds) *Handbook of Research on Multicultural Education*, San Francisco, CA: Jossey-Bass.

Kunjufu, J. (2005) *Countering the Conspiracy to Destroy Black Boys Series*, Chicago, IL: African American Images. (This is a revised and expanded version of a four-volume series first published between 1982 and 1994.)

Kysel, F. (1988) 'Ethnic background and examination results', *Educational Research*, 30(2): 83–9.

Labour Party (1997) 'New Labour: because Britain deserves better', Labour Party manifesto, London: Labour Party.

Labour Party (2005) 'Britain forward not back: Labour Party manifesto 2005', London: Labour Party.

Ladson-Billings, G. (1998) 'Just what is critical race theory and what's it doing in a *nice* field like education?', *International Journal of Qualitative Studies in Education*, 11:7–24.

Ladson-Billings, G. (1999) 'Preparing teachers for diverse student populations: a critical race theory perspective', in A. Iran-Nejad and P.D. Pearson (eds) *Review of Research in Education*, 24, Washington: American Educational Research Association, pp. 211–47.

Ladson-Billings, G. (2004) 'New directions in multicultural education: complexities, boundaries, and critical race theory', in J.A. Banks and C.A.M. Banks (eds) *Handbook of Research on Multicultural Education*, 2nd edn, San Francisco, CA: Jossey-Bass, pp. 50–65.

Ladson-Billings, G. (2005) 'The evolving role of critical race theory in educational scholarship', *Race Ethnicity and Education*, 8(1), 115–9.

Ladson-Billings, G. (2006a) 'They're trying to wash us away: the adolescence of critical race theory in education', in A.D. Dixson and C.K. Rousseau (eds) *Critical Race Theory in Education: All God's Children Got a Song*, New York: Routledge, pp. v–xiii.

Ladson-Billings, G. (2006b) 'From the achievement gap to the educational debt: understanding achievement in US schools', *Educational Researcher*, 35(7): 3–12.

Ladson-Billings, G. and Tate, W.F. (1995) 'Toward a critical race theory of education', *Teachers College Record*, 97 (1), 47–68.

Lane, C. (1999) 'The tainted sources of *The Bell Curve*', in A. Montague (ed.) *Race and IQ*, expanded edition, New York: Oxford University Press, pp. 408–24.

Lawrence, Daniel (1974) *Black Migrants, White Natives: a Study of Race Relations in Nottingham*, Cambridge: Cambridge University Press.

Lawrence, Doreen (2006) *And Still I Rise: Seeking Justice for Stephen*, London: Faber & Faber.

Lee, S.J. (2006) 'Additional complexities: social class, ethnicity, generation, and gender in Asian American student experience', *Race Ethnicity and Education*, 9(1): 17–28.

Leonardo, Z. (2002) 'The souls of white folk: critical pedagogy, whiteness studies, and globalization discourse', *Race Ethnicity and Education,* 5 (1): 29–50.

Leonardo, Z. (2004) 'The color of supremacy: beyond the discourse of "white privilege"', *Educational Philosophy and Theory*, 36(2): 137–52.

Lepkowska, D. (1998) 'Muslims gain equality of funding', *Times Educational Supplement*, 16 January, p. 18.

Levit, N. (1999) 'Critical of race theory: race, reason, merit, and civility', *Georgetown Law Journal*, 87: 795–822.

Liddle, R. (2005) 'It's not race that keeps black boys back', *The Times*, 17 March, http://www.timesonline.co.uk/tol/comment/article426390.ece (last accessed 11 May 2007).

Limburg, V.E. (no date) 'Fairness Doctrine', the Museum of Broadcast Communications, http://www.museum.tv/archives/etv/F/htmlF/fairnessdoct/fairnessdoct.htm (last accessed 13 July 2007).

Littlejohn, R. (2005) 'Don't destroy the morale of the poor bloody infantry', *The Sun*, 19 August, p. 11.

Lowe, R. (1997) *Schooling and Social Change 1964–1990*, London: Routledge.

Mabey, C. (1986) 'Black pupils' achievement in inner London', *Educational Research*, 28(3): 163–73.

Mac an Ghaill, M. (1999) *Contemporary Racisms and Ethnicities: Social and Cultural Transformations,* Buckingham: Open University Press.

McIntosh, P. (1992) 'White privilege and male privilege: a personal account of coming to see correspondences through work in women's studies', in R. Delgado and J. Stefancic (eds) (1997) *Critical White Studies: Looking Behind the Mirror*, Philadelphia, PA: Temple University Press, pp. 291–9.

McKenley, J. (2005) *Seven Black Men: an Ecological Study of Education and Parenting*, Bristol: Aduma Books.

Macpherson, W. (1999) 'The Stephen Lawrence Inquiry', CM 4262-I, London: The Stationery Office, http://www.archive.official-documents.co.uk/document/cm42/4262/4262.htm (last accessed 2 May 2007).

Maeroff, G.I. (1991) 'Assessing alternative assessment', *Phi Delta Kappan*, 73(4): 273–81

Magowan, C. (1999) 'Victims of "racist" system', *Times Educational Supplement*, 12 March.

Major, J. (1997) 'Britain – the best place in the world', Text of a speech to the Commonwealth Institute, 18 January, London: Conservative Central Office.

Mansell, W. (2007) 'Stunted progress for white pupils', *Times Educational Supplement*, 9 February, http://www.tes.co.uk/search/story/?story_id=2341930 (last accessed 14 May 07).

Mason, D. (2000) *Race and Ethnicity in Modern Britain*, 2nd edn, Oxford: Oxford University Press.

Mathiason, N. (2005) 'Lawrence: you have let my son down', *The Observer*, 16 October, p. 9.

Matsuda, M.J., Lawrence, C.R., Delgado, R. and Crenshaw, K.W. (eds) (1993) *Words that Wound: Critical Race Theory, Assaultive Speech, and the First Amendment*, Boulder, CO: Westview Press.

Matthews, D. (2004) 'Academic failure, a contempt for authority, and violence – we can't blame it *all* on racism!', *Daily Mail*, 19 August, p. 30.

Maughan, B. and Rutter, M. (1986) 'Black pupils' progress in secondary schools: II. examination achievements', *British Journal of Developmental Psychology*, 4(1): 19–29.

Meikle, J. (2007) 'Half school "failures" are white working-class boys, says report', *The Guardian*, 22 June, http://education.guardian.co.uk/raceinschools/story/0,, 2108863,00.html (last accessed 27 June 2007).

Mills, C.W. (1997) *The Racial Contract*, London: Cornell University Press.

Mills, C.W. (2003) *From Class to Race: Essays in White Marxism and Black Radicalism*, New York: Rowman & Littlefield.

Min, P.G. (2004) 'Social science research on Asian Americans', in J.A. Banks and C.A.M. Banks (eds) *Handbook of Research on Multicultural Education*, 2nd edn, San Francisco, CA: Jossey-Bass, pp. 332–48.

Ministry of Education (1954) 'Language', pamphlet no. 26, London: HMSO.

Mirza, H.S. and Reay, D. (2000) 'Spaces and places of black educational desire: rethinking black supplementary schools as a new social movement', *Sociology*, 34: 521–44.

Modood, T. (1989) 'Religious anger and minority rights', *Political Quarterly*, July, pp. 280–4

Modood, T. (1997) 'Conclusion: ethnic diversity and disadvantage', in T. Modood, R. Berthoud, J. Lakey, J. Nazroo, P. Smith, S. Virdee and S. Beishon (eds) *Ethnic Minorities in Britain: Diversity and Disadvantage*, London: Policy Studies Institute.

Modood, T. (2005) *Multicultural Politics: Racism, Ethnicity and Muslims in Britain*, Edinburgh: Edinburgh University Press.

Modood, T. (2007) *Multiculturalism*, Cambridge: Polity Press.

Morris, N. (2007) 'Dispersal policy "put asylum-seekers at risk"', *Independent*, 16 March, http://news.independent.co.uk/uk/politics/article2362749.ece (accessed 23 August 2007).

Mullard, C. (1982) 'Multiracial education in Britain: from assimilation to cultural pluralism', in J. Tierney (ed.) *Race, Migration and Schooling*, London: Holt, Rinehart & Winston, pp. 120–33.

Mullin, J. (1994) 'CPS says new evidence on race killing is insufficient', *The Guardian*, 16 April, http://www.guardian.co.uk/lawrence/Story/0,,941266,00.html.

National Academy for Gifted and Talented Youth (NAGTY)(2007) 'Gifted education: the English model in full', http://www.nagty.ac.uk/about/english_model_full.aspx (last accessed 29 April 2007).

National Statistics (2007) 'Household income', http://www.statistics.gov.uk/cci/nugget.asp?id=334 (last accessed 24 January 2007).

Nazroo, J.Y. (1997) 'Racial harassment', in T. Modood, R. Berthoud, J. Lakey, J. Nazroo, P. Smith, S. Virdee and S. Beishon (eds) *Ethnic Minorities in Britain: Diversity and Disadvantage*, London: Policy Studies Institute, pp. 259–89.

Neisser, U., Boodoo, G., Bouchard, T.J., Boykin, A.W., Brody, N., Ceci, S.J., Halpern, D.F., Loehlin, J.C., Perloff, R., Sternberg, R.J. and Urbina, S. (1995) 'Intelligence: knowns and unknowns. Report of a task force established by the Board of Scientific Affairs of the American Psychological Association', released August 7, http://www.gifted.uconn.edu/siegle/research/correlation/intelligence.pdf (last accessed 26 November 2005). An edited version was later published in *American Psychologist*, February 1996.

Newitz, A. and Wray, M. (1997) Introduction to M. Wray and A. Newitz (eds) *White Trash: Race and Class in America*, New York: Routledge, pp. 1–12.

Ngo, B. (2006) 'Learning from the margins: the education of Southeast and South Asian Americans in context', *Race Ethnicity and Education*, 9(1): 51–65.

Norwood Report (1943) 'Curriculum and examinations in secondary schools. Report of the Committee of the Secondary School Examinations Council appointed by the president of the Board of Education in 1941', London: HM Stationery Office. http://www.dg.dial.pipex.com/documents/docs2/norwood01.shtml (last accessed 24 August 2007).

O'Hear, A. (1999) 'Slur on teachers reveals the real bigotry', *Daily Mail*, 11 March.

Oakes, J. (1990) *Multiplying Inequalities: The Effects of Race, Social Class, and Tracking On Students' Opportunities to Learn Mathematics and Science*, Santa Monica, CA: Rand Corporation.

Oakes, J., Joseph, R. and Muir, K. (2004) 'Access and achievement in mathematics and science: inequalities that endure and change', in J.A. Banks and C.A.M. Banks (eds) *Handbook of Research on Multicultural Education*, 2nd edn, San Francisco, CA: Jossey-Bass, pp. 69–90.

The Observer (1997) 'Goodbye xenophobia', 4 May, p. 1, http://observer.guardian.co.uk/politics/story/0,,920356,00.html (last accessed 5 March 2007).

The Observer (2006) 'Can airlines recover after terror ordeal?', 20 August, Business section, p. 38.

The Observer (2007) *The Observer Book of Film*, London: Observer Books.

Office for Standards in Education (Ofsted) (1996) 'Exclusions from secondary schools 1995/6', London: Ofsted.

Office for Standards in Education (Ofsted) (2001) 'Improving attendance and behaviour in secondary schools', London: Ofsted.

Office for Standards in Education (Ofsted) (2004) 'National Academy for Gifted and Talented Youth: summer schools 2003', HMI 2073, London: Ofsted.

Office for Standards in Education (Ofsted) (2005) 'National Academy for Gifted and Talented Youth: summer schools 2004', HMI 2303, London: Ofsted.

Omi, M. and Winant, H. (1993) 'On the theoretical status of the concept of race', in G. Ladson-Billings and D. Gillborn (eds) (2004) *The RoutledgeFalmer Reader in Multicultural Education*, London: RoutledgeFalmer, pp. 7–15.

Orwell, G. (1949) *Nineteen Eighty-four*, Harmondsworth: Penguin.

Osajima, K. (1988) 'Asian Americans as a model minority: an analysis of the popular press image in the 1960s and 1980s', in G.Y. Okihiro, S. Hune, A. Hansen and J. Liu (eds) *Reflections on Shattered Windows*, Pullman: Washington University Press, pp. 165–74.

Osler, A. and Morrison, M. (2000) *Inspecting Schools for Racial Equality: Ofsted's Strengths and Weaknesses*, a report for the CRE, Stoke-on-Trent: Trentham.

Osler, A., Watling, R., Busher, H., Cole, T. and White, A. (2001) 'Reasons for exclusion from school', DfEE research brief no. 244, London: DfEE.

Oxford English Dictionary (1989) *Oxford English Dictionary*, 2nd edn, Oxford: Clarendon Press.

Pallister, D. (2006) 'Man took own life to save son from deportation', *The Guardian*, 20 September, http://www.guardian.co.uk/immigration/story/0,,1876442,00.html (last accessed 16 May 2007).

Parker, D. (1995) *Through Different Eyes: the Cultural Identities of Young Chinese People in Britain*, Aldershot: Ashgate.

Parker, L. (1998) '"Race is … race ain't": an exploration of the utility of critical race theory in qualitative research in education', *International Journal of Qualitative Studies in Education*, 11(1), 43–55.

Parsons, C., Godfrey, R., Annan, G., Cornwall, J., Dussart, M., Hepburn, S., Howlett, K. and Wennerstrom, V. (2004) 'Minority ethnic exclusions and the Race Relations (Amendment) Act 2000', research report no. 616 London: DfES.

Parsons, S., Simmons, W., Shinhoster, F. and Kilburn, J. (1999) 'A test of the grapevine: an empirical examination of conspiracy theories among African Americans', *Sociological Spectrum*, 19(2): 201–22.

Paton, G. (2007) 'White boys "let down by education system"', *Daily Telegraph*, 22 June, http://www. telegraph.co.uk/news/main.jhtml?xml=/news/2007/06/22/nschools322.xml (last accessed 27 June 2007).

Phillips, M. (1999) 'The enemy within doing for Woodhead by stealth', *Sunday Times*, 14 March.

Phillips, M. (2004) 'For years anyone who said multiculturalism didn't work was branded a racist. Guess what? Now the Left admit they got it all wrong', *Daily Mail*, 5 April, p. 10, http://www.melaniephillips.com/articles-new/?m=200404 (last accessed 6 March 2007).

Phillips, M. (2005) 'The deadly intelligence gap', *Daily Mail*, 25 July, http://melaniephillips.com/articles/archives/2005_07.html (last accessed 5 September 2006).

Phillips, M. (2006) 'The fight for the west', *Daily Mail*, 16 October, http://www.melaniephillips.com/articles-new/?p=457 (last accessed 7 March 2007).

Phillips, T. (2005) 'After 7/7: sleepwalking to segregation', speech to the Manchester Council for Community Relations, 22 September.

Pilkington, A. (2003) *Racial Disadvantage and Ethnic Diversity in Britain*, London: Palgrave.

Pioneer Fund (2007) 'About us', http://www.pioneerfund.org/ (last accessed 27 April 2007).

Pyke, N. (2003) 'Gifted and talented', *Times Educational Supplement*, 10 October, http://www.tes.co.uk/search/story/?story_id=385108 9 (last accessed 31 October 2007).

Qualifications and Curriculum Authority (QCA) (2000) 'Pupil grouping and its relationship with gender, ethnicity and social class: a summary of the research literature', London: QCA.

Qualifications and Curriculum Authority (QCA) (2003) 'Foundation Stage Profile: Handbook', London: QCA.

Raffe, D. and Spours, K. (eds) (2007) *Policy-making and Policy Learning in 14–19 Education*, London: Institute of Education, University of London.

Ramdin, R. (1987) *The Making of the Black Working Class in Britain*, Aldershot: Wildwood House.

Rampton, A. (1981) 'West Indian children in our schools', Cmnd 8273, London: HMSO.

Ramsay, R. (2006) *Conspiracy Theories*, Harpenden: Pocket Essentials.

Raphael Reed, L. (1999) 'Troubling boys and disturbing discourses on masculinity and schooling: a feminist exploration of current debates and interventions concerning boys in school', *Gender and Education*, 11(1): 93–110.

Ratcliffe, P. (1994) *'Race', Ethnicity and Nation: International Perspectives on Social Conflict*, London: UCL Press.

Ratcliffe, P. (2004) *'Race', Ethnicity and Difference: Imagining the Inclusive Society*, Maidenhead: Open University Press.

Ratcliffe, S. (ed.) (1994) *The Little Oxford Dictionary of Quotations*, Oxford: Oxford University Press.

Reay, D. and Mirza, H.S. (1997) 'Uncovering genealogies of the margins: black supplementary schooling', *British Journal of Sociology of Education*, 18(4): 477–99.

Rich, M.D. and Cargile, A.C. (2004) 'Beyond the breach: transforming white identities in the classroom', *Race Ethnicity and Education*, 7(4): 351–65.

Richardson, B. (ed.) (2005) *Tell It Like It Is: How Our Schools Fail Black Children*, London: Bookmarks.

Richardson, R. and Wood, A. (1999) *Inclusive Schools, Inclusive Society: Race and Identity on the Agenda*, report produced for Race on the Agenda in partnership with Association of London Government and Save the Children, Stoke-on-Trent: Trentham.

Robins, R.S. and Post, J.M. (1997) *Political Paranoia: the Psychopolitics of Hatred*, New Haven: Yale University Press.

Roediger, D.R. (1992) *The Wages of Whiteness: Race and the Making of the American Working Class*, New York: Verso.

Roediger, D.R. (1994) *Towards the Abolition of Whiteness*, London: Verso.

Roithmayr, D. (1998) 'Deconstructing the distinction between merit and bias', *California Law Review*, 85: 1,449–507.

Roithmayr, D. (2000) 'Barriers to entry: a market lock-in model of discrimination', *Virginia Law Review*, 86: 727–99.

Roithmayr, D. (2003) 'Locked in inequality: the persistence of discrimination', *Michigan Journal of Race and Law*, 9: 31–75.

Roithmayr, D. (2004) 'Locked in segregation', *Virginia Journal of Social Policy and the Law*, 12(2): 197–259.

Rollock, N. (2006) 'Legitimate players? An ethnographic study of academically successful Black pupils in a London secondary school', unpublished PhD thesis, Institute of Education: University of London.

Rollock, N. (2007) 'Why black girls don't matter: exploring how race and gender shape academic success in an inner city school', *British Journal of Learning Support*, 4.

Ruffins, P. (1998) 'The Tuskegee Experiment's long shadow', *Black Issues in Higher Education*, October 29, pp. 26–8.

Runnymede Trust (1997) *Islamophobia: Its Features and Dangers*, London: Runnymede Trust.

Runnymede Trust (2000) *The Future of Multi-ethnic Britain*, report of the Commission on the Future of Multi-ethnic Britain chaired by Bhikhu Parekh (the Parekh Report), London: Profile Books/Runnymede Trust.

Rushton, J.P. (1997) *Race, Evolution, and Behaviour: a Life History Perspective*, London: Transaction Books.

Sacks, K.B. (1997) 'How did Jews become white folks?', in R. Delgado and J. Stefancic (eds) *Critical White Studies: Looking Behind the Mirror*, Philadelphia, PA: Temple University Press, pp. 395–401.

Said, E.W. (1978) *Orientalism: Western Conceptions of the Orient*, London: Penguin.

Saltmarsh, S. and Youdell, D. (2004) '"Special sport" for misfits and losers: educational triage and the constitution of schooled subjectivities', *International Journal of Inclusive Education*, 8(4): 353–71.

Sanders, W.L. and Horn, S.P. (1995) 'Educational assessment reassessed: the usefulness of standardized and alternative measures of student achievement as indicators for the assessment of educational outcomes', *Education Policy Analysis Archives*, 3(6), http://epaa.asu.edu/epaa/v3n6.html (last accessed 30 October 2007).

Sassoon, T. (1995) 'African American conspiracy theories and the social construction of crime', *Sociological Inquiry*, 65: 265–84.

Schneider-Ross (2003) 'Towards racial equality: an evaluation of the public duty to promote race equality and good race relations in England and Wales', London: Commission for Racial Equality.

Searchlight (2001) editorial, October.

Sellers, S. (ed.) (1994) *The Hélène Cixous Reader*, London: Routledge.

Sewell, T. (2004) 'How political correctness is betraying (and killing) young black men', *Daily Mail*, 25 June, p. 13.

Shain, F. (2003) *The Schooling and Identity of Asian Girls*, Stoke-on-Trent: Trentham.

Shaw, M. (2003) 'English racism hits volcano refugees', *Times Educational Supplement*, 21 March, http://www.tes.co.uk/search/story/?story_id=377179 (last accessed 24 May 2007).

Sheets, R.H. (2000) 'Advancing the field or taking center stage: the white movement in multicultural education', *Educational Researcher*, 29(9): 15–21.

Sheets, R.H. (2003) 'Competency vs. good intentions: diversity ideologies and teacher potential', *International Journal of Qualitative Studies in Education*, 16(1): 111–20.

Shotte, G. (2003) 'Education, migration and identities among relocated Montserratian students in British schools', paper presented at the Montserrat Country Conference, 13–14 November 2002, http://www.cavehill.uwi.edu/bnccde/montserrat/conference/papers/shotte.html (last accessed 8 March 2007).

Shotte, G. (2006) 'Diasporic transnationalism: relocated Montserratians "in the Docks"', unpublished manuscript.

Sivanandan, A. (1990) *Communities of Resistance: Writings on Black Struggles for Socialism*, London: Verso.

Skelton, C. (2001) *Schooling the Boys*, Maidenhead: Open University Press.

Slavin, R.E. (1996) *Education for All*, Lisse: Swets & Zeitlinger.

Sleeter, C.E. (ed.) (2007) *Facing Accountability in Education: Democracy and Equity at Risk*, New York: Teachers College Press.

Smith, A. (2006) 'Lecturer at centre of race row takes early retirement', *The Guardian*, 12 July, http://education.guardian.co.uk/racism/story/0,,1818873,00.html (last accessed 15 July 2007).

Smith, P. (1999) letter, *Times Educational Supplement*, 2 April, http://www.tes.co.uk/search/story/story_id=312705 (last accessed 31 October 2007).

Smithers, R. (2002) 'Racism rife says school expert', *The Guardian*, 12 March, http://education.guardian.co.uk/racism/story/0,,666029,00.html (last accessed 25 November 2005).

Smithers, R. and Carvel, J. (1999) 'Britain's schools dubbed racist', *The Guardian*, 11 March, p. 4.

Snipp, C.M. (2004) 'American Indian studies', in J.A. Banks and C.A.M. Banks (eds) *Handbook of Research on Multicultural Education*, 2nd edn, San Francisco, CA: Jossey-Bass, pp. 315–31.

Social Exclusion Unit (1998) 'Truancy and school exclusion report by the Social Exclusion Unit', Cm 3957, London: SEU.

Song, M. (1999) *Helping Out: Children's Labor in Ethnic Businesses*, Philadelphia, PA: Temple University Press.

Sony Radio Academy Awards (2007) 'The News and Current Affairs Programme Award', http://www.radioawards.org/winners07/win07.htm (last accessed 13 July 2007).

Spann, G.A. (1990) 'Pure politics', *Michigan Law Review*, 88: 1,971–2,033.

Stefancic, J. and Delgado, R. (1996) *No Mercy: How Conservative Think Tanks and Foundations Changed America's Social Agenda*, Philadelphia, PA: Temple University Press.

Sternberg, R.J. (1998) 'Abilities are forms of developing expertise', *Educational Researcher*, 27(3): 11–20.

Sternberg, R.J. (2001) 'Giftedness as developing expertise: a theory of the interface between high abilities and achieved excellence', *High Ability Studies*, 12(2): 157–79.

Steven, S. (1999) 'Don't they know we're no longer a racist society?', *Mail on Sunday*, 28 February, p. 35.

Stevens, J. (2006) 'Heroes should get medals not face murder rap', *News of the World*, 22 January, p. 20.

Stovall, D. (2006) 'Forging community in race and class: critical race theory and the quest for social justice in education', *Race Ethnicity and Education*, 9(3): 243–59.

Sukhnandan, L. and Lee, B. (1998) 'Streaming, setting and grouping by ability', Slough: NFER.

The Sun (1999) 'Editorial', 25 February, p. 8.

The Sun (2003) 'OFFICIAL: asylum rush causes crisis for schools', 6 February, pp. 14–15.

The Sun (2007a), 'Veil ban on kids: schools' health & safety blitz', 20 March, p. 1.

The Sun (2007b), 'School minister's verdict: face veils stop girls learning', 20 March, p. 2.

Sunday Times (2005a) 'Race chief warns of ghetto crisis', 18 September, p.1.

Sunday Times (2005b) 'Are we sleepwalking towards apartheid?', 18 September, pp. 14–15.

Swain, C.M. and Nieli, R. (eds) (2003) *Contemporary Voices of White Nationalism in America*, Cambridge: Cambridge University Press.

Swann, Lord (1985) 'Education for all: final report of the committee of inquiry into the education of children from ethnic minority groups', Cmnd 9453, London: HMSO.

Takagi, D.Y. (1992) *The Retreat from Race: Asian American Admissions and Racial Politics*, New Brunswick, NJ: Rutgers University Press.

Takaki, R. (1993) *A Different Mirror: a History of Multicultural America*, New York: Little, Brown.

Talbert, J.E. and Ennis, M. (1990) 'Teacher tracking: exacerbating inequalities in the high school', Center for Research on the Context of Teaching, Stanford University, http://www.stanford.edu/group/CRC/publications_files/Teacher_Tracking.pdf (last accessed 19 April 2007).

Tate, W.F. (1997) 'Critical race theory and education: history, theory, and implications', in M.W. Apple (ed.) *Review of Research in Education*, 22, Washington DC: American Educational Research Association, pp. 195–247.

Tate, W.F. (1999) Conclusion in L. Parker, D. Deyhle and S. Villenas (eds) *Race Is…Race Isn't: Critical Race Theory and Qualitative Studies in Education*, Boulder, CO: Westview Press, pp. 251–71.

Tate, W.F. (2005) 'Ethics, engineering and the challenge of racial reform in education', *Race Ethnicity and Education*, 8(1): 123–9.

Taylor, E. (1998) 'A primer on critical race theory: who are the critical race theorists and what are they saying?', *Journal of Blacks in Higher Education*, 19: 122–4.

Taylor, E. (1999) 'Critical race theory and interest convergence in the desegregation of higher education', in L. Parker, D. Deyhle and S. Villenas (eds) *Race Is… Race Isn't: Critical Race Theory and Qualitative Studies in Education*, Boulder, CO: Westview Press, pp. 181–204.

Thatcher, M. (1993) *The Downing Street Years*, London: HarperCollins.

Tikly, L., Haynes, J., Caballero, C., Hill, J. and Gillborn, D. (2006) '*Evaluation of Aiming High: African Caribbean Achievement Project*', research report RR801, London: DfES.

Tippeconnic, J.W. and Saunders, S.R. (2007) 'Policy issues in the education of American Indians and Alaska natives', in R. Joshee and L. Johnson (eds) *Multicultural Education Policies in Canada and the United States*, Vancouver: UBC Press, pp. 69–82.

Tolson, A. (2006) *Media Talk: Spoken Discourse on TV and Radio*, Edinburgh: Edinburgh University Press.

Tomlinson, S. (1977) 'Race and education in Britain 1960–77: an overview of the literature', *Sage Race Relations Abstracts*, 2(4): 3–33.

Tomlinson, S. (2005) *Education in a Post-welfare Society*, 2nd edn, Maidenhead: Open University Press.

Tooley, J. with Darby, D. (1998) 'Educational research: a critique', London: Office for Standards in Education.

Troyna, B. (1994) 'The "everyday world" of teachers? Deracialised discourses in the sociology of teachers and the teaching profession', *British Journal of Sociology of Education*, 15(3): 325–39.

Troyna, B. and Carrington, B. (1990) *Education, Racism and Reform*, London: Routledge.

Turner, P.A. (1993) *I Heard it Through the Grapevine – Rumor in African American Culture*, London: University of California Press.

Twomey, J. and Pilditch, D. (2005) 'It was just a tragic mistake: why the police should NEVER face murder charges over shot Brazilian', *Daily Express*, 18 August, pp. 1, 6–7.

United States Senate (1976) 'Final report of the select committee to study governmental operations with respect to intelligence activities: COINTELPRO: The FBI's covert action programs against American citizens', http://www.icdc.com/~paulwolf/cointelpro/churchfinalreportIIIa.htm (last accessed 1 Dec 2006).

Valli, L., Cooper, D. and Frankes, L. (1997) 'Professional development schools and equity: a critical analysis of rhetoric and research', in M.W. Apple (ed.) *Review of Research in Education*, 22, Washington DC: American Educational Research Association, pp. 251–304.

Vandenberghe, L. (2006) 'I was the Jean Charles de Menezes whistleblower', *The Guardian*, July 22, http://www.guardian.co.uk/menezes/story/0,,1825038,00.html. (last accessed 10 August 2006).

Verhoeven, J.C. (1989) *Methodological and Matascientific Problems in Symbolic Interactionism,* Leuven: Departement Sociologie, Katholieke Universiteit Leuven.

Vevers, S. (2005) 'Special report: Foundation Stage Profile: without prejudice?', *Nursery World*, 20 October, pp. 10–11.

Villenas, S., Deyhle, D. and Parker, L. (1999) 'Critical race theory and praxis: Chicano(a)/Latino(a) and Navajo struggles for dignity, educational equity, and social justice', in L. Parker, D. Deyhle and S. Villenas (eds) *Race Is… Race Isn't: Critical Race Theory and Qualitative Studies in Education*, Boulder, CO: Westview Press, pp. 31–52.

Wall Street Journal (1994) 'Mainstream science on intelligence', 13 December, p. A18.

Waterhouse, R. (1997) 'British schools are second rate say the volcano island refugees', *Mail on Sunday*, 30 November, p. 5.

Weissinger, T. (2002) 'Black studies scholarly communication', *Collection Management*, 27(3/4): 45–56.

Weissinger, T. (2007) 'Roots of conspiracy theory in the black community', University of Illinois at Urbana-Champaign, Afro-Americana Library Unit, http://www.library.uiuc.edu/afx/Conspiracy%20Theory.htm (last accessed 19 August 2007).

Werbner, P. (2000) 'Who sets the terms of the debate? Heterotopic intellectuals and the clash of discourses', *Theory, Culture and Society*, 17(1): 147–56.

West, C. (1995) Foreword in K. Crenshaw, N. Gotanda, G. Peller, and K. Thomas (eds) *Critical Race Theory: the Key Writings that Formed the Movement*, New York: New Press, (pp. xi–xii).

White, P. and Gorard, S. (1999) 'Ethnicity, attainment and progress: a cautionary note regarding percentages and percentage points', *Research in Education*, November, http://www.findarticles.com/p/articles/mi_qa3765/is_199911/ai_n8867365/pg_1 (last accessed 23 January 07).

Whitty, G. (2006) 'Education(al) research and education policy making: is conflict inevitable?', *British Educational Research Journal*, 32(2): 159–76.

Whitty, G., Power, S. and Halpin, D. (1998) *Devolution and Choice in Education*, Buckingham: Open University Press.

Wiliam, D. and Bartholomew, H. (2004) 'It's not which school but which set you're in that matters: the influence of ability grouping practices on student progress in mathematics', *British Educational Research Journal*, 30(2): 279–93.

Williams, D. and Wright, S. (2005) 'Tragic trail of police blunders over shooting', *Daily Mail*, 17 August, http://www.dailymail.co.uk/pages/live/articles/news/news.html?in_article_id=359494andin_page_id=1770 (last accessed 7 June 2007).

Williams, P.J. (1987) 'Alchemical notes: reconstructing ideals from deconstructed rights', *Harvard Civil Rights – Civil Liberties Law Review*, 22: 401–33.

Wilson, D., Burgess, S. and Briggs, A. (2005) 'The dynamics of school attainment of England's ethnic minorities', working paper no. 05/130, Bristol: Centre for Market and Public Organisation, University of Bristol.

Wilson, G. (2007) 'Brown: make migrants do community jobs', *Daily Telegraph*, 28 February, p. 8.

Wing, A.K. (ed.) (1997) *Critical Race Feminism: a Reader*, New York: New York University Press.

Wing, A.K. and Smith, M.N. (2005) 'Critical race feminism lifts the veil?: Muslim women, France, and the headscarf ban', *U.C. Davis Law Review*, 39: 743–85.

Wolmar, C. (2005) 'Who do we search? Well, it isn't little old white ladies, says police chief', *Mail on Sunday*, 31 July, p. 9.

Wright, C., Weekes, D. and McGlaughlin, A. (2000) '*Race*', *Class and Gender in Exclusion from School*, London: Falmer.

Yates, L. (1997) 'Gender equity and the boys debate: what sort of challenge is it?', *British Journal of Sociology of Education*, 18(3): 337–47.

Yosso, T.J. (2005) 'Whose culture has capital? A critical race theory discussion of community cultural wealth', *Race Ethnicity and Education*, 8(1): 69–91.

Yosso, T.J., Parker, L., Solórzano, D.G. and Lynn, M. (2004) 'From Jim Crow to Affirmative Action and back again: a critical race discussion of racialized rationales and access to higher education', in R.E. Floden (ed.) *Review of Research in Education*, Washington DC: American Educational Research Association, pp. 1–25.

Youdell, D. (2000) 'Schooling identities: an ethnography of the constitution of pupil identities', unpublished PhD thesis, London: Institute of Education, University of London.

Youdell, D. (2003) 'Identity traps or how black students fail: the interactions between biographical, sub-cultural and learner identities', *British Journal of Sociology of Education*, 24(1): 3–20.

Youdell, D. (2004a) 'Engineering school markets, constituting schools and subjectivating students: the bureaucratic, institutional and classroom dimensions of educational triage', *Journal of Education Policy*, 19(4): 408–31.

Youdell, D. (2004b) 'Wounds and reinscriptions: schools, sexualities and performative subjects', *Discourse*, 25(4): 477–94.

Youdell, D. (2004c) 'Bent as a ballet dancer: the possibilities and limits for a legitimate homosexuality in school', in M.L. Rasmussen, E. Rofes and S. Talburt (eds) *Youth and Sexualities: Pleasure, Subversion and Insubordination in and out of Schools*, Basingstoke: Palgrave Macmillan, pp. 201–22.

Youdell, D. (2006) *Impossible Bodies, Impossible Selves: Exclusions and Student Subjectivities*, Dordrecht, Netherlands: Springer.

YouGov (2005) 'Press gazette poll: the most trusted news brands', London: YouGov.

Younge, G. (2005) 'Please stop fetishising integration. Equality is what we really need', *The Guardian*, 19 September, http://www.guardian.co.uk/Columnists/Column/0,,1573186,00.html (last accessed 7 March 2007).

Zoric, T. in C. Cornbleth, R. Walcott, C.J. Ovando and T. Zoric (2007) 'Multicultural policies and practices in North America: a dialogue with the view from England', in R. Joshee and L. Johnson (eds) *Multicultural Education Policies in Canada and the United States*, Vancouver: UBC Press, pp. 241–7.

Index

Page references to non-textual information such as Exhibits, Figures or Tables will be in italic print. Titles of publications beginning with 'A' or 'The' will be filed under the first significant word.